RIDING *for* LIFE

RIDING *for* LIFE

A Horsewoman's Guide to Lifetime Health & Fitness

RALLIE MCALLISTER, M.D.

ECLIPSE PRESS

Lexington, Kentucky

Library of Congress Control Number: 2007926929
ISBN: 978-1-58150-170-4
Printed in China
First Edition: 2007

a division of
Blood-Horse Publications
PUBLISHERS SINCE 1916
ECLIPSE PRESS

contents

To my mother, Maureen Murray Horton:

a Scottish girl who crossed the Atlantic to become

a great American horsewoman

introduction

For women with a passion for horses, remaining strong, supple, and healthy is essential. As a physician and an equestrian, I understand the importance of good health in maintaining a full and active life. As a wife and mother of three sons, I know how challenging it can be to fit good health habits into an overcrowded schedule. With this in mind, I've designed a one-of-a-kind program that helps busy horsewomen create and maintain optimal health while remaining true to their priorities in life. Key components of the program include:

* A comprehensive questionnaire that enables horsewomen to identify and overcome common barriers to optimal health and fitness. Throughout their lives, women are vulnerable to a number of potentially devastating conditions that can threaten their emotional and physical well-being, ranging from depression to diabetes and heart disease. By following a few simple strategies, horsewomen can sidestep many problems that can interfere with the enjoyment of horses, as well as good health.

* The Riding for Life Diet, a wholesome, balanced eating program designed to support the unique nutritional demands of the female equestrian. Every diet comprises three key nutrients, and although each is necessary for good health, it is the balance of these nutrients that is most important. Short-term benefits of an optimally balanced diet include enhanced moods and energy levels; long-term benefits include better health and greater longevity.

* A special section on nutritional supplements and functional foods. Although Americans are rarely considered to be malnourished, a significant proportion of women are at heightened risk for various nutritional deficiencies. Supplementing a well-balanced diet with a few crucial vitamins, minerals, and beneficial foods can reduce the risk for a variety of common medical conditions and can revitalize a woman's health.

* The Riding for Life Fitness Program, a step-by-step guide to maximizing performance as an equestrian and in every other aspect of life. Specifically designed for the female rider, the Riding for Life Fitness Program allows women to improve their strength, stamina, and flexibility at any stage of life, regardless of their current fitness levels.

* Effective time management tools for busy horsewomen with demanding schedules. The roles and responsibilities of daily life can seem overwhelming, but it is critically important for women to make time to invest in their health

and happiness. It's not about being selfish; it's a matter of survival.

* Sound strategies for overcoming obstacles standing in the way of riding and enjoying horses. As women strive to become better equestrians, most face a number of challenges. Whether these potential roadblocks are self-imposed or created by relationships or circumstances, there is always a way around them.

* Creative solutions for aspiring equestrians who strive to make horses a part of their lives — without breaking the bank. While there's no doubt that horse ownership can be expensive, women can enjoy all the benefits and pleasures of horses and riding, regardless of their financial status.

Riding for Life inspires and empowers women of all ages and stages of life to follow their hearts and pursue their passion for horses. By nurturing body, mind, and spirit, every horsewoman can achieve her dreams and create a lifetime of happiness and good health.

women and horses

PERKS FOR THE MIND, BODY, AND SOUL

There's something special — perhaps even spiritual — about the connection between a woman and her horse. Although the relationship has long been celebrated and frequently analyzed, it's unlikely anyone will ever fully understand it.

If asked why you are drawn to horses, you might find it difficult to express in words. Many of us have felt the lure of horses for as long as we can remember — our passion precedes even our earliest awareness. It's as if we simply were born this way, with a love for horses inexplicably encoded in our DNA or somehow rooted in our souls.

It could be the special connection between women and horses stems from the similarities in our natures. We are kindred spirits, with strength and intelligence tempered by grace and understanding; independence and self-reliance balanced by a solid sense of community and a nurturing disposition. In their presence, we are more compassionate and competent. On their backs, we are swift, sure, and powerful.

I can't explain the gravitational pull between women and horses, but I do know it fosters a relationship unlike any other. No human being can ever hope to see you as clearly as your horse does. People may judge you on your appearance and all your material trappings — clothes, car, house. Your horse doesn't know about these things, and even if he did, they wouldn't sway him. Your horse holds you accountable only for what lies in your heart.

You can use words to color how others perceive you, but the complexities of conversation will never help or hinder communication between you and your horse. With a nuzzle, a glance, or perhaps even a telepathic tap on your subconscious mind, your horse knows the real you, and through his eyes you begin to know yourself.

The moment you begin sharing your life with a horse you embark on a journey of self-discovery that is virtually impassable by any other means. Your horse mirrors the essence of who you are and reveals to you your strengths and your weaknesses, your promise and your potential.

With exquisite sensitivity, your horse not only intuits your emotions and intentions but embodies them. If you are anxious or afraid, your horse is fearful and tense. If you are preoccupied, your horse is distracted. If you are uncaring, your horse is indifferent. The more time you spend with your horse, the more clearly you see your reflection in him and the greater your self-awareness and understanding become.

With each encounter, whether on the ground or in the saddle, you become a better horsewoman. You understand that you must give to your horse exactly what you expect to get in return and that you must communicate your intentions honestly and openly. You learn to acknowledge your weaknesses, correct your mistakes, and strive for continuous improvement. Although you become more determined and decisive, you realize that you can only advance through the constant give and take of teamwork. Anyone can buy a horse, but there isn't enough money in the world to buy a good relationship with a horse — it must be earned. In the process of earning the trust and respect of your horse, you learn to trust and respect yourself. With each goal you set and attain, you gain confidence and self-esteem that spill into every other area of your life. In time, you are empowered to become not only a better horsewoman but also a better human being.

While horses guide us through a life-altering self-improvement course, they also dramatically enhance our emotional well being. In spite of all the modern conveniences of the 21st century, women are working harder than ever, and the stress of our daily lives is exponentially greater. It's true most of us no longer have to wash our clothes on a rock by the stream or milk the family cow before breakfast, but we're toiling in other ways that are far more taxing. In addition to putting in long hours at demanding jobs, many women simultaneously manage incredibly busy households, raise active children, care for aging parents, and make substantial contributions to their communities.

Although we are nurturers and caretakers by nature, even the most compassionate and committed among us can easily become overwhelmed and stressed to the breaking point. Many women are so busy taking care of everyone and everything around them that they often find themselves with little time or energy left to pursue their own dreams or even to attend to their own spiritual and emotional needs. It's easy to understand how some women can end up feeling as if they've been pushed out of their own lives.

Spending time with a horse gives you a chance to step back and take stock of yourself and your circumstances and allows you to restore a measure of emotional and spiritual balance to your life. You may be troubled by the past or concerned about the future, but you can connect with your horse only in the present moment — the here and now of life.

In a horse's presence, time has a way of standing still, giving you a much-needed respite from the frantic pace of life in the fast lane. When you are with your horse, you enter a world of open space and fresh air, which comes with an incredible sense of release and freedom. You're able to appreciate the beauty and the wonder of nature and to revel in the miracle of life.

Not only does a relationship with a horse enhance your emotional well being, it also contributes to your physical health. While riding may relax your mind, it is a rigorous sport that challenges your body. For women who don't enjoy exercise for its own sake, horses provide both the means and the end to becoming more active and physically fit. They give us the opportunity and the inspiration we need to become athletes at any age.

Virtually every task you undertake as you care for your horse benefits your physical health: mucking stalls and pushing wheelbarrows; lifting bales of hay, bags of feed, and buckets of water. As you push and pull, lift and lug, you improve your strength and stamina. With every bending and stretching motion, you enhance your body's flexibility and balance. The end results are a higher level of conditioning, better health, and a reduced risk for the diseases that represent the greatest threat to women: osteoporosis, obesity, diabetes, cancer, and heart disease.

If you're like most horsewomen, you probably can't imagine a life without horses. How long and to what extent you're able to ride and remain actively involved with horses depends not only on your desire but also on your health. Because horsewomen will always seek out the comfort and companionship of horses, desire is rarely the limiting factor. By default, health is usually the primary determinant.

To some degree, our genes determine our health, but in most cases the influence of heredity is far outweighed by the impact of our everyday habits and activities. Among American women, most ailments and illnesses are related to our lifestyles. Our lifestyles, in turn, are determined by our choices: whether we choose to exercise regularly and eat properly; whether we choose to indulge in or abstain from practices hazardous to our health.

Because every choice you make ultimately impacts your health, it is important to choose wisely. Regardless of your age, it's never too late to start making small, positive changes that will dramatically improve your chances of enjoying a life filled with horses, good health, and happiness.

starting here, starting now

A HEALTHIER YOU

Your health is influenced by a number of factors — your genes and your gender as well as your diet and level of activity. The Riding for Life Self-Assessment is designed to help you uncover any problems that may interfere with your ability to enjoy good health now or in the future. It's divided into 10 phases, and each phase evaluates a different aspect of your health. For the questions included in the self-assessment, simply answer "yes" or "no." Following the self-assessment, you'll find information about a number of disorders and diseases that frequently plague women, especially as we grow older. It's worth the effort to acquaint yourself with these ailments, so that you'll be on the lookout for their earliest signs and symptoms. It's even more important to learn about the steps you can take to postpone — or even prevent — these conditions.

RIDING FOR LIFE SELF-ASSESSMENT

PHASE I

YES	NO	
YES	NO	Are you menopausal?
YES	NO	Do you have a family history of heart disease?
YES	NO	Do you smoke?
YES	NO	Do you have high cholesterol levels?
YES	NO	Do you have high blood pressure?
YES	NO	Would you describe yourself as someone who seldom or only occasionally engages in physical activity?
YES	NO	Are you more than 20 pounds overweight?
YES	NO	Is your waist circumference greater than 35 inches?
YES	NO	Do you have diabetes?
YES	NO	Do you experience shortness of breath or chest discomfort with exertion?

PHASE II

YES	NO	
YES	NO	Do you have diabetes?
YES	NO	Do you eat junk food on a regular basis?
YES	NO	Do you eat red meat more than three times a week?
YES	NO	Do you usually eat whole dairy products instead of the low-fat or reduced-fat varieties?
YES	NO	Do you have high blood pressure?
YES	NO	Are you overweight?
YES	NO	Do you rarely engage in physical activity?
YES	NO	Has it been more than three years since you had your cholesterol levels checked?

PHASE III

YES	NO	
YES	NO	Are you overweight?
YES	NO	Are you older than 35?
YES	NO	Did your mother or sister suffer a heart attack or stroke before the age of 55?

RIDING FOR LIFE SELF-ASSESSMENT

PHASE III   (CONTINUED)

YES   NO   Did your father or brother suffer a heart attack or stroke before the age of 45?

YES   NO   Do you exercise less than 30 minutes a day three times a week?

YES   NO   Do you smoke?

YES   NO   Do you consume more than a teaspoon of salt each day?

YES   NO   Do you drink more than two alcoholic beverages each day?

YES   NO   Do you experience frequent, pulsating headaches?

PHASE IV

YES   NO   Does diabetes run in your family?

YES   NO   Are you more than 15 pounds overweight?

YES   NO   Do you experience excessive thirst or hunger?

YES   NO   Do you urinate frequently?

YES   NO   Do you have blurred vision?

YES   NO   Do you feel extremely fatigued on a regular basis?

YES   NO   Do you have skin wounds that are slow to heal?

YES   NO   Do you suffer frequent infections of your skin, urinary tract, or vagina?

YES   NO   Do you experience numbness or tingling of your hands or feet?

YES   NO   Does you mouth frequently feel dry?

PHASE V

YES   NO   Are you 40 years old or older?

YES   NO   Do you have a mother, sister, or daughter with breast cancer or ovarian cancer?

YES   NO   Are you overweight?

YES   NO   Have you taken or are you currently taking estrogen and/or progestin hormone therapy?

YES   NO   Do you smoke?

YES   NO   Do you consume more than one alcoholic drink on most days?

RIDING FOR LIFE SELF-ASSESSMENT

PHASE VI

YES	**NO**	Are you over age 45?
YES	**NO**	Do you have hot flashes?
YES	**NO**	Do you have breast tenderness?
YES	**NO**	Are you frequently fatigued?
YES	**NO**	Do you suffer from vaginal dryness?
YES	**NO**	Do you have urine leakage with coughing or sneezing?
YES	**NO**	Do you have night sweats?
YES	**NO**	Do you have mood swings?
YES	**NO**	Do you have difficulty sleeping?

PHASE VII

YES	**NO**	Have you experienced menopause?
YES	**NO**	Have you had your ovaries surgically removed?
YES	**NO**	Do you rarely eat dairy products?
YES	**NO**	Do you rarely exercise?
YES	**NO**	Do you smoke?
YES	**NO**	Do you drink more than two alcoholic beverages on most days?
YES	**NO**	Is your bone structure small?
YES	**NO**	Do you weigh less than 127 pounds?
YES	**NO**	Are you fair-skinned (Caucasian or Asian)?
YES	**NO**	Have you been diagnosed with hyperthyroidism (over-active thyroid gland)?
YES	**NO**	Do you take oral steroid medications on a regular basis?

PHASE VIII

YES	**NO**	Are you overweight?
YES	**NO**	Do you suffer from joint pain, especially in your hips, knees, and fingers?
YES	**NO**	Does one or more of your joints feel stiff, especially first thing in the morning or after periods of rest?
YES	**NO**	Does one or more of your joints seem to be enlarged or misshapen?
YES	**NO**	Have you ever suffered an injury to one or more of your joints?

RIDING FOR LIFE SELF-ASSESSMENT

PHASE IX

YES NO   Do you feel sad or down most of the day, nearly every day?
YES NO   Do you have less interest in the activities that you normally enjoy?
YES NO   Have you lost or gained weight or noticed a change in appetite?
YES NO   Are you sleeping too much or too little?
YES NO   Do you often feel hopeless or worthless?
YES NO   Do you think about dying or ending your life?
YES NO   Do you cry easily?
YES NO   Do you have trouble remembering things?
YES NO   Do you have a family history of depression?

PHASE X   AROUND THE TIME OF YOUR MENSTRUAL PERIOD:

YES NO   Do you experience bloating or weight gain?
YES NO   Are your breasts tender?
YES NO   Do you feel anxious or irritable?
YES NO   Do you cry more easily than usual?
YES NO   Do you feel excessively tired?
YES NO   Do you experience food cravings or changes in your appetite?
YES NO   Do you sleep more or less than you usually do?
YES NO   Do you have trouble concentrating or remembering things?
YES NO   Do you experience abdominal pain or changes in bowel habits?

PHASE XI

YES NO   Have you gained more than 20 pounds since high school?
YES NO   Does your waist circumference measure more than 35 inches?
YES NO   Do you tend to gain weight around your mid-section, as opposed to around your hips and thighs?
YES NO   Is your body mass index (BMI) greater than 24.9 (see page 37)

RIDING FOR LIFE SELF-ASSESSMENT:

WHAT YOUR ANSWERS MEAN The questions for Phase I through Phase XI of the Riding for Life

Self-Assessment pertain to risk factors for the following diseases and conditions:

Phase I:	Cardiovascular Disease	**Phase VII:**	Osteoporosis
Phase II:	High Cholesterol	**Phase VIII:**	Osteoarthritis
Phase III:	High Blood Pressure (Hypertension)	**Phase IX:**	Depression
Phase IV:	Diabetes	**Phase X:**	Premenstrual Syndrome (PMS)
Phase V:	Breast Cancer	**Phase XI:**	Overweight and Obesity
Phase VI:	Menopause		

Each of these diseases and conditions is discussed in the remaining pages of this chapter. While even a single "yes" answer to any one of the questions in the Riding For Life Self-Assessment can increase your likelihood of having or developing the relevant disease or disorder, the more questions you answered in the affirmative, the greater your chances of having the related condition. Be sure to discuss your findings and your concerns with your physician, because each of these conditions has the potential to diminish your health, your quality of life, and your ability to continue to enjoy riding and working with your horse. In the following pages you'll find information about each condition and learn about the steps you can take to reduce its impact on your health.

Phase I: Cardiovascular Disease

Although cardiovascular disease is often considered to be a male affliction, it is truly an equal opportunity condition. American women are far more likely to die from cardiovascular disease than from any other cause. Many women believe that cancer, especially breast cancer, is a greater threat to their health and their lives, but that isn't the case. Nearly twice as many American women die of heart disease and stroke as from all types of cancer combined. Currently, heart disease is the leading killer of men and women over 65. Although the condition typically makes its unwelcome appearance about 12 to 15 years later in women than it does in men, it makes up for its late arrival with a vengeance. In older women the severity of heart disease accelerates dramatically with age, surpassing that of men by the time women reach their late 70s or early 80s. After suffering a heart attack, women are more likely to die than men.

Several risk factors boost a woman's risk of having a heart attack or stroke, including high blood pressure, obesity, diabetes, and high levels of triglycerides and cholesterol. Lifestyle factors — including cigarette smoking, excessive consumption of alcohol, and lack of exercise — also increase the likelihood that a woman will develop cardiovascular disease. You can reduce your chances of acquiring this devastating disease by staying physically active, eating a low-fat diet, and maintaining a desirable body weight. For women who smoke, quitting is one of the best ways to cut the chances of having a heart attack or stroke. Because diabetes, high blood pressure, and high cholesterol levels can be dangerous — and even deadly — women with these conditions should work closely with their physicians to stay as healthy as possible.

Phase II: High Cholesterol

A high cholesterol level is a major risk factor for heart disease and stroke. Cholesterol is a soft, waxy substance found among the fats in your bloodstream and in every cell in the body. Thanks to our penchant for high-fat foods, a significant portion of the U.S. population has high cholesterol. Heredity undoubtedly contributes to the disorder, but eating a fat- and cholesterol-laden diet is primarily to blame.

Although cholesterol has several important functions, including serving as the raw material for hormones and vitamin D, you really don't have to go out of your way to add any extra to your diet. Mother Nature has assigned your liver the task of producing all that your body needs. When you force-feed your body excessive amounts of cholesterol by eating too many high-fat and high-cholesterol foods, the excess cholesterol begins to accumulate along the walls of your blood vessels. Eventually, the buildup can cause the arteries to become narrow, a process called atherosclerosis, or hardening of the arteries. Large deposits of cholesterol, or plaques, can slow or block the flow of blood to the heart or brain. If oxygen-rich blood isn't able to penetrate a blockage in the coronary arteries that lead to the heart, the heart muscle begins to suffer damage, and even death, resulting in a heart attack. When the same phenomenon occurs in the brain, the result is a stroke.

Because cholesterol and other types of fat in the human body cannot dissolve in the blood, they are transported to and from the cells by special carriers called lipoproteins, especially low-density lipoprotein (LDL) and high-density lipoprotein (HDL). Low-density lipoprotein, also known as the "bad" cholesterol, is the major cholesterol carrier in the blood, and when present in excess, it contributes to the formation of cholesterol plaques in the arteries. A high level of LDL cholesterol is a risk factor for cardiovascular disease. High-density lipo-protein, also known as the "good" cholesterol, carries cholesterol away from the arteries and back to the liver. For this reason, a high level of HDL cholesterol reduces the risk of cardiovas-cular disease.

Triglycerides are the chemical form in which most fat exists in food, as well as in your body. Triglycerides in your body are derived from the fats in food or manufactured from the carbo-hydrates in your diet. After you have eaten a meal, any calories not immediately used for energy by the body are converted to triglycer-ides and then delivered to fat cells for storage. Between meals the triglycerides are released from fat cells to be used for energy. A high tri-glyceride level is often the result of a diet that is too rich in fat, carbohydrates, and calories, although it may be a consequence of another disease or disorder, including diabetes. Regard-less of the cause, an elevated triglyceride level increases your risk for heart disease.

One way to lower your blood levels of triglyc-erides and cholesterol is to limit the amount of fat in your diet. While most of the cholesterol in your body is manufactured by your liver from saturated fats in your diet, some of your body's cholesterol comes directly from animal-based foods, including meat, poultry, fish, egg yolks, and whole-milk dairy products. Plant foods, including fruits, vegetables, grains, nuts, and seeds, are cholesterol-free.

Because consuming too much cholesterol is bad for your health, it's a good idea to keep an eye on your daily cholesterol intake. Most healthy adult women should limit their con-sumption to less than 300 milligrams (mg) a day. If you've been diagnosed with high blood cholesterol levels or heart disease, you should strive to limit your daily intake to less than 200 mg. One way to reduce your cholesterol con-sumption is to avoid eating foods that are rich in saturated fat, since they generally contain substantial amounts of cholesterol. Whenever possible, you should choose fat-free and low-fat dairy products, and substitute high-quality plant proteins for some of the animal proteins in your diet. Since even small amounts of alcohol can lead to big changes in triglyceride levels, it's important to consume alcohol in moderation. For women, this means drinking no more than one alcoholic beverage each day. Engaging in regular physical activity can lower LDL cholesterol and triglyceride levels and boost HDL levels. If you smoke, quitting will likely result in higher levels of heart-healthy HDL cholesterol as well.

Because high cholesterol typically produces no symptoms, women should have their levels checked periodically, starting no later than age 45. If you have one or more risk factors for cardiovascular disease, you may need to have your cholesterol levels checked earlier in life. Your physician can help you decide on a schedule that is best for you.

What the Results Mean

When physicians order a blood lipid profile, they're checking levels of HDL, LDL, and total cholesterol, as well as the level of triglycerides in the bloodstream. As far as reducing your risk for cardiovascular disease, a total cholesterol level of below 200 milligrams per deciliter (mg/dL) is best. A total cholesterol level between 200 mg/dL and 239 mg/dL is considered to be borderline high, while a level of 240 mg/dL is considered to be high and significantly increases your risk for cardiovascular disease.

As far as LDL cholesterol is concerned, a level below 130 mg/dL is ideal. A level between 130 mg/dL and 159 mg/dL is considered to be borderline high, while a level of 160 mg/dL or greater means that you're at higher risk for cardiovascular disease. If your HDL level is below 40 mg/dL, it's considered to be too low, putting your health at risk. An HDL level of 60 mg/dL or higher is ideal, as it reduces your cardiovascular risk.

A cholesterol profile typically includes a measure of your triglyceride level. A normal level is considered to be one lower than 150 mg/dL, while a result of 150 to 199 mg/dL is considered to be borderline high. A triglyceride reading in the range of 200 to 499 mg/dL is

high, while one greater than 500 mg/dL is classified as very high.

Phase III: High Blood Pressure

High blood pressure, also known as hypertension, is a relatively common problem in the United States, affecting nearly a quarter of American adults. Blood pressure is the force of blood against the arteries measured in millimeters mercury (mm/Hg). It's recorded in two parts: a top and bottom number. The top number reflects the systolic pressure, measured when the heart muscle squeezes, or contracts, to deliver blood throughout the body. The bottom number reflects the diastolic blood pressure, which is measured when the heart muscle relaxes between beats.

A normal blood pressure is considered to be 120/80 mmHg. If your systolic blood pressure usually falls between 120 and 139 mmHg, and your diastolic blood pressure falls between 80 and 89 mmHg, you're considered to have pre-hypertension. If your numbers are usually higher than these, you meet the criteria for a diagnosis of high blood pressure, or hypertension.

When your blood pressure is normal, your heart contracts in an appropriate manner, causing blood to flow through your blood vessels without undue effort. Elevated blood pressure increases the workload of the heart, placing a significant strain on the muscle of the heart and the blood vessels throughout the body. Over time, these vessels can narrow and lose their natural elasticity. When blood vessels grow stiffer and harder, they exert more pressure, and the heart must work even harder to overcome the increasing resistance. High blood pressure not only strains your heart, it also can lead to damage of other organs, including your kidneys, brain, and eyes. Although hypertension is a dangerous and potentially life-threatening condition, you probably won't know that you have it unless you have your blood pressure checked. In most cases, there are no symptoms — that's why high blood pressure is often referred to as the "silent killer."

Many people are under the misconception that having high blood pressure is caused by being tense or nervous, but in reality, in about 90 percent to 95 percent of cases, the cause of the condition is unknown. It is entirely possible for a calm, cool, and collected individual to have abnormally high blood pressure. The only way to know for sure is to have it checked, either at your doctor's office or elsewhere. Many pharmacies make electronic blood pressure cuffs available for their customers, and in this setting, having your blood pressure checked is as simple as sitting down, placing your arm in a cuff, and pressing a button.

Hypertension increases the risk of heart disease and stroke, especially when it's present along with other conditions. If you have high blood pressure and diabetes, a common combination, your risk for cardiovascular disease doubles. If you have high blood pressure and obesity, a smoking habit, or high blood cholesterol levels, the risk of heart attack or stroke is even greater.

There's no quick and easy cure for high blood pressure, but it can be managed. Weight control and regular physical activity are of primary importance. Limiting alcohol consumption to no more than one drink a day and eating a nutritious, plant-based diet low in saturated fat, cholesterol, and salt also helps lower blood pressure. If lifestyle measures aren't sufficient, your physician may recommend taking prescription medication. Keeping your blood pressure within a normal range — and protecting your health from the devastating consequences of uncontrolled hypertension — can be as simple as taking one pill a day.

Phase IV: Diabetes

Diabetes is a disease that affects the way in which the body controls blood sugar. There are two types of diabetes, conveniently dubbed type I and type II. Type I diabetes occurs when the body is incapable of producing insulin, a hormone manufactured by the pancreas, while type II diabetes is the result of the body's inability to use insulin properly.

In healthy people without diabetes, the body transforms food in the diet into glucose, a sugar that supplies energy to the millions of cells throughout the body. To gain access to those cells, glucose must travel through the bloodstream on the coattails of insulin. In individuals with diabetes, the body is either unable to use insulin properly or to manufacture it in the first place. As a result, glucose is denied access into the body's cells and instead accumulates in the bloodstream, often reaching dangerously high levels. Over time, chronically elevated blood sugar can damage cells and tissues, including those of the veins, arteries, and nerves in virtually every part of the body. Because the blood vessels of the eyes, kidneys, heart, and lower limbs are especially vulnerable, diabetes is a leading cause of blindness, heart and kidney disease, and amputation.

Type I diabetes, once called juvenile onset or insulin-dependent diabetes, occurs when the pancreas is rendered incapable of producing insulin, necessitating daily injections of a synthetic form of the hormone for survival. The condition, which typically strikes in childhood, adolescence, or early adulthood, is believed to occur when the immune system of the body attacks and permanently disables the insulin-making cells of the pancreas.

Far more common is type II diabetes, resulting from the body's inability to make enough insulin or to use the insulin that it produces properly, a condition known as insulin resistance. The end result is an elevated blood sugar level and a greater risk for diabetes-related conditions. People with type II diabetes are often able to control their disease with oral medications, although occasionally, insulin injections eventually become necessary. In some cases, type II diabetes may be managed with diet and exercise alone.

In recent years, type II diabetes has become an epidemic in the United States, striking a rapidly growing number of adults. Even more alarming, it is now rampant among our nation's children and teenagers. Type II diabetes tends to creep up on its victims, often taking

years to develop. It is estimated that a third of the people suffering from type II diabetes aren't even aware they have the disease. For this reason, if you have any risk factors for the condition, it is especially important to have your blood sugar tested on a regular basis. Starting at age 45, you should have your blood-glucose levels measured every three years or so, even if you don't have any diabetic symptoms.

Some women should be tested more frequently and earlier in life. If you experience symptoms of the disease, including excessive thirst or hunger, frequent urination, fatigue, or recurrent, slow-to-heal infections, you should be tested immediately. Women who are overweight, have high triglyceride levels, or have a family history of the condition may be advised to have the appropriate blood tests performed annually. Women who developed diabetes during a pregnancy, a condition known as gestational diabetes, will want to keep a close eye on their blood sugar levels continually. Nearly a third of women with gestational diabetes eventually develops type II diabetes later in life.

Ironically, type II diabetes is largely preventable. Although your genes may influence whether you develop type II diabetes in your lifetime, heredity definitely takes a backseat to behavioral and lifestyle factors. About 90 percent of diabetes cases in women can be attributed to five lifestyle factors: excess weight, lack of exercise, smoking, drinking excessive amounts of alcohol, and a diet high in fat, calories, and sugar.

Diet plays a tremendous role in the development of type II diabetes. While excessive consumption of calories, fat, and sugar contributes to the disease, plant-based diets high in fiber and low in fat and sugar reduce the risk of developing type II diabetes. Maintaining a desirable weight is especially important, because excess weight is the single most important risk factor. Being overweight increases your chances of developing the condition seven-fold. Being obese, on the other hand, makes you 20 to 40 times more likely to develop type II diabetes than someone of normal weight.

Not only does losing excess weight reduce the risk of developing diabetes, it also is critical to managing the condition successfully. Studies show that losing just 10 pounds and walking a half hour most days of the week can reduce the risk of developing type II diabetes by nearly 60 percent.

Increasing physical activity also can lower your risk. When you're actively working your muscles, you're improving their ability to use insulin and absorb glucose properly. When you allow your muscles to be idle much of the time, you diminish their ability to use insulin and glucose effectively and dramatically increase your risk of developing type II diabetes.

Phase V: Breast Cancer

Many women fear breast cancer more than heart disease or stroke, even though the latter two are much more pervasive than all forms of cancer combined. Still, breast cancer represents a very real risk to our health: It is second only to lung cancer as a cause of cancer deaths in American women. Each year in the United States, more than 200,000 women develop the disease.

With recent advances in diagnostic tests and cancer treatments, women with breast cancer, especially detected in the early stages, have every reason to be optimistic. More women with breast cancer are not only beating the disease and surviving but also continuing to live rich and productive lives.

Signs and Symptoms

Recognizing the signs and symptoms of breast cancer can help save your life. When diagnosed early, women with breast cancer have a wider variety of treatment options and a far better chance of being cured.

Although the vast majority of breast lumps aren't cancerous, the most common sign of breast cancer is a lump or a thickened area in the breast. In many cases, the lump is painless, and it may be accompanied by a change in the size or shape of the breast. Other signs of breast cancer include flattening or indentation of the skin, redness, or pitting of the skin, similar to the pitting of an orange peel. Clear or bloody discharge from the nipple or a retraction or indentation of the nipple may also be warning signs. If you discover a lump or any of the other warning signs of breast cancer, it's important to discuss these changes with your doctor as soon as possible.

Risk Factors for Breast Cancer

In women with breast cancer, some of the

cells in the breast begin dividing more rapidly than they should and growing abnormally. The most common type of breast cancer begins in the milk-producing ducts, but cancer may occur in various types of tissues anywhere in the breast. In most cases, it isn't known exactly what triggers abnormal cell growth and division in breast cancer.

Inherited genetic mutations cause between 5 percent and 10 percent of breast cancers. Defects in one of two genes, known as breast cancer gene 1 (BRCA1) or breast cancer gene 2 (BRCA2), not only elevate the risk of developing breast cancer but also increase the risk of developing ovarian cancer. In most women, these genes help ward off cancer by manufacturing proteins that prevent cells from growing abnormally, but when these genes are affected by a mutation, they aren't able to offer full protection against cancer.

Most genetic mutations related to breast cancer aren't inherited but rather develop over time. These mutations may be the result of exposure to radiation or other cancer-causing agents. Exposure to carcinogens called polycyclic aromatic hydrocarbons in tobacco and charred red meats also increases the risk of developing breast cancer. A woman who received radiation treatments of the chest as a child or young adult is more likely to develop breast cancer later.

Every woman's chances of developing breast cancer increase with age. Women younger than 25 rarely develop the disease; and nearly 80 percent of breast cancers occur in women over 50. At age 40, you have about a one in 250 chance of developing the condition, but by the time you're 85, your chance is one in eight. Women with a mother, sister, or daughter with breast or ovarian cancer have greater chances of developing the disease. The more relatives you have that are affected, the higher your risk. If, for example, you have a close relative with the disease, your risk is doubled, and if you have two or more relatives with breast cancer, your risk is even greater.

A relationship between excess weight and breast cancer is known to exist, but it is complex and not yet fully understood. In general, carrying excess weight increases your risk. If you've gained the extra weight as an adult, especially after menopause, your risk for breast cancer is greater. Where women carry their excess weight also influences the risk of developing breast cancer. The risk is higher if fat is stored predominantly in the upper body, around the chest and abdomen, as opposed to the lower body, around the hips and thighs.

Exposure to estrogen, which begins in earnest with your first menstrual period and dramatically slacks off following menopause, also increases the chances of developing breast cancer. The longer you're exposed to the hormone, the greater your risk. If, for example, you had your first menstrual period before the age of 12, and you experienced menopause after the age of 55, you have a slightly higher risk of developing breast cancer than women who started their periods later in life and experienced menopause before age 55. Women who have never had children or had a first pregnancy at the age of 35 or older also have a greater risk than women who became pregnant when they were younger.

While exposure to your body's natural estrogen can increase your risk of developing breast cancer, exposure to estrogen and progestin in hormone therapy also can increase the risk. Although hormone therapy was once considered the standard treatment for menopausal symptoms, recent research reveals the risks of taking the medication on a long-term basis outweigh the benefits. Women taking hormone therapy consisting of estrogen plus progestin are known to have a slightly higher risk of developing breast cancer than women not taking the medication.

Women who consume more than one alcoholic drink a day have about a 20 percent greater risk of breast cancer than women who don't consume alcohol at all. The National Cancer Institute recommends that women limit alcohol intake to a maximum of one drink daily.

Screening

Unless you have a family history of cancer or other factors that place you at high risk for breast cancer, the American Cancer Society recommends having clinical breast exams performed by a physician once every three years until you reach age 40. Afterward, a yearly exam is recommended. While these examinations are useful and important, the screening mammogram is currently the best imaging technique for detecting tumors before you or your doctor can feel them. All women over age 40 should have screening mammograms annually.

Phase VI: Menopause

Because menopause can produce a wide variety of disturbing symptoms, it can significantly interfere with your enjoyment of your horse and your riding. It's hard to focus on the finer points of horsemanship when you're besieged by hot flashes. If menopausal symptoms are making life difficult for you — and in turn for your horse — be sure to discuss them with your doctor. A number of treatment options are available, and one of them might help make you feel more like yourself again.

No matter how prepared you think you are for the change of life, menopause still can sneak up on you. Menopause, which occurs when the ovaries' production of the female hormone estrogen begins to diminish, is defined as the absence of menstruation for one year. This definition is a source of great frustration to many women, as the diagnosis can only be made in retrospect. Fortunately, most women are so sufficiently in tune with their bodies that they don't need anyone to tell them that they're going through the change of life. If you're around age 50, you've ceased menstruating, and you're experiencing hot flashes, the diagnosis of menopause is a shoo-in. Still, if you are uncertain or have questions, your doctor can help provide answers.

Before declaring you menopausal, your physician will likely consider several factors, including your age, symptoms, and the result of blood tests that measure hormone levels.

Because menopause is merely a normal stage of life rather than an illness or a disease, you may opt to deal with the hot flashes, night sweats, fatigue, and other symptoms without the help of pills or potions. This strategy is fine, as long as your symptoms are tolerable. If, on the other hand, your symptoms interfere with riding and other activities that are important to you, there's no reason to be a menopausal martyr. One of several prescription medications or natural remedies might be worth taking until your menopause-related miseries subside.

Less than a decade ago, the quick and easy solution for easing menopausal symptoms came in the form of a prescription for hormone therapy, usually consisting of estrogen and progestin. Of all the menopausal remedies, estrogen has consistently proven itself the most effective in symptom relief. As a result, hormone therapy was one of the most commonly used medical regimens in the United States, prescribed to an estimated 38 percent of postmenopausal women in 2000.

That percentage took a hard nosedive in 2002 after data from the now famous Women's Health Initiative (WHI) study were released. Of the women enrolled in the study, those taking estrogen plus progestin were found to have an increased risk of developing breast cancer within just three years of starting the regimen. The WHI study also soundly disproved the long-held theory that hormone therapy reduces a woman's risk for heart disease. In fact, estrogen plus progestin was shown to boost the risk of cardiovascular disease in postmenopausal women. So compelling were the findings supporting the negative effects of hormone therapy that women enrolled in the WHI study were taken off the medication earlier than scheduled. Researchers felt it would be unethical to allow women to continue taking the drugs, as the risks clearly outweighed the benefits.

In April 2007, the results of secondary analyses of findings from the Women's Health Initiative were released. After reanalyzing previously collected data, scientists concluded that the risk of developing heart disease related to hormone therapy varies, depending on a woman's age and the number of years that have passed since the onset of menopause.

Women who begin taking hormone therapy within 10 years of experiencing menopause appear to have a lower risk of developing heart disease due to hormone therapy than women who begin taking it 15 or 20 years after the onset of menopause. Even after reanalyzing the data, researchers still agree that hormone therapy offers no overall benefit for prevention of heart disease.

Based on the WHI findings, hormone therapy is now cautiously recommended for short-term relief of menopausal symptoms. Fortunately, there are a few alternative prescription medications that your doctor may recommend for relief of hot flashes, insomnia, and fatigue. In addition, you can choose one of dozens of nutritional supplements designed to alleviate menopausal symptoms, although scientific evidence supporting their effectiveness is limited.

Herbal Help for Menopausal Symptoms

One of the most popular natural remedies for menopause is an herbal preparation of the black cohosh root. In the body, black cohosh has been shown to behave like a weak estrogen and is reported to relieve many menopausal symptoms, including hot flashes and irritability.

When taken as directed, the herb is generally well tolerated, with stomach upset being the most common side effect. In higher doses, it can be hazardous to your health, causing dizziness, nausea, and headaches. Because the long-term effects of black cohosh aren't known, most experts recommend taking it for six months or less, allowing a few weeks or months between uses.

Chasteberry is another herb frequently used for treating menopausal symptoms, although it is generally believed to be less effective than black cohosh. The plant medicine appears to be safe for women taking the recommended doses, but at higher doses, skin rashes may develop.

For centuries Chinese women have used the herb dong quai to promote the health of the female reproductive tract. Dong quai seems to have pain-relieving effects on the uterus and may act as a mild laxative and diuretic. When taken alone, the herb doesn't appear to be especially effective in relieving hot flashes and night sweats, but it is believed to complement other herbs in natural preparations designed for menopausal women. When taken in moderation, dong quai appears to be safe, but because it can increase your skin's sensitivity to the sun, it's a good idea to wear sunscreen.

The herb ginseng is often included in natural preparations for menopause, as its estrogen-like behavior in the body is thought to help alleviate many menopausal symptoms. Ginseng also is known to exert a stimulant effect, which makes it useful in combating the fatigue that frequently accompanies menopause. While taking the recommended dose may help invigorate you, taking excessive amounts can lead to insomnia.

Licorice root is reported to reduce hot flashes and irritability in menopausal women and is included in many natural menopause remedies. The herb contains plant compounds that mimic the effects of estrogen in the body. At recommended doses, licorice root may safely alleviate some of the symptoms of menopause, but it can be deadly in high doses. When taken in excess, licorice root can lead to dangerous elevations in blood pressure and serious heart problems.

Vitamin E isn't an herb, but results of a few small studies have shown it to relieve hot flashes. On a molecular level, vitamin E is structurally similar to estrogen, and this similarity may account for its beneficial effects.

Soy products are rich in phytoestrogens, plant substances similar to human estrogen. Although the effects of soy foods have been examined in numerous studies, the results are conflicting. While soy products may offer minor relief of menopausal symptoms and a small measure of protection against osteoporosis and heart disease, there is some speculation that they may actually trigger cancers of the reproductive tract in women. In any case, most women in the United States simply don't eat enough soy products to derive either major benefits or major risks to their health. If you're thinking about taking a soy supplement for the relief of menopausal symptoms, be sure to talk it over with your physician ahead of time.

With or without prescription medications or herbal remedies, the majority of your menopausal symptoms will eventually be gone. Menopause is like a mini-marathon — you'll feel much better once you've crossed the finish line. Remember, no matter how unwelcome menopausal symptoms may be, they can serve as an excellent wake-up call. If you've been thinking about making some positive, much-needed changes in your diet and exercise habits, there's no better time than now. It's also a great time to see your doctor for a head-to-toe check up.

Phase VII: Osteoporosis

Improving your diet and increasing your activity not only help prevent heart disease and diabetes but also protect your bones, especially as you grow older. A healthy skeleton is a must-have for every horsewoman, given the fact that she regularly faces the very real possibility of sustaining bumps, bruises, and falls.

As a young adult, you might not have given your bones much thought. After all, they seem like pretty permanent structures, and they make a nice hanger for your skin. In reality, bones have many vital functions. In addition to providing a structural framework for the body, they're also responsible for the production of blood cells, and they store important minerals.

Bones are metabolically active, just like your organs, including your muscles, kidneys, and liver. Living bone tissue is constantly being broken down and rebuilt, and if you're an active young adult and have adequate amounts of calcium and vitamin D in your diet, the remodeled bone is as good as new. Sometime around your mid-30s, however, your bones reach their maximum size and strength, a condition referred to as peak bone mass. At this point, your body stops adding mass to your bones and simply works to maintain the mass it has accumulated. If you don't get plenty of regular exercise or if your diet is lacking in vitamin D or calcium, the rate of bone destruction may exceed the rate of reconstruction, and your bones may begin to thin and weaken.

Menopause worsens the problem. The female hormone estrogen is partly responsible for maintaining the delicate balance between bone destruction and reconstruction. With the estrogen deficiency that occurs at menopause or after the surgical removal of the ovaries, bones begin to break down a bit more than they build up. Because the mineral loss from bones is accelerated, the skeleton becomes progressively weaker and thinner. This condition, known as osteoporosis, leaves bones brittle and easily fractured, even by minor bumps and bangs.

Osteoporosis affects more than a third of all postmenopausal women, and those over age 50 have a 50 percent chance of sustaining an osteoporosis-related bone fracture at some point in their lives. As a woman, you're much more likely to suffer a debilitating fracture than a heart attack, stroke, or breast cancer. If you're unfortunate enough to suffer a hip fracture, you have a 50 percent chance of becoming severely disabled. Women with osteoporosis who fracture a hip have a 10 percent to 20 percent chance of dying in the year following the fracture, and fewer than half are able to regain their previous level of mobility and independence. For this reason, prevention and treatment of osteoporosis are critical.

Are you at risk for osteoporosis? If you're a postmenopausal woman, the answer is yes. Caucasian women are at greater risk than African-Americans, as are women who have diabetes or a petite bone structure, and those who have never had children. Smoking, drinking alcohol, and maintaining a sedentary lifestyle and a diet deficient in calcium or vitamin D also heighten your risk. Although lifestyle choices are important, the greatest risk factor for osteoporosis is the estrogen deficiency that accompanies menopause. In the first five years following menopause, a woman may experience as much as a third of her lifetime bone loss.

In the past, there was very little women could do to stop the progression of osteoporosis. Fortunately, the development of new prescription drugs has made it possible to slow, or even reverse, bone loss in menopausal women. These drugs work by slowing or stopping the destruction of bone tissue while promoting rebuilding. In women currently diagnosed with osteoporosis, these medications can significantly reduce the risk of sustaining a debilitating bone fracture.

As devastating as osteoporosis can be, there are very few warning signs. For many women, a broken bone may be the first hint of trouble. To find out if you have the condition, your doctor can order a painless, non-invasive diagnostic test to determine your bone mineral density. Using X-rays or ultrasound technology to measure the thickness of your bones, the test can help your physician evaluate the soundness of your skeleton.

The Role of Calcium in Osteoporosis

Although osteoporosis typically doesn't strike women until the fifth decade of life, it's never too early to start taking good care of your skeleton. Boning up on your calcium is one of the most important steps. While the typical American diet provides only about 600 mg of calcium a day, your body needs far more to keep your bones in good shape. Most healthy adult women require at least 1,000 mg daily, and menopausal women should aim for an intake of about 1,500 mg a day.

While calcium supplements are helpful, eating a diet naturally rich in the mineral is your best bet. In most cases, calcium from food sources is better absorbed and metabolized by the human body. Dairy products, including the reduced-fat varieties, are loaded with calcium, as are dried beans, sardines, and broccoli. You'll want to include several servings of these foods in your daily diet.

Just getting enough calcium in your diet doesn't necessarily mean that your body will use the mineral to your skeleton's advantage

— you have to give it a reason. Engaging in regular, weight-bearing exercise, such as walking, jogging, strength training, or just working around the barn is usually all it takes to stimulate calcium absorption and utilization.

The Role of Vitamin D in Osteoporosis

While adequate calcium intake has long been considered the cornerstone of bone health, vitamin D is also important because the body requires it to use calcium effectively. Vitamin D allows calcium to leave the intestine and enter the bloodstream, and it also works in the kidneys to help absorb calcium that would otherwise be excreted from the body.

Although the National Academy of Sciences has not established a recommended daily allowance for vitamin D, the organization has specified "adequate intakes" of the vitamin for healthy adults. Women ages 19 to 50 are advised to obtain at least 200 international units (IU) of vitamin D daily while those ages 51 to 70 should strive for an intake of 400 IU per day. For women ages 71 and older, the adequate daily intake of vitamin D is considered to be 600 IU. Although these dosages are likely adequate for good health, newer evidence suggests that menopausal women should aim for a daily vitamin D intake of at least 800 IU to lower fracture risk. While the ideal dose is still being determined, it's safe to take up to 2,000 IU daily.

Vitamin D is manufactured in the skin following direct exposure to sunlight. The amount produced in the skin varies, depending on a number of sun-related factors, including time of day, season, and latitude. Your skin pigmentation also affects vitamin D production: The fairer you are, the more you make. In most cases, getting 10 to 15 minutes of sun exposure on the face, arms, hands, or back two to three times each week is enough to satisfy the body's requirement for vitamin D. Darker-skinned women may not derive this benefit, and wearing sunscreen can interfere with the absorption of sunlight necessary to manufacture vitamin D.

To boost your intake, you can turn to foods like vitamin D-fortified dairy products, egg yolks, saltwater fish, cod liver oil, and liver. From dietary sources alone, it's relatively difficult to exceed the safe upper limit of 2,000 IU of vitamin D per day.

While you're increasing your intake of vitamin D- and calcium-containing foods, it's important to refrain from smoking, which increases your chances of developing osteoporosis, and to limit your consumption of alcohol and caffeine-containing beverages. Drinking more than two alcoholic beverages a day can decrease bone formation and interfere with your body's ability to absorb calcium. While enjoying a couple of cups of coffee every day won't turn your bones to dust, regularly drinking too many caffeinated beverages can hinder calcium absorption. As long as you're getting an adequate amount of calcium in your diet, you can drink two to three cups of coffee or other caffeinated beverages a day without sabotaging your skeleton.

Phase VIII: Osteoarthritis

Osteoarthritis is a common condition that can make riding difficult, or even impossible. It is the leading cause of disability and activity limitation among American adults. In the face of increasing life expectancy, it's likely that osteoarthritis will soon become the most prevalent and expensive disease in our aging society. In most cases, the disease makes its presence known in middle age, and by age 70, nearly every woman will be affected.

Osteoarthritis is a disease of the joints, affecting mainly the fingers, hips, and knees. Normally, the bones that form these joints are separated and cushioned by a layer of healthy cartilage. When osteoarthritis is present, the cartilage begins to disintegrate. The process may take decades to evolve, but, eventually, the cartilage may become so damaged that the bones grind against each other, causing considerable pain.

Several factors are involved in the development of osteoarthritis. It's likely that your genes set the stage for the condition, and then joint stress or injury sets the process in motion. Obesity is strongly linked to osteoarthritis, especially in the knees and hips. People who are overweight as young adults have a good chance of developing the condition as they grow older.

Once you develop osteoarthritis, it's yours for life. Most people with the condition suffer some degree of joint pain, which is usually described as a deep, dull ache. The pain tends to wax and wane throughout the day, worsening with joint use and improving with rest. Nighttime discomfort or joint pain that persists during rest usually indicates the disease is advanced. Stiffness is another common problem, usually lasting for about a half hour after awakening. Sitting still can cause the stiffness to return, but it usually disappears after a few minutes of activity. As the disease progresses, the diseased joints may become deformed and debilitated.

As there's no cure for osteoarthritis, prevention is especially important. If you're overweight and you don't currently have the condition, losing just 12 pounds can reduce your chances of developing it by 50 percent. Every pound lost can have a dramatic effect, since the weight carried by the knee during walking is equivalent to approximately three times your body weight. Losing 5 pounds can lead to the equivalent of a 15-pound reduction in the weight on the knee, significantly reducing joint stress and pain. In addition to weight loss, regular activity can help alleviate pain and improve the function of affected joints. Drinking plenty of water each day is also important for the health of your joints. Water is a major component of cartilage, and when properly hydrated, cartilage can change shape in response to movement and stress.

Natural supplements, such as glucosamine and chondroitin sulfate, have been touted as cures for arthritis. Some evidence suggests glucosamine can stimulate growth of cartilage, and chondroitin sulfate may protect cartilage. In spite of these attributes, neither supplement can cure the disease. Eating a diet rich in antioxidants, including beta-carotene and vitamins C and E, may help prevent or slow the progression of osteoarthritis. Some studies have found a significant reduction in the progression of osteoarthritis of the knee in people with high intakes of antioxidants. Vitamin D also may have a protective effect on the joints. Recent research indicates progression of osteoarthritis is markedly accelerated in people with low intakes of the vitamin.

Phase IX: Depression

No matter how much you love riding and being around your horse, depression can make going to the barn seem like drudgery. If you think you're suffering from depression, getting help from your physician as soon as possible is critically important because the condition rarely goes away on its own.

Depression isn't the same as feeling a little blue on occasion. As you journey through life, you'll undoubtedly experience sadness from time to time, and in most cases these feelings will be perfectly normal. Feeling a little low or down in the dumps every once in a while is to be expected. Being depressed, on the other hand, is not something you should accept as a natural part of life.

Although the exact biochemical changes that occur with depression aren't completely understood, it is thought that the condition results from an imbalance of neurochemicals in the brain. When you don't have enough of the "feel good" types of neurochemicals or when your brain doesn't respond to them normally you may become depressed. While depression can be hereditary, it is commonly linked to stressful life events, including the death of a loved one, an illness, a divorce, or the loss of a job.

Women are nearly twice as likely to develop depression as men. About 20 percent to 25 percent of women will experience depression at least once in their lives, compared to just 7 percent to 12 percent of men. The gender gap first appears during adolescence and then peaks during the menopausal period.

In spite of common misconceptions to the contrary, depression isn't a sign of weakness nor is it a personality flaw. People with the condition aren't able to just "shake it off" or "get over it," no matter how hard they might try. Fortunately, depression can be treated, just like other medical conditions, including diabetes and high blood pressure. If your doctor diagnoses you with depression, she'll probably offer you a prescription antidepressant medication, with the goal of correcting the chemical imbalances in your brain and alleviating your symptoms. Your job is to take the medication as prescribed. You may not experience the maximum beneficial effects of the drug for a couple of weeks, or even a month or two, so it's important not to give up on your medication — or yourself — before it's had a chance to work. Most doctors recommend continuing the medication for at least six months, even if your symptoms improve in the first couple of weeks of treatment.

Once you feel more like yourself, try to engage in some sort of enjoyable physical activity, such as riding, as often as possible. Exercise triggers the release of endorphins in the body, and these compounds are known to elevate mood and promote a sense of well-being.

Phase X: Premenstrual Syndrome

If you believe that you have premenstrual syndrome, you're probably right. For years, the monthly monster known as premenstrual syndrome — or PMS for those on a first-name basis with the condition — was dismissed as nothing more than an ugly figment of an over-active female imagination. Although the sci-entific community has only recently acknowl-edged the condition, PMS sufferers have always known that it is very real and, furthermore, can make life miserable at times.

Now that physicians have seen the light, PMS has achieved the status of a respectable medi-cal disorder. Although the actual prevalence of the condition is unknown, an estimated 75 percent of women report regularly experienc-ing PMS symptoms. More than a third of these women have symptoms severe enough to dis-rupt their daily lives, and about 7 percent have a form of PMS so disabling that it has earned its own psychiatric designation: premenstrual dysphoric disorder, or PMDD for short.

If you suffer premenstrual miseries, you've probably learned to brace yourself for the onslaught of physical and emotional changes that strike the week before your period. Moods can turn on a dime, and within the space of 24 hours, you may experience a bewildering array of emotions ranging from weepy despair to rip-roaring rage. You may have trouble concentrat-ing and remembering, and fatigue, food crav-ings, and sleep disturbances only make matters worse. Constipation, abdominal bloating, and ankle swelling are also part of PMS.

It's important to remember that PMS isn't all in your head, and it certainly isn't your fault. If you think about it, it's not surprising that women have so many physical and emotional changes during or around the time of their periods. Menstruation is a time of complete hormonal upheaval, and the hormones doing all the up-heaving have major impacts on the female brain, as well on the body.

Although you may not have signed up for PMS, it's yours to deal with. You can let it rob you of a week of your life every month of the year until you hit menopause, or you can take steps to make life more pleasant for your-self — and possibly the horses and humans around you. The best strategy to relieve PMS symptoms is one that involves a few simple lifestyle changes. Engaging in regular exercise and adopting a sensible, nutritious diet are important first steps. Physical activity regulates blood-sugar levels, boosts energy, and helps keep you from feeling down in the dumps.

Although you may find yourself longing for foods loaded with simple carbohydrates, such as chips, cookies, and candy, it's better to avoid them. Foods rich in fiber and complex carbohy-drates, such as whole grains, cereals, and veg-etables, help keep your moods on an even keel because they boost levels of the mood-elevating brain chemical serotonin. It's also a good idea to hold the salt around the time of your period. Too much salt in the diet elevates sodium levels in the bloodstream, where it attracts and holds water in your body like a sponge.

While you're steering clear of salt and simple-carbohydrate foods, you might also want to give alcohol a wide berth around the time of your period. Alcohol may seem to make you feel better in the short-term, but, in reality, it can worsen fatigue and deepen a blue mood. As caffeine can contribute to breast tenderness, anxiety, and fatigue, you also should consider going easy on the coffee and colas for a week or so around your period.

Some evidence suggests that adding a few key vitamins and minerals to your diet can banish the symptoms of PMS. Many women experience a reduction in PMS symptoms when they take 400 IU of vitamin E each day. Vitamin E may dampen the effects of prostaglandins, the hormone-like chemicals that are blamed for many PMS-related miseries, including irritability, breast tenderness, and bloating.

Calcium has been shown to improve symptoms of PMS. One study found that women who took a daily supplement of 1,200 mg of chewable calcium carbonate experienced a 50 percent reduction in most of their PMS symptoms by the third month of treatment.

Another study found that taking 200 mg of magnesium daily reduced PMS symptoms by 40 percent. Magnesium seems especially beneficial in reducing uterine cramping, pain, and bloating. Vitamin B-6 may be another nutrient worth taking. Recent research suggests that the vitamin reduces PMS-related fatigue, insomnia, and irritability.

If lifestyle changes and supplements don't ease your suffering, your doctor might be able to help. Relief often comes in the form of a pill — the Pill, to be exact. Oral contraceptives help regulate menstrual cycles and reduce your body's state of hormonal upheaval. If you don't like the idea of taking hormones to control your hormones — or your PMS symptoms — antidepressant drugs belonging to the selective serotonin reuptake inhibitor (SSRI) class may seem like a better solution. These drugs have been shown to cut PMS symptoms in half in most of the women who take them.

Although there are no surefire diagnostic tests for PMS, a litany of symptoms may be all your physician requires to recognize the condition. Keeping a monthly diary of your symptoms will help your doctor make the correct diagnosis, and, more importantly, to recommend the most effective treatment for you.

Phase XI: Overweight and Obesity

Being overweight is a condition that not only affects you but also affects your horse. In addition to making riding uncomfortable, excess weight can make riding effectively very difficult.

If you're carrying a few extra pounds, you're in very good company. More than 60 percent of American women are currently overweight or obese, and this percentage is expected to continue to rise in the coming years. As women, we often tend to think of obesity as a cosmetic issue, but, in reality, it is a tremendous threat to our health. Obesity is responsible for more than 300,000 preventable deaths in the United States each year, second only to cigarette smoking, which causes approximately 400,000 preventable deaths annually.

In addition to causing physical harm, obesity inflicts a large measure of emotional suffering. In a culture in which thinness is equated with beauty, intelligence, success, and a number of other positive attributes, carrying even a few extra pounds can cause virtually any woman to feel unattractive at one time or another, and it can wreak havoc with her happiness and self-esteem. It's important to remember that your weight is not — by any stretch of the imagination — a measure of your worth. Beautiful, smart, hard-working, talented, and successful women come in all shapes and sizes.

Although your weight is not a reflection of your character, it is a reasonably good predictor of your current and future health, and even your longevity. Emotional issues aside, being overweight isn't good for you. Carrying even 15 extra pounds can significantly increase your risk of developing more than 30 different diseases. While all of these obesity-related conditions are capable of dramatically reducing your enjoyment of riding and other activities, many of them can actually end your life.

Most of us don't need a high-tech diagnostic tool to know if we're overweight: A hard look in the mirror is usually all it takes. Physicians, on the other hand, prefer to use a more scientific approach when diagnosing a weight problem

or obesity, and most use a tool called the body mass index on the following page. Body mass index, or BMI for short, plots your weight against your height to determine if you are of normal weight, overweight, or obese. It's also used to determine whether your weight is putting your health at risk.

While the BMI is a useful tool, it isn't entirely foolproof. For starters, it doesn't take into account the muscle-to-fat ratio of your body. If you're a large-framed, muscle-bound athlete, you could end up being classified as "overweight" on the basis of BMI, when in fact your buff bod doesn't have an ounce of excess body fat. If on the other hand, you haven't exercised a lick since the last physical education class of your senior year in high school, your body might contain far more flab than muscle, and you could still end up scoring a normal BMI. In spite of these shortcomings, the BMI is usually sufficient to assess the weight status of the vast majority of women.

By current standards, the optimal BMI for good health falls in the range of 19 to 21 for women. If your BMI is a little higher, don't panic. Any woman with a BMI of 18.5 to 24.9 is still considered to be of normal weight. If your BMI falls in the range of 25 to 29, you're considered to be overweight, and if your BMI is 30 or greater, you meet the criteria for obesity. If this is the case, it's time to get serious about your diet and exercise program.

In general, a BMI of 24 or lower is consistent with good health as it relates to weight while a BMI of 27 or greater is associated with a

BODY MASS INDEX CHART

DETERMINING YOUR BODY MASS INDEX (BMI). To determine your BMI, find your height in the left-hand column, and then move across the row to find your weight. Your BMI is listed in the top row above the point that these two numbers intersect.

IF YOUR BMI IS:	YOUR WEIGHT STATUS IS:
18.5 to 24.9	Normal
25 to 29.9	Overweight
30 or greater	Obese

BMI	19	20	21	22	23	24	25	26	27	28	29	30	31	32	33	34	35
HEIGHT (inches)							**BODY WEIGHT** (pounds)										
58	91	96	100	105	110	115	119	124	129	134	138	143	148	153	158	162	167
59	94	99	104	109	114	119	124	128	133	138	143	148	153	158	163	168	173
60	97	102	107	112	118	123	128	133	138	143	148	153	158	163	168	174	179
61	100	106	111	116	122	127	132	137	143	148	153	158	164	169	174	180	185
62	104	109	115	120	126	131	136	142	147	153	158	164	169	175	180	186	191
63	107	113	118	124	130	135	141	146	152	158	163	169	175	180	186	191	197
64	110	116	122	128	134	140	145	151	157	163	169	174	180	186	192	197	204
65	114	120	126	132	138	144	150	156	162	168	174	180	186	192	198	204	210
66	118	124	130	136	142	148	155	161	167	173	179	186	192	198	204	210	216
67	121	127	134	140	146	153	159	166	172	178	185	191	198	204	211	217	223
68	125	131	138	144	151	158	164	171	177	184	180	197	203	210	216	223	230
69	128	135	142	149	155	162	169	176	182	189	196	203	209	216	223	230	236
70	132	139	146	153	160	167	174	181	188	195	202	209	216	222	229	236	243
71	136	143	150	157	165	172	179	186	193	200	208	215	222	229	236	243	250
72	140	147	154	162	169	177	184	191	199	206	213	221	228	235	242	250	258
73	144	151	159	166	174	182	189	197	204	212	219	227	235	242	250	257	265
74	148	155	163	171	179	186	194	202	210	218	225	233	241	249	256	264	272
75	152	160	168	176	184	192	200	208	216	224	232	240	248	256	264	272	279
76	156	164	172	180	189	197	205	213	221	230	238	246	254	263	271	279	287

significantly higher risk of developing dozens of debilitating medical conditions, including type II diabetes, heart disease, stroke, and some types of cancer.

Body Shape Matters, Too

For women, excess body fat is undoubtedly a health hazard, but the location of that fat may be the best predictor of future health risks. A growing body of research suggests that the larger a woman's waist becomes, the greater her risk for developing many deadly diseases. As unglamorous as it may seem, all women can be categorized as either pear-shaped or apple-shaped, depending upon where they tend to accumulate body fat. Women who store excess fat around their waists are said to have apple-shaped bodies, because like the fruit, their weight collects around their middles. Women who tend to deposit fat around their hips, buttocks, and thighs, on the other hand, are said to have pear-shaped bodies, because like pears, they are widest at the bottom.

How do you know which fruit you most resemble? The answer lies in a measurement called the waist-to-hip ratio (WHR). To determine your WHR, all you need is a tape measure and a calculator. Start by standing erect and measuring your waist at a point about one inch above your navel. Next, measure your hips by placing the tape measure around your buttocks. To determine your WHR, divide your waist measurement by your hip measurement.

If your WHR is .80 or less, your body can be classified as pear shaped. If your WHR is higher than .80, your body shape falls into the apple category. To a large degree, the shape of your body determines which type of fat you'll accumulate when you gain weight.

Body fat comes in two main varieties: subcutaneous fat, which lies just under the skin, and visceral fat, which lies deep in the torso, surrounding the organs in the abdomen. While pear-shaped women tend to have more subcutaneous fat, apple-shaped women tend to have more visceral fat.

Subcutaneous fat is the soft fat you can pinch with your fingers. It's stuff that jiggles when you move. This type of fat may be visible and annoying, but as far as your health is concerned, it is relatively harmless. Some of it, in fact, is necessary for good health. Excessive visceral fat is another story: It can be hazardous to your health.

Visceral fat is packed away in the abdomen, so it isn't always visible from the outside. This type of fat acts like a gland with a self-serving agenda, and most of its actions are harmful to the body.

After collecting information about the health of more than 120,000 women for nearly three decades, researchers involved in the Nurses' Health Study identified a strong link between body shape, fat distribution, and certain medical conditions. While pear-shaped women appeared to be more likely to develop osteoporosis after menopause, the apple-shaped women in the study were found to be more susceptible to diabetes, stroke, and heart disease.

Subcutaneous body fat that collects around

the hips, thighs, and buttocks of pear-shaped women has been shown to increase levels of high-density lipoprotein (HDL), the "good" type of cholesterol that helps fend off heart disease. In apple-shaped women, excess visceral fat works to increase levels of unfriendly fats, including triglycerides and low-density lipoprotein (LDL), while it lowers levels of heart-healthy HDL cholesterol. Regardless of total body weight, research shows that apple-shaped women have triple the risk of heart disease of pear-shaped women.

Apple-shaped women are also significantly more likely to develop diabetes. Unlike sub-cutaneous fat, visceral fat reduces a woman's sensitivity to insulin, the hormone responsible for maintaining normal blood sugar levels.

Pear-shaped women have their own health risks to contend with. With less metabolically active visceral fat around their midsections, they produce lower levels of bone-strengthening hormones, putting them at greater risk for developing osteoporosis after menopause than apple-shaped women. While pear-shaped women have some protection against heart disease and diabetes, their risk of developing these conditions increases with every inch they add to their midsections. Conversely, losing

---

KEY RECOMMENDED SCREENING EXAMS FOR WOMEN

AGE 18

If you've ever had a sexual relationship, you should begin having annual Pap smears to screen for cervical cancer. Plan on having a Pap smear every year, unless your physician recommends otherwise. Each time you visit your physician's office, you should have your blood pressure checked to screen for hypertension. Weighing in regularly is also important, as it allows your doctor to determine if your body mass index (BMI) is within the normal range.

AGE 40

Although some women will begin having mammograms earlier in life, almost every woman should receive annual mammograms after age 40. Mammograms can reveal breast changes that may be indicative of breast cancer, even before they're noticeable to you during self-examinations or to your doctor during clinical breast exams.

KEY RECOMMENDED SCREENING EXAMS FOR WOMEN

AGE 45

At no later than age 45, you should have your doctor take a blood sample and obtain a fasting lipid profile to make sure that your cholesterol levels are within normal limits, because abnormally high levels increase your risk of developing cardiovascular disease. In this screening blood test, total cholesterol, low-density lipoprotein (LDL), high-density lipoprotein (HDL), and triglycerides are measured. At the same time, your physician will likely check your blood sugar to screen for diabetes.

AGE 50

Even if you're healthy and don't have a family history of colorectal cancer, you should be screened for the disease beginning no later than age 50. Diagnostic tests include a rectal exam and collection of a stool smear for occult (hidden) blood, a sigmoidoscopy, or a colonoscopy. The latter two examinations involve inserting a thin, flexible tube equipped with a light and a tiny camera into the intestinal tract via the rectum.

AGE 65

As long as you don't have any signs, symptoms, or outstanding risk factors for osteo-porosis, your doctor may wait until you're 65 to begin screening you for bone loss. If you're younger than 65 and feel that you're at risk for the disease, be sure to ask your physician about having a screening test sooner.

---

just two inches from the midsection has been shown to lower total cholesterol levels and blood pressure, and to reduce the risk of heart disease and diabetes significantly. While it is always a good idea to keep an eye on your weight, it's just as important to monitor the size of your waist. Keeping your waist circum-ference below 35 inches is an excellent way to protect your body from a number of serious diseases and to increase your chances of living a long and healthy life.

Losing excess weight is by no means the easiest task you'll undertake, but it is certainly possible for virtually every woman who is determined to make changes in her diet and activity level. Following the Riding for Life diet, featured in Chapter 4, can help you lose excess weight. Because it is a low-fat, plant-based diet rich in wholesome foods, fiber, and important nutrients, it also can help improve your overall health.

Avoid Tetanus — Get the Vaccine

At various stages in your life, your doctor may advise you to be vaccinated against one of several illnesses, including influenza or pneumonia. As a horsewoman who spends time tromping around barns, paddocks, and pastures, one vaccine that is especially important for you is the tetanus vaccine. Although it's highly unlikely that you'll ever contract tetanus, or "lockjaw" as it's commonly known, it is critical that you take steps to protect yourself against the disease. You may not think about getting a tetanus shot until you've stepped on a rusty nail or been snagged by a strand of barbed wire, but if it's been more than ten years since you had your last tetanus booster, you need to make an appointment with your doctor — today — to schedule one as soon as possible.

Most cases of tetanus follow cuts, scrapes, and puncture wounds sustained outdoors during farming and gardening chores, but indoor injuries — even those involving sewing needles — have been known to cause tetanus as well. The injuries leading to tetanus are often so trivial that medical attention isn't sought.

Tetanus is a deadly disease. It's caused by bacteria, *Clostridium tetani*, that live in the soil of backyards and barnyards around the world. Contamination of wounds with the tetanus-causing bacteria is more common than we'd like to think, but actual infection is relatively rare. *Clostridium tetani* require low levels of oxygen to thrive, which is why puncture or penetrating wounds are riskier than open lacerations. In wounds that involve punctured or penetrated skin, bacteria can be driven deep into body tissues where oxygen levels are lower.

After gaining entrance to the body, tetanus-producing bacteria can begin producing symptoms in three days to two weeks. By the time symptoms develop, the injury or illness responsible for the infection may have been forgotten. The tetanus-producing bacteria don't cause swelling or redness by themselves, and if the wound isn't infected with other organism, their point of entry into the body may be hard to find.

The bacteria responsible for tetanus infection wreak havoc in the body by producing a powerful and deadly poison called tetanospasmin, similar to the one responsible for botulism. In the body, tetanospasmin blocks the nerves' ability to relax. As a result, the affected nerves fire almost nonstop, causing muscles to contract spasmodically and forcefully enough to break bones.

Tetanus infection may first cause stiffness in the face and jaw — thus the name lockjaw. The muscles of the neck, shoulders and back also stiffen, and swallowing becomes difficult or impossible. Breathing muscles are paralyzed, and asphyxiation is often the cause of death.

In the United States, tetanus is relatively rare, but not because tetanus-causing bacteria have been eradicated — they're still abundant in the world around us. Immunization programs have helped reduce the number of tetanus infections, and fewer than 50 cases are reported in this country every year.

The majority of tetanus infections in the United States occurs in people 60 years of age and older — especially those who were never immunized against tetanus in the first place. Of all the cases of tetanus reported to the Centers for Disease Control and Prevention each year, over half involve people age 70 and older. It's estimated that about two-thirds of Americans age 70 and older are not protected against tetanus. Many of these vulnerable elderly people were never immunized as children while others were previously immunized but didn't receive regular tetanus boosters.

Vaccination with tetanus toxoid is virtually 100 percent effective in preventing tetanus infection. The vaccine works by alerting the body's immune system to the tetanus-causing bacteria. If those same bacteria should invade the body at a later time, the immune system is armed and ready to fight back by producing antibodies that will recognize and destroy them.

If you've never had a tetanus shot, you'll need to take the primary series, which consists of three doses of tetanus toxoid. A month after your first dose, you'll receive your second dose, and the third dose follows in six to 12 months. Because the protective effects of the vaccine tend to fade with time, adults should receive booster doses at least once every decade.

If you haven't had a tetanus shot in the past ten years, you shouldn't wait for an injury to get one. The discomfort of the shot is minor and short-lived, and it's a small price to pay for a decade of protection against a deadly disease.

eat smart, ride well

NUTRITION FOR HORSEWOMEN

As an equestrian, you know the importance of your horse getting good nutrition. You realize the quality of the feed and forage is key in determining how he looks, feels, and performs. You probably invest in high-quality grain, hay, and nutritional supplements to maximize your horse's health. If your non-equestrian friends ever caught a glimpse of your feed bill, they might shake their heads in disbelief.

Not only do you pay close attention to *what* your horse eats, you're also careful about *when* he eats. You feed him on a schedule, and you wouldn't dream of asking him to skip a meal. You'd never intentionally underfeed or overfeed your horse, nor would you give him anything detrimental.

While you're working hard to ensure that your horse eats a perfectly balanced, nutritionally complete, and irresistibly tasty ration, is it possible you're fueling your own body with foods full of fat, sugar, and empty calories? This isn't an uncommon occurrence. Many perfectly sensible, highly intelligent women who obsess about every single micro-nutrient that passes their horses' lips think nothing of filling their own bodies with burgers, fries, and soft drinks. If you fall into this category, it's time to rethink your nutritional strategy.

Fueling the Female Athlete

The female body is a miracle in motion. As the owner of such a miraculous machine, you have an opportunity to improve its performance and increase its longevity by supplying it with wholesome, nutritious foods.

Nutrition dramatically impacts not only your health but also your ability to function, both intellectually and physically. To a large extent, your diet dictates the way you look and feel. The foods you eat determine your weight, your moods, and your energy levels. A substandard diet can leave you irritable, zap your energy, and rob you of strength and stamina.

Even if you're not competing in equestrian events, the fact that you're riding, handling, or caring for horses qualifies you as an athlete, with specific nutritional needs. Your diet can either enhance or impede your motivation to ride and, ultimately, your ability to ride effectively.

Fuel or Filler?

When you fully appreciate the importance of good nutrition in all areas of your life, you realize that every bite matters. Because you can consume only a finite number of calories each day, it's essential to make those calories count.

This strategy may require you to analyze your eating habits. Many women — ever conscious of their weight — have trained themselves to evaluate foods only in caloric terms. Frequently, this leads us to adopt a mentality in which we consider low-calorie foods to be good and high-calorie foods to be bad. In reality, many relatively high-calorie foods are extremely healthy, making them well worth the caloric investment.

The opposite also is true. Many low-calorie foods are hardly worth eating. While there's no harm in snacking on a serving of pretzels or a handful of animal crackers, there's also no benefit. These foods may fill your stomach to some degree, but they offer little more than empty calories because neither is a rich source of vitamins, minerals, fiber, or high-quality protein. A serving of fruit or vegetables or a handful of nuts would be a far better choice because these foods contribute to your health.

As you're making decisions about what to eat to optimize your health, it's a good idea to look closely at some of the foods you normally choose. Before you dig in, ask yourself whether the food you've chosen is merely filler or if it truly a source of high-quality fuel, worthy of consumption.

If your diet and eating habits are less than desirable, it's time to start choosing foods that support you as a hard-working female athlete, so that you'll feel and perform better, in and out of the saddle. Even better, you'll increase your chances of living a longer, healthier, and happier life.

The Three Key Nutrients

No matter what foods you eat, your diet contains varying amounts of the three nutrients: carbohydrates, proteins, and fats. Although each is necessary for good health, it is the *balance* of these three nutrients that is of primary importance. By getting the proper proportions of carbohydrates, proteins, and fats in your daily diet, your body is better able to ward off common ailments and illnesses, while keeping you as strong and energetic as possible. As an added bonus of eating a nutritious, balanced diet, you'll notice that your hunger is suppressed, your food cravings are quieted, and your metabolism is maximized. You'll find it far easier to achieve and maintain an appropriate weight than you might have thought possible.

Carbohydrates

In years past, when the low-carb diet craze was at its frenetic peak, millions of otherwise rational Americans began slashing most — and in some cases virtually all — carbohydrate-containing foods from their diets. It was good riddance to high-carb items such as pizza, spaghetti, chips, and French fries. But in a classic example of throwing the baby out with the bath water, many hardcore carb-cutters also banished the most nutritious sources of carbohydrates from their diets. Fruits, vegetables, and whole grains frequently became off limits, despite their obvious — not to mention scientifically proven — contributions to good health.

Carbohydrates are not, of course, the dietary villains they've been portrayed as. Nor are they the root of all weight- and health-related woes. In reality, carbohydrates are essential to a healthy diet, no matter your age, weight, or health status.

Carbohydrates as Energy

Carbohydrates provide a readily available, easily accessible form of energy, especially for the brain, muscles, and nervous system. Elite endurance athletes have known this for years, which is why they routinely engage in a practice known as carbohydrate loading in preparation for rigorous training and competition.

To function optimally, your brain requires a steady supply of glucose, or sugar, from the blood. This, in turn, is dependent on a regular intake of carbohydrate-containing foods. If you've ever experienced a serious case of brain-drain, characterized by the inability to concentrate, remember, or think clearly, you know that one of the best ways to reverse the condition is to eat something, pronto. If you're like most people, you naturally turn to foods or beverages that are packed with carbohydrates to refuel your sputtering brain.

Getting adequate amounts of carbohydrates in your diet is important, but it's even more important to choose the right kinds. As it turns out, there are two types: simple carbohydrates and complex carbohydrates.

Simple Carbohydrates

Both simple and complex carbohydrates are made of smaller building blocks, which are sugar molecules, linked by chemical bonds.

Simple-carbohydrate foods comprise either monosaccharides, which are one-sugar units, or disaccharides, which are two-sugar units. Because of their small structure, they are quickly and easily broken down in the digestive tract. As a result, simple-carbohydrate foods are rapidly converted to single-sugar molecules in the stomach, and these sugar molecules are almost instantly released into the bloodstream.

When you eat simple carbohydrates, such as a sugar cookie, digestion begins with your first bite. In the presence of enzymes in your saliva and your stomach, the bonds holding the individual sugar molecules together rapidly disintegrate. Free of their bonds, these sugar molecules make a beeline for your bloodstream, and the result is a rapid spike in your blood-sugar level and an immediate, intense surge of energy.

Unfortunately, the energy rush is rather short-lived. In response to the sugar overload in your bloodstream, your pancreas is primed to pump out insulin, the hormone responsible for regulating blood-sugar levels. To fulfill its duties, insulin attaches itself to sugar molecules in the bloodstream and escorts them to various cells and tissues in the body, where they will be used as energy to fuel thousands of life-sustaining processes.

When you take in a sizeable load of simple carbohydrates in a short period, as you would if you devoured two or three sugar cookies on your way to the barn, you create big problems for your body. Spurred into action by a hefty dose of sugar, your pancreas may overshoot the mark and release too much insulin. The excess insulin clears your bloodstream of more blood sugar than it should, resulting in a below-normal blood-sugar level. This, in turn, can leave you feeling weak, shaky, and irritable. It's quite possible that you'll feel far worse after eating the sugar cookies than you did beforehand. In the presence of low blood-sugar levels, your brain attempts to restore normalcy by activating the hunger signal, sending you in search of another sugary snack. This destructive cycle can repeat itself dozens of times every day.

A sub-optimal blood-sugar level not only stimulates hunger but also creates a strong preference for sweet-tasting foods. The more sweets you eat, the more sweets you'll want. In addition, elevated insulin levels affect the storage of body fat. The longer and more frequently blood-insulin levels remain high, the more likely you are to accumulate excess body fat.

When you consume too many simple carbohydrates in a single sitting, your blood-sugar can climb to above-normal levels over a period of about 10 to 15 minutes. Within a half-hour to 45 minutes of eating the simple-carbohydrate treat, your blood-sugar levels may plummet to below normal levels, leaving you feeling tired, grumpy, and, even worse, hungry again. Because simple-carbohydrate foods can wreak havoc on your body and your life in so many ways, it's important to choose them with great care.

Sources of Simple Carbohydrates

Simple carbohydrates are abundant in most products that fall into the category of junk food. Any food that tastes delightfully sweet or seems to just melt in your mouth with very little chewing is likely a simple-carbohydrate food. This includes cookies, candies, sodas, pastries, potato chips, and just about every type of pseudo-food with a name that ends in "ito." White and brown sugar, molasses, corn syrup, and maple syrup also make the list of simple carbohydrates.

Empty Calories

While they're typically packed with sugar and calories, and may offer a hefty dose of fat to boot, most simple-carbohydrate junk foods are virtually devoid of anything that's even remotely good for you, including fiber, vitamins, and minerals. Because they contain very few substances that contribute to your health, calories from these foods are appropriately referred to as "empty" calories. You'll be doing yourself a huge favor if you eliminate these simple-carbohydrate foods. If this isn't possible, they probably should be eaten only in the case of a *dire* emergency, like impending starvation.

Some simple-carbohydrate foods are a little harder to recognize, because they don't fall into the traditional junk-food category. White rice and pastas, breads, and cereals made from refined grains are composed of simple carbohydrates. Although we tend to think of these foods as being far better for us than chips or cookies, their basic structures are similar, and they can similarly affect blood sugar and insulin, as well as energy levels and mood.

While white bread and highly refined cereals and pastas are typically lower in fat and contain more vitamins and minerals than traditional junk foods, they're still lacking in fiber and are relatively high in sugar. These carbohydrate-rich foods should be eaten in moderation, if at all. Whenever possible, you should substitute whole-grain products, such as oat cereal and whole-wheat varieties of bread and pasta.

Not all simple-carbohydrate foods are bad for you — many are not only desirable but also necessary for good health. Some examples are many varieties of fruit, which contain the sugar fructose, and dairy products, which contain the sugar lactose.

Complex Carbohydrates

As their name suggests, complex carbohydrates have a more complex chemical structure. Like simple carbohydrates, they're made up of individual sugar molecules, but instead of consisting of just one or two sugar molecules (monosaccharides or disaccharides), complex-carbohydrate foods are made up of polysaccharides, which contain hundreds or thousands of sugar molecules.

Time-Released Energy

Because they're so large, the polysaccharides in complex-carbohydrate foods are broken down slowly in the digestive tract, and the individual sugar molecules that form them are very gradually released into the bloodstream. This slow, steady release of sugar doesn't spike blood-sugar levels, and, as a result, it doesn't trigger a dramatic insulin response from your pancreas.

As the individual sugar molecules enter the bloodstream in a leisurely fashion over a period of one to four hours, insulin levels rise slowly and gently. The overall effect is a gradual, sustained rise in blood sugar, which is reflected in your mood and energy level. Because they fuel your body and your brain for hours after you eat them, you can think of complex carbohydrates as time-released energy foods.

Mood Food

Complex carbohydrates play another vital role in your diet. They stimulate your body's production of a neurotransmitter called serotonin and a hormone known as norepinephrine. Norepinephrine is structurally similar to adrenaline, and like adrenaline, it is an energy booster. Even better, it revs up your body's metabolism, so you burn more calories, even at rest.

The brain chemical serotonin has a number of functions in the human body. It helps calm and ward off depression. Severely depressed and anxious individuals have lower levels of serotonin than happier, calmer folk. Many antidepressants reduce anxiety and depression by increasing serotonin in the central nervous system. If you've ever found yourself eating in response to anxiety, depression, or stress, you may have noticed you crave foods rich in carbohydrates. This is your body's built-in mechanism to bolster serotonin in your brain.

Not only is serotonin an important mood-stabilizer, it also regulates appetite. Some prescription appetite suppressants work by increasing serotonin levels. Simply boosting your daily intake of complex carbohydrates can have the same effect. A diet rich in complex carbohydrates not only makes you feel good physically, but also enhances your sense of emotional well-being.

Sources of Complex Carbohydrates

While simple-carbohydrate foods are easily identified by their sweet taste, complex-carbohydrate foods are pleasant to the taste buds, but they aren't exceptionally sweet. Complex carbohydrates are found in whole-grain products, such as brown rice and whole-grain breads, pastas, and cereals. Legumes, including dozens of varieties of dried beans and peas, are also good sources. Some fruits, including prunes, apples, and grapefruit, contain complex carbohydrates, as do some vegetables, such as okra, celery, corn, and spinach.

Most complex-carbohydrate foods are rich in vitamins, minerals, and fiber, and in their natural forms, they're usually low calorie. A simple, unadulterated bowl of oatmeal, for example, has about 100 calories, with no fat or cholesterol. But if you pile butter and sugar on your oatmeal, it ceases to be a low-fat, low-calorie food. Now it may have as many as 200 calories and up to 18 grams of fat; and it's no longer such a great nutritional bargain. Whenever possible, you should try to eat fruits, vegetables, and whole grains in their original states. Virtually anything you add, whether it's butter, gravy, or creamy sauces, will end up detracting from the food's overall nutritional value.

Carbohydrate Requirements

Calories from carbohydrate foods — both simple and complex — should comprise about 50 percent of your daily caloric intake. This means that if your body requires 1,600 calories a day, 800 of these calories should come from carbohydrate foods. Ideally, the bulk of your carbohydrate calories will come from fruits, vegetables, whole-grain foods, and legumes; and when you eat simple carbohydrates, the vast majority will be in the form of fruits, vegetables, and low-fat dairy products. Both simple and complex carbohydrates have four calories per gram, so if you're eating 800 carbohydrate calories a day, you'll be getting a total of 200 grams of carbohydrates, the majority of which are complex.

Protein

Regardless of your age or activity level, getting an adequate amount of high-quality protein in your diet is essential to your health. If you discount the water in your body, about three-quarters of your weight is protein. Most of it is stored in your muscles, but it's also an important component of your bones, teeth, cartilage, skin, organs, and even blood and body fluids. Protein is a critical ingredient of virtually every cell, tissue, and substance in your body. Body tissues that are very active, including glands, organs, and muscles, have lots of protein, while less active body tissues, such as fat, have far less.

Your immune system is made up entirely of proteins, and it depends on replacement proteins from the foods in your diet to effectively fend off minor infections and major illnesses. Proteins serve as the catalysts for countless life-sustaining biochemical reactions and physiological processes that occur throughout your body each and every day. Although you probably haven't noticed, your body naturally loses millions of protein-containing cells daily — they're used up, worn out, and even rubbed off. To replace these and repair others, you need a steady source of protein from your diet.

Not only does dietary protein perform important maintenance in the body, it also serves as a long-lasting source of energy. Eating protein-rich foods doesn't lead to dramatic spikes in blood-sugar and insulin levels, and it won't wreak havoc with your energy levels and moods. When you eat a mixture of protein and complex carbohydrates, such as a grilled chicken breast on whole-wheat bread, blood sugar rises gradually and remains steady for as long as three to four hours.

Complete Versus Incomplete Proteins

Like carbohydrates, proteins are made up of smaller building blocks. While the building blocks of carbohydrates are individual sugars, the building blocks of protein are amino acids. Because the body doesn't store amino acids as it does fats and carbohydrates, it needs a daily supply of these substances from dietary sources to make new proteins.

The body uses 20 amino acids to build hundreds of different proteins, similar to the way letters of the alphabet are used to build words. Of the 20 different amino acids, nine are considered essential, because the human body isn't capable of manufacturing them. These must be obtained from food. The remaining 11 amino acids are known as nonessential amino acids because the body is able to manufacture them.

Any food that contains all nine of the essential amino acids your body needs to build new proteins is known as a complete protein. Animal sources of protein, including meat, milk, and eggs, are considered complete proteins. Foods that lack one or more of the essential amino acids are known as incomplete proteins. Incomplete proteins include those found in fruits, vegetables, grains, and nuts. To supply your body with all the amino acids it needs to make new proteins, it's important to include a wide variety of plant and animal products in your daily diet.

Sources of Protein

If you're an avid meat eater, getting enough protein in your diet probably isn't a problem for you. If you don't consider yourself an enthusiastic carnivore, you may have to work a little harder to meet your body's protein requirements.

Almost all foods have some protein. Fruits and vegetables have relatively little: a half-cup serving typically provides just a gram or two of protein. Meats, nuts, and beans are protein-rich, and many types provide 15 to 30 grams of protein per serving.

Protein-rich foods aren't hard to find, but sometimes nutritious, low-fat sources of high-quality protein can seem a little scarce or expensive. While animal products of all types are generally protein rich, there's a downside to eating them. Many are loaded with fat, cholesterol, and calories. A 6-ounce serving of broiled beef ribs is a great source of protein — it offers about 36 grams. But since the same serving of beef ribs also packs a whopping 72 grams of fat and 800 calories, it's obviously not the healthiest source. If you choose 6 ounces of baked salmon instead, you'll get 44 grams of protein, 22 grams of fat, and only about 385 calories.

Because many high-protein foods are also high-fat, high-cholesterol foods, it's important to choose them wisely, with an emphasis on low-fat dairy products, skinless poultry, fish, and lean meats trimmed of all visible fat. In the produce department, nuts, dried beans, peas, and other legumes are excellent sources. Smaller amounts of protein also can be found in corn, brown rice, and whole-wheat pasta.

Protein Requirements

In the era of the low-carb craze, dieters routinely ate far more protein than needed. The documented dangers of a high-protein, very low-carbohydrate diet are varied, numerous, and occasionally scary. When someone drastically lowers carbohydrate intake, blood sugar becomes scarce. Interpreting this as a

sign of starvation, the brain activates a rescue mode called ketosis. In this precarious metabolic state, the body is forced to burn some of its own tissues — not just fat, but also muscle — to produce the energy it needs to survive. The fat-burning part may sound great, but unfortunately, ketosis can cause a few problems, ranging from merely annoying to downright life threatening.

Ketosis can unfavorably alter the concentrations of electrolytes in the blood, leading to weakness, dizziness, and fainting spells, all of which can be problematic if they happen while you're riding or handling a horse. Ketosis also taints the breath, perspiration, and urine with a particularly unpleasant odor, which frequently is likened to rotten apples or sewer gas. Because the odor emanates from the lungs and pores, there's no disguising it with breath mints or perfumes. Clipping an air freshener to one's breeches may be the only practical solution.

Because high-protein, low-carbohydrate foods are notoriously lacking in fiber, eating too many of them can lead to constipation. High-protein diets are known to contribute to osteoporosis, because they steal calcium from the bones and reroute the mineral directly to the toilet bowl via the urine. They also can trigger flare-ups of gout in people who are prone to the condition. Last but not least, high-protein diets lacking in fruits, vegetables, and whole grains increase the risk for heart disease and many types of cancer. Fortunately, most folks have come to realize that these high-protein, low-carbohydrate diets may not be so great after all.

While eating a diet containing excessive amounts of protein is definitely asking for trouble, consuming an adequate amount of protein is vital to your good health. Calories from protein foods should make up 30 percent of your total daily intake. If, for example, your body requires 1,600 calories a day to support itself, 480 of those calories should come from protein-rich foods. Like carbohydrates, proteins have 4 calories per gram, so a well-balanced diet consisting of 1,600 calories a day includes about 120 grams of protein.

Fats

If you're old enough, you may remember the era of the low-fat diets. In those times, prevailing wisdom held that dietary fats — as opposed to carbohydrates — were the root of all weight- and health-related evils. As a result, many Americans developed an unhealthy degree of fat-phobia that still lingers to this day.

It's a fact that too much fat in the diet contributes to a thousand ills, such as obesity, high cholesterol levels, heart disease, and cancer of the breast and colon. Some fat in your diet, however, not only is beneficial but also absolutely essential. Fat is found in every cell in the body and is an important source of stored energy. It also helps keep your skin soft and supple, while it cushions, supports, and protects your internal organs. This feature comes in very handy when you are riding at the trot, or when you're hurling yourself and your horse around barrels or over fences.

Like carbohydrates and proteins, dietary fat is a nutrient that is critical for proper growth and development, as well as maintaining good health. It aids in the body's absorption and circulation of the fat-soluble vitamins, A, D, E, and K. Fat can enhance the taste and improve the texture of the foods you eat and contribute to feeling full and satisfied after eating.

With that said, not all fats are created equally. While the unsaturated fats, including monounsaturated and polyunsaturated fats, are beneficial when consumed in moderation, saturated fat, trans fat, and dietary cholesterol are not. These three types of fat are known to raise levels of LDL (low-density lipoprotein) cholesterol in the blood, a phenomenon that contributes to heart disease. For this reason, it's important to choose foods that are low in cholesterol, trans fat, and saturated fat as a part of a healthy diet.

The Good Fats

Monounsaturated and polyunsaturated fats are the dietary good guys, since neither of these types elevates LDL cholesterol levels. In addition, consumption of polyunsaturated and monounsaturated fats has been shown to lower the risk of developing diabetes.

Polyunsaturated fats are found in oils made from plants, including soybeans, corn, and sunflower seeds. They're especially abundant in a variety of fatty fish, including tuna and salmon, as well as in nuts and seeds. Sources of monounsaturated fats include olive oil, peanut oil, and canola oil, and avocados.

The Bad Fats

Saturated fat is commonly referred to as a "bad" fat, because consuming it in excess can raise cholesterol levels and contribute to heart disease and other chronic illnesses. It's found primarily in foods from animal sources, including fatty beef, veal, pork, and poultry. Dairy products made from whole milk, including butter, cream, milk, and cheese, tend to be high in saturated fat, as well as cholesterol. A few plant foods that are rich in saturated fat include cocoa butter and the tropical oils, specifically coconut oil, palm oil, and palm kernel oil.

Trans Fat

Some foods with low levels of saturated fat and cholesterol can appear deceptively benign, when in fact they harbor the most dangerous type of fat of all: trans fat.

Very low levels of trans fat occur naturally in our diets. Because small quantities are produced in the gastrointestinal tracts of cattle, folks who eat beef and dairy products are likely to consume small amounts. The vast majority of trans fat in the American diet, however, is intentionally added to the foods that we eat.

These trans unsaturated fatty acids, or trans fats for short, are solid fats that are produced artificially by heating liquid vegetable oils in the presence of metal catalysts and hydrogen. The process, called partial hydrogenation, causes fats to remain in a solid state at room temperature. Food manufacturers like this property. When used as an ingredient in baked goods and other products, solid fats slow spoilage and dramatically extend shelf life. When trans fat is included as an ingredient, many baked goods remain not only edible, but also "fresh" and "delicious" for months on end.

The process of partial hydrogenation not only creates dangerous types of fat but also destroys some beneficial fatty acids. Because these fatty acids are rather unstable and tend to oxidize in the presence of air, they're prone to become rancid without refrigeration. Although these heart-healthy fats may contribute to a longer lifespan in humans, they definitely shorten the shelf-life of baked goods.

In terms of your health, trans fat acts more like saturated fat, the kind that can elevate LDL cholesterol levels and clog your arteries. At the same time, trans fat can lower levels of heart-healthy HDL (high-density lipoprotein cholesterol), increasing the risk for heart disease. This double whammy makes the negative health effects of trans fat twice as bad as those of saturated fat. In addition, consumption of excess quantities of trans fat is linked to elevated triglyceride levels and an increased risk of developing diabetes.

Sources of Trans Fats

Trans fat turns up in many types of margarine and vegetable shortenings, deep fried fast foods and snack foods, and many commercially baked goods such as pies, cookies, crackers, and other packaged items. There are a few notable exceptions: potato chips, pretzels, and salad dressings generally aren't made with partially hydrogenated oils, so they typically don't contain trans fat.

While many brands of peanut butter include small amounts of hydrogenated oil, they contain only traces of trans fat. French fries and other fried fast foods are typically prepared with partially hydrogenated oils, and as a result, they're usually loaded with trans fat. With 8 grams of trans fat, 7 grams of saturated fat, and 27 grams of total fat, a large order of French fries is not exactly a health food — it's more like a health hazard.

Cholesterol

Cholesterol is a waxy, fat-like substance found in every cell of your body. It insulates nerve cells and makes up a significant part of your brain, and it is involved in the formation of cell membranes, hormones, and vitamin D. While some cholesterol is necessary for life, too much is dangerous. Excess cholesterol in the bloodstream accumulates along the interior walls of arteries. This buildup, known as plaque, can narrow arteries enough to slow or block the flow of blood. Narrowing of arteries, a condition called atherosclerosis, commonly occurs in the coronary arteries that supply blood to the heart and can contribute to heart attacks.

Because your liver manufactures all the cholesterol your body needs, you don't need to consume a lot of extra cholesterol in your diet. Animal products, including meat, poultry, fish, eggs, and dairy products provide varying amounts while vegetables, fruits, nuts, seeds, cereals, and grains have no cholesterol.

On average, American women eat about 240 milligrams (mg) a day, and that's a reasonable intake for those with normal cholesterol levels and no history of heart disease. If you have heart disease, or if your latest blood test revealed that your levels of total cholesterol and low-density lipoprotein cholesterol (LDL) are too high, you might want to reduce your cholesterol intake to about 200 mg a day.

Fat Requirements

Getting enough dietary fat isn't a problem for most folks. American adults routinely consume as much as twice the amount their bodies need. As part of a nutritious and well-balanced diet, calories from fat should make up roughly 20 percent of your daily intake. For women consuming a diet of 1,600 calories a day, fat should contribute about 320 calories. Unlike carbohydrates and proteins, which have just 4 calories per gram, fat has a whopping 9 calories per gram, and that's precisely what makes it so fattening. If you consume 320 calories of fat each day, you'll be getting about 36 grams of fat.

While you're watching your fat intake, be sure to pay attention to the types of fats that are working their way into your diet. Most Americans consume far more saturated fat than trans fat, and both should be limited. Your intake of trans fat should be as low as possible and should never exceed 1 percent of your total calories, or about 1.7 grams per day in a 1,600-calorie diet. You should try to restrict the total amount of saturated fats and trans fats to no more than 7 percent of your daily calories, which translates to about 12 grams in a 1,600-calorie diet. The remainder of your fat intake should come from the healthier varieties, including monounsaturated and polyunsaturated fats.

Fiber

Although fiber is a type of carbohydrate, it isn't considered to be a true nutrient because it cannot be digested or absorbed by the body. Still, fiber is a critical component of a healthy, well-balanced diet. In years past, fiber didn't get nearly the respect it deserved: Its greatest claim to fame was its ability to promote gastrointestinal regularity and ward off constipation. Recent research has elevated fiber to its rightful position in the food chain.

Fiber, also known as roughage or bulk, forms the structural framework of all food plants, including fruits, vegetables, grains, legumes, and nuts. Because humans lack the enzymes necessary to digest it, fiber travels through the gastrointestinal tract pretty much unchanged, and that's exactly what makes it so beneficial.

Soluble Versus Insoluble Fiber

Not all fiber is the same, and one of the most common ways of categorizing the various types is by how easily they dissolve in water. Those that dissolve in water are considered to be soluble fiber; those that do not are classified as insoluble fiber. The difference is important when it comes to determining fiber's beneficial effects on reducing your risk of certain diseases.

Soluble Fiber

Soluble fiber, like the pectin in many fruits, dissolves in water to form a gel-like material. This substance has been shown to help lower levels of cholesterol and blood sugar in the body, reducing the risk for heart disease and diabetes. You can find generous quantities of soluble fiber in oats, peas, beans, apples, citrus fruits, carrots, barley, and psyllium.

Insoluble Fiber

Unlike soluble fiber, fiber of the insoluble type doesn't dissolve in water to form a gel. Insoluble fiber increases stool bulk, facilitating the movement of material through your digestive system. These properties are what make insoluble fiber so beneficial in the prevention and treatment of constipation. Whole-wheat flour, wheat bran, nuts, and many vegetables are good sources of insoluble fiber.

High-Fiber Diets Promote Weight Loss

You probably know from experience that eating a bowl of bran cereal or a serving of beans can fill you up pretty fast. Not only do high-fiber foods make you feel full, they also can help you lose weight. They're bulky and filling; and ounce for ounce, they're typically far lower in calories than low-fiber foods.

Because they require some serious chewing, high-fiber foods take longer to eat, and this property dramatically increases their ability to make you feel full and satisfied. Time spent chewing slows the pace at which you eat, giving your brain a chance to notice when your stomach is full and you're no longer hungry. As a result, eating high-fiber foods makes it more difficult to overeat. Numerous studies have shown that people who consume high-fiber diets tend to be thinner and healthier than those whose diets lack in roughage. One study demonstrated that the addition of 14 grams of fiber to the daily diet was associated with an average weight loss of 4.2 pounds over a four-month period.

There's no doubt that the sheer bulk of high-fiber foods helps make you feel full, but there's another important reason for their ability to satisfy. Foods rich in fiber trigger the release of a specific hormone in the bloodstream called cholecystokinin, or CCK, known to produce feelings of satiety.

In the body, CCK is released not only when high-fiber foods are eaten but also when fatty foods are consumed. This hormone is the chemical messenger that notifies the brain that the stomach is getting full and it's time to push away from the table. As with fat, the consumption of fiber not only stimulates the release of CCK but also prolongs the hormone's presence in the bloodstream after eating.

Women appear to be particularly sensitive to the effects of this hormone. Compared to men, women eating high-fat and high-fiber meals have significantly higher levels of CCK and report greater feelings of satiety. We can use this little gift of nature to our advantage. Instead of feeding on high-fat, high-calorie foods, such as cheeseburgers and fries, to feel full and satisfied, we can get the same feeling by feasting on fiber-rich foods, such as big, beautiful salads or delicately steamed vegetables served over a bed of brown rice.

Health Benefits of Fiber

Most women are aware of fiber's ability to prevent or treat constipation. If you want to stay regular, it's important to eat fiber regularly, especially the soluble variety.

Soluble fiber also reduces the risk of heart disease. Water-soluble gums and pectin interfere with the absorption of cholesterol so that less of the substance is deposited on artery walls and more is excreted as waste. As a bonus, most fiber-rich foods are high in potassium and magnesium, two minerals that help regulate blood pressure.

Dozens of studies have demonstrated a strong link between high intakes of dietary fiber and lower risks of heart disease. In some cases, the reduction in risk is as great as 40 percent.

High-fiber diets also improve health by reducing the risk of developing type II diabetes. In people with the disease, fiber-rich foods can significantly improve blood-sugar control. Fiber slows the absorption of sugar from foods, minimizing the dramatic spikes in blood sugar and insulin that can occur after eating. While this action is especially helpful for people with diabetes, it is also beneficial to individuals without the disease.

Sources of Fiber

Fiber is found only in plant foods. Animal

products, such as meat and dairy foods, are completely fiber-free. Only traces of roughage are found in heavily refined or processed foods, including white rice, white bread, refined breakfast cereals, and most types of cookies, crackers, and pasta. With every phase of processing that occurs during the manufacture of food, fiber content is diminished. A whole orange, for example, has 3 grams of fiber, but when oranges are processed to make juice, fiber is lost.

A serving of orange juice has less than 1 gram of fiber per serving. While a baked potato with skin offers 3 grams of fiber, a serving of mashed potatoes or French fries has none.

Rich sources of roughage include bran and multigrain cereals, whole-grain bread products, oatmeal, and dried beans and other legumes. Fiber-rich fruits include apples, berries, figs, pears, and prunes; fiber-rich vegetables include broccoli, Brussels sprouts, carrots, and cauliflower.

HIGH-FIBER FOODS

FOOD	FIBER CONTENT IN GRAMS
Split peas, cooked, 1 cup	16.3
Lentils, 1 cup	15.6
Black beans, 1 cup	15.0
Lima beans, 1 cup	13.2
Red kidney beans, boiled, 1 cup	13.1
Raspberries, raw, 1 cup	8.0
Whole-wheat spaghetti, 1 cup	6.3
Bran flakes, 3/4 cup	5.3
Oat bran muffin, medium	5.2
Broccoli, boiled, 1 cup	5.1
Pear, 1 medium	5.1
Oatmeal, regular or instant, cooked, 1 cup	4.0
Green beans, cooked, 1 cup	4.0
Brown rice, cooked, 1 cup	3.5
Almonds, 24 nuts	3.3
Apple, medium with skin	3.3
Whole-wheat bread, 2 slices	3.8
Brussels sprouts, cooked, 1 cup	6.4
Corn, 1 cup	4.2

Fiber Requirements

If you aren't getting enough fiber each day, you definitely need to boost your intake. You don't have to eat a bale of alfalfa or a bag of oats to meet your daily requirement, but you may have to partake of a wider variety of plant foods, including whole grains, fruits, vegetables, and legumes. Eating the typical American diet, most adults get only about 11 to 15 grams of fiber a day, less than half the recommended amount. For optimum health, women 19 to 50 years old should get about 25 grams of fiber a day and those older should aim for at least 21 grams daily. Pregnant women should consume 28 grams a day.

When you're increasing the fiber in your diet, be sure to start slowly and work your way up gradually. It's a good idea to drink plenty of water while you're at it because fiber absorbs water in the digestive tract. If you switch abruptly from a low-fiber diet to one rich in roughage, you may suffer bloating, cramping, and gas. These symptoms will resolve as your body adjusts, but adding fiber to your diet slowly will allow you to avoid the gastrointestinal distress altogether.

Water

Although it's not nutritious in the true sense of the word, water is vital to life, second only in importance to oxygen. In terms of composition, water makes up the vast majority of the human brain and body. Because water is the primary ingredient of our very beings, it's easy to see why drinking it is so critical. A loss of

just 5 percent of body water results in weakness and irritability and impairs concentration while a loss of just 15 percent to 20 percent can be fatal.

You need to drink plenty of water throughout the day to stay healthy and fight disease. The mucous membranes that line your nose and throat are your body's first-line defense against invading viruses and bacteria. When these membranes are moist, they act like sticky flypaper, trapping and destroying germs before they can cause infection. Blood, which is roughly 85 percent water, delivers the cellular soldiers of the immune system throughout your body to help destroy disease-causing organisms. Water helps lubricate your joints, cushion your internal organs, moisten your eyes, and keep your skin soft and supple. It carries food through your digestive tract, delivering nutrients and removing wastes from cells and tissues.

Drinking water also can help with weight control and can improve energy levels. Many women feel hungry when in reality they're thirsty. Drinking a glass of water before and between meals helps fill your stomach and reduces your chances of overeating. As fatigue is one of the first signs of mild dehydration, increasing your fluid intake may give you a boost of energy and help you avoid turning to food for a quick pick-me-up.

Staying well hydrated may protect your heart and reduce your risk of having a heart attack. One study demonstrated that women who drank more than five glasses of water each day were 41 percent less likely to die from a heart attack than those who drank fewer than two glasses daily. Water may protect against heart attacks because it is quickly and easily absorbed into the bloodstream. Once there, it helps prevent blockages in the heart's arteries by reducing the clotting potential of the blood.

Drink up

If you don't drink enough liquid, your body will remind you by signaling you that you're thirsty. Unfortunately, your built-in sensation of thirst isn't a very reliable indicator of your body's state of hydration, and you may feel thirsty only after your body is considerably dehydrated. Because even a few swallows of water can quench your thirst, you may stop drinking long before you've fully met your body's fluid requirements. As it isn't an ideal indicator of your body's state of hydration, you shouldn't count on thirst alone to regulate your fluid intake. Most healthy women require about a quart of water a day for every 50 pounds of body weight. As an active, working athlete, your water requirements are likely greater.

While you're riding or working at the barn, it's especially important to stay well hydrated. Drinking adequate amounts of fluid can enhance performance and delay fatigue and muscle weakness or soreness. An hour or two before you head to the barn is a good time to get a jump-start on your fluid intake, pre-hydrating your body with 12 to 16 ounces of water. While you're working or riding, you need to drink 4 to 6 ounces of water for every 15 to 20 minutes of exercise. On days that you're less active, a water intake of 48 to 64 ounces, or six to eight glasses, will allow you to meet your fluid requirements.

the riding for life diet

Now that you understand the importance of carbohydrates, proteins, and fats in your diet, it's time to chart your course to a healthier way of eating. You're ready for some solid numbers.

The first number you'll need is the total number of calories you should eat every day to achieve and maintain your goal weight. The exact number varies from person to person, depending on level of activity, body composition, metabolism, age, and gender, but most moderately active women need somewhere in the neighborhood of 11 calories to support each pound of body weight on a daily basis.

If, for example, you weigh 150 pounds, you'll need to eat about 1,650 calories every day to maintain that weight (150 x 11 = 1,650). What if your goal weight is 150 pounds, but you currently weigh 200 pounds? If you weigh 200 pounds right now, it's likely that your daily diet consists of around 2,200 calories (200 x 11 = 2,200), as it takes about 2,200 calories a day to support and maintain 200 pounds of body weight for a reasonably active person.

If you want to weigh 150 pounds, you have to start eating like a 150-pound person. The good news is that if you feed only 150 pounds of your body, the extra, unwanted 50 pounds will eventually get lost. By feeding your 200-pound body 1,650 calories a day instead of 2,200 calories a day, you'll be cutting your daily intake by 550 calories, enough to net you a weight loss of little more than a pound a week. As you continue to slim down, the rate at which you lose weight will gradually slow, but, ultimately, you'll reach your goal of 150 pounds.

It sounds too simple to be true, but it works. All you have to do is feed the pounds you want to keep. When you eat like the person you want to become, you'll eventually become that person. If you want to lose your excess weight and keep it off forever, you have to change your eating habits permanently.

Determining your own personal nutrient needs for a nutritious, balanced diet is as easy as performing some simple calculations and filling in the blanks on the following page, so grab your calculator and let's get started!

RIDING FOR LIFE DIET WORKSHEET

DAILY CALORIC NEEDS

GOAL WEIGHT:

GOAL WEIGHT X 11 =
DAILY CALORIC INTAKE:

Your daily caloric intake is the number of calories your body needs to support itself at your goal weight.

DAILY NUTRIENT NEEDS

A nutritious, balanced diet consists of 50 percent carbohydrates, 30 percent protein, and 20 percent fat.

Since 50 percent of your daily calories will come from carbohydrate foods, multiply your daily caloric intake by .50 to determine the total number of carbohydrate calories you should eat every day:

CARBOHYDRATE CALORIES:

There are 4 calories in each gram of carbohydrate, so divide this number by 4 to get the total number of carbohydrate grams you should eat each day:

CARBOHYDRATE GRAMS:

Proteins make up 30 percent of the Riding for Life Diet. Multiply your daily calorie intake by .30 to determine the number of protein calories you should eat every day:

PROTEIN CALORIES:

Since there are 4 calories in each gram of protein, divide this number by 4 to get the total number of protein grams you should eat each day:

PROTEIN GRAMS:

Fat makes up 20 percent of the Riding for Life Diet. Multiply your daily caloric intake by .20 to determine the number of fat calories you should eat every day:

FAT CALORIES:

Each gram of fat has 9 calories, so divide this number by 9 to get the number of fat grams you should eat every day:

FAT GRAMS:

From this point on, the only numbers you'll need to remember are the numbers of grams for carbohydrates, protein, and fat. If you eat foods that allow you to approximate these numbers on a daily basis, everything else will take care of itself. You'll be eating a nutritious, well-balanced diet, and you'll find that your energy levels soar. Because you'll be maximizing your metabolic rate and quieting food cravings in the process, losing weight or maintaining your current weight will be practically effortless. Write your numbers here:

GRAMS CARBOHYDRATE:

GRAMS PROTEIN:

GRAMS FAT:

It's time to design your own Riding for Life daily menus, featuring only the foods that you like, and none that you don't. Designing your meals and snacks will a take little effort at first because you might not be familiar with the nutrient contents of various foods. Fortunately, nearly every packaged food in America now comes with a handy nutrition facts panel attached.

If you look at the sample nutrition label on the following page, you'll find all the information you need. The first thing you'll want to know is the suggested serving size. According to the sample label, a single serving size of the food inside the package is 1 cup. Next, you'll need to know how many grams of carbohydrates, protein, and fat that a cup of this food contains. As you can see, 1 cup contains 31 grams of carbohydrates, 5 grams of protein, and 12 grams of fat.

Determining the nutrient content of the food you eat is no great feat when it comes packaged with a nutrition facts panel. But it's not quite as simple to figure out the nutrient content of the foods that you prepare from scratch or that are served to you in restaurants. For these types of foods, you can use a reference book that features the nutrient content of many popular foods. Most supermarkets, health food stores, and bookstores sell these books, and many are available at your public library or online.

Nutrition Facts

Serving Size 1 cup (228g)
Servings Per Container 2

Amount Per Serving

Calories 250   Calories from Fat 110

	% Daily Value*
Total Fat 12g	**18%**
Saturated Fat 3g	**15%**
Trans Fat 3g	
Cholesterol 30mg	**10%**
Sodium 470mg	**20%**
Total Carbohydrate 31g	**10%**
Dietary Fiber 0g	**0%**
Sugars 5g	
Protein 5g	
Vitamin A	**4%**
Vitamin C	**2%**
Calcium	**20%**
Iron 4%	

* Percent Daily Values are based on a 2,000 calorie diet. Your daily values may be higher or lower depending on your calorie needs.

		Calories	2,000	2,500
Total Fat	Less than		65g	80g
Sat Fat	Less than		20g	25g
Cholesterol	Less than		300mg	300mg
Sodium	Less than		2,400mg	2,400mg
Potassium	Less than		3,500mg	3,500mg
Total Carbohydrate			300g	375g
Dietary Fiber			25g	30g

You won't have to consult a reference book every time you open your mouth for a morsel of food, but it is very important to do it initially while you're still getting the hang of it. Before long you'll get a feel for the nutrient values of your favorite foods, and eating a nutritious, balanced diet will become second nature.

Deciphering Label Lingo

To make sure you're getting the biggest bang for your nutritional buck, it's important to read the nutrition information listed on the packages of the foods that you choose to include in your daily diet. In an effort to attract conscientious consumers, manufacturers often put enthusiastic nutritional claims on the front of product packages — statements such as "Contains no trans fats!" or "Cholesterol-free!" While these attributes are undoubtedly important dietary virtues, they don't necessarily absolve some foods of their nutritional sins. A serving of potato chips may be free of trans fats and cholesterol, for example, but that doesn't exactly elevate the potato chip to the status of superfood. Many low-fat foods are high in sugar and calories, while some sugar-free items are loaded with fat and cholesterol.

The Food and Drug Administration requires food manufacturers to provide evidence to support nutritional claims on their products' packaging. These claims must meet strict government definitions to ensure that they're not only accurate but also consistent from one product to another. "Reduced fat," for instance, means that a product has 25 percent less fat than the manufacturer's "regular" version of the same product, while "light" means that the product has 50 percent less fat than the regular version. For a food manufacturer to proclaim a food "low-fat," the product must have fewer than 3 grams of fat per serving.

While these claims can be helpful, the best source of information is the nutrition facts panel on the side or back of the package. Deciphering this information is easier if you understand the language used.

Serving Size

At the top of the nutrition facts panel, you'll find the manufacturer's suggested serving size. Whether the suggested serving size is a reasonable portion may be debatable, but it is intended to reflect the amount that people generally eat, according to standards set by the Food and Drug Administration. The nutrition information included in the nutrition facts panel is based on the stated serving size, so if you eat more or less, be sure to make adjustments. Simply multiply the amount of fat, calories, and other nutrients by the number of servings you eat.

Calories

A calorie is a standard unit that measures the amount of energy that food provides to your body. The number listed on the nutrition facts panel tells you how many calories you'll get in a single serving. Although daily caloric requirements vary from person to person, food labels are based on a diet of 2,000 calories per day.

Calories From Fat

This figure gives the number of calories provided by fat in a single serving, making it easier for you to keep track of the amount of fat in your daily diet.

Percent Daily Value (% Daily Value)

Percent daily values, listed in the right-hand column of the panel, reveal the percentage of various nutrients you'll get by eating a single serving. Ideally, of course, the goal is to consume 100 percent of each of these nutrients every day. If, for example, a serving offers 20 percent calcium, it provides enough calcium to meet a fifth of your daily requirement for the mineral, based on a 2,000-calorie daily diet. After eating a serving of this food, you'll still need to get the remaining 80 percent of your calcium requirement from other foods.

Percent daily value is most useful for determining whether a food is a good source of a particular nutrient. If a food has 5 percent or less of a nutrient, it is considered to be low in that nutrient. A food is considered to be a good source of a nutrient if the percent daily value listed is between 10 percent and 19 percent. If a food has more than 20 percent of a particular nutrient, it is considered to be high in that nutrient.

Total Fat

This number indicates the amount of fat in a single serving of food.

Although eating too much fat can be hazardous to your health, fat is an important source of energy. It also cushions internal organs, keeps skin soft and supple, and helps circulate and store the fat-soluble vitamins, A, D, E, and K.

Saturated Fat and Trans Fat

The FDA requires manufacturers to list separately the amounts of saturated and trans fats contained in a serving of food. Saturated fats and trans fats are the dietary bad guys. When eaten in excess, they can lead to high cholesterol levels and hardening of the arteries, increasing the risk for heart disease and stroke. Saturated fats should contribute less than 10 percent of the total calories in your daily diet, while the amount of trans fat should be as low as possible.

Unsaturated Fats

Unsaturated fats are often referred to as "good fats" because when eaten in moderation, they don't elevate blood cholesterol levels or increase the risk for heart attack and stroke.

Cholesterol

Cholesterol is a fat-like substance that is necessary for the production of vitamin D and hormones. It's important to pay attention to the amount of dietary cholesterol in the foods you eat because when consumed in excess, it can lead to high cholesterol levels in the bloodstream and increase the risk of cardiovascular disease.

Sodium

Sodium is a component of salt. Small amounts of sodium are necessary to maintain the body's fluid balance and to aid in the transmission of electrical signals throughout the nervous system. Too much sodium, on the other hand, can contribute to high blood pressure and kidney problems.

Total Carbohydrate

This number includes several types of carbohydrates, including dietary fibers, sugars, and others. Carbohydrates are an important source of energy for the body, but eating them in excess can contribute to weight gain.

Dietary Fiber

Listed under total carbohydrate, dietary fiber has no calories. Still, it is a necessary part of a balanced diet. High-fiber diets promote gastrointestinal health and reduce the risk of diabetes, heart disease, and certain cancers.

Sugars

Also listed under total carbohydrate on food labels, sugars provide energy for the body. It's important to make sure that they're packaged in nutritious foods, such as fruits, vegetables, and legumes, rather than junk foods and sodas. Sugars obtained from junk foods and sodas typically provide lots of empty calories and few beneficial nutrients.

Protein

Muscles, skin, and the immune system are made up of protein. In addition to carbohydrates and fat, the body can use protein as a source of energy.

Vitamin A and Vitamin C

The amount of each of these vitamins in a single serving of food is listed in terms of percent daily value. Vitamin C, found mainly in citrus fruits, is used by the body to heal wounds and fight infection. Vitamin A, found in orange and green vegetables, is important for eyesight and healthy skin. While food manufacturers are required to state amounts of vitamins A and C on the nutrition facts panel, listing amounts of other vitamins is optional.

Calcium and Iron

These two important minerals are listed in terms of percent daily values. Food manufacturers are required to list the amounts of calcium and iron and may list the amounts of other minerals their products contain. Calcium, found primarily in dairy products, has many important roles in the body but is best known for its role in building healthy bones and teeth. Iron helps the body produce new, healthy red blood cells to transport oxygen throughout the body. While iron from red meat is most easily absorbed and used by the body, the mineral is also found in iron-fortified cereals, raisins, and dark green, leafy vegetables.

List of Ingredients

Manufacturers are required to include the ingredients contained in the food on the nutritional facts panel. Ingredients are listed by amount, from greatest to least.

Calories per Gram

This information is printed on food labels for reference, to remind you that each gram of fat contains 9 calories while each gram of protein and carbohydrate contains 4 calories.

Your Favorite Foods

To familiarize yourself with the nutrient content of the foods you normally eat, try this simple exercise on page 66. List the foods that you enjoy eating for breakfast, and look up their nutrient contents in your reference book, online, or simply consult the nutrition facts panel of the package.

Completing this exercise will give you a good start toward designing your Riding for Life eating program.

Now it's time to put it all together in a daily diet plan. Remember, you don't have to limit yourself to certain foods every day. You just have to make wise choices, so that at the end of each day, your actual nutrient intake roughly matches your ideal intake of carbohydrates, proteins, and fats.

If you want to see how close your old way of eating comes to a well-balanced diet, try listing everything you ate yesterday for breakfast, lunch, dinner, and snacks, and then list the number of carbohydrate, protein, and fat grams they provided.

Now it's time for the acid test — compare yesterday's totals with the recommended values on your Riding for Life Diet Worksheet. How close did you come to eating a nutritious, balanced diet?

YOUR FAVORITE FOODS

LIST THE FOODS THAT YOU ENJOY EATING for breakfast, lunch, and dinner followed by their nutrient contents.

BREAKFAST

Food	Carbohydrate Grams	Protein Grams	Fat Grams

LUNCH

Food	Carbohydrate Grams	Protein Grams	Fat Grams

DINNER

Food	Carbohydrate Grams	Protein Grams	Fat Grams

The Physiology of Weight Loss

Although weight loss may often seem elusive, there's really nothing magical about it. It all boils down to the simple, irrefutable principles of mathematics. To lose weight, you must consume fewer calories than your body needs to support itself at your current weight.

Like your bank account, your body weight is a reflection of the deposits and withdrawals that you make. When you deposit excess cash into your bank account, it swells. As you withdraw funds, it shrinks. The same is true of your body: Whenever you deposit excess calories, your weight increases, and when you make withdrawals, your weight decreases.

A pound of body weight represents 3,500 calories. When you consume 3,500 calories more than your body needs to support itself at your current weight, you gain a pound. When you consume 3,500 fewer calories than your body needs to support itself at your current weight, or when you expend 3,500 additional calories, you lose a pound.

Here's an example of how weight loss works. Let's say that my current weight has recently climbed to 150 pounds. My ideal body weight is 140; naturally, I'm interested in dropping those extra 10 pounds. I know that to maintain a weight of 140, I need to consume about 1,540 calories a day because each pound of body weight requires about 11 calories a day.

Because I'm carrying 10 extra pounds, it's obvious that I've been consuming too many calories for quite some time. I've probably been consuming at least 1,650 calories a day, since 150 pounds x 11 calories per pound is 1,650 calories. Those extra caloric deposits are reflected in the "savings accounts" on my hips, thighs, and trunk. I need to make some regular caloric withdrawals to get back to my ideal weight.

There are several ways I can make the necessary caloric withdrawals. At the very least, I can return to my old way of eating. I can stop eating like a 150-pound person and start eating like a 140-pound person again. To do this, I'll no longer consume 1,650 calories a day: I'll go back to consuming 1,540 calories daily. When I follow this plan, I'll be getting 110 fewer calories each day. At the end of the week, I will have created a caloric deficit of 770 calories. At this rate, it will take me approximately four and a half weeks to create a total caloric deficit of 3,500 calories; enough to lose a pound of body weight.

Naturally, I'll want to lose those extra 10 pounds a little faster, so here's what I'll do: I'll create an even greater caloric deficit. Instead of consuming 1,540 calories a day, I'll consume 1,250 calories a day — that's still enough to ensure I get all the nutrients my body needs for good health. When I consume 1,250 calories a day, I create a daily deficit of 290 calories. After seven days, my total deficit is 2,030 calories. At this rate, it will only take 12 days to drop a pound of my excess body weight.

If I want to lose those extra 10 pounds even faster, I can always step up my level of physical activity. If I put in an extra half-hour of

WEIGHT LOSS WORKSHEET

A Multiply your current body weight by 11 to determine the approximate number of calories you are currently consuming daily, and write that number here:

B Next, decide on the number of calories you plan to consume each day. (Keep in mind that it's never wise to consume fewer than 1,000 calories a day without a physician's supervision.) Write that number here:

C Subtract the number on line B from the number on line A to determine your daily caloric deficit, and write that number here:

D If you plan to create an even greater caloric deficit by exercising, write the number of calories you plan to expend exercising each day here:

E Add the numbers on line C and D to get your total daily caloric deficit created by dietary changes and physical activity. Write this number here:

F To determine your total weekly caloric deficit, multiply the number on line E by 7, and write the number here:

G To determine how many pounds you will lose in one week, divide the number on line F by 3,500, and write that number here:
(If this number is more than two pounds per week, you may want to increase your daily caloric consumption. If you plan to engage in rapid weight loss of more than two pounds a week, consult your doctor first.)

H To determine how long it will likely take you to lose your total excess weight, simply subtract your goal weight from your current weight, and write that number here:

I Now, divide H by G, and you'll have the approximate number of weeks it will take you to achieve your goal weight.

riding on a daily basis, I'll expend an extra 120 calories each day. When I add this 120-calorie deficit to the 290-calorie deficit created by my dietary changes, the end result is a daily caloric deficit of 410 calories. When I follow this regimen, it will take me only about 8½ days to lose a pound of excess body weight.

If you're interested in finding out roughly how long it will take you to lose your excess body weight, use the worksheet opposite.

If losing your excess weight will take longer than you'd like, don't be discouraged. With every pound you lose, you'll feel better and stronger, both physically and emotionally. Your self-confidence will grow by leaps and bounds. As you get into the habit of eating a nutritious, well-balanced diet and getting plenty of exercise, you'll find that achieving and maintaining your desired body weight are easier than you ever thought possible.

Foods To Include

A Plant-based Diet Is a Healthy Diet

You don't have to become a devout vegetarian to eat a healthy diet, but, ideally, the majority of foods in your daily diet should come from plant sources, including fruits, vegetables, and whole grains. Women who deprive themselves of important plant nutrients not only leave themselves open to a variety of diseases but also may feel less vibrant and energetic than they might otherwise.

Fruits and Vegetables

One of the smartest strategies to improve dra-matically the quality of your diet — and your health — is to eat five to nine servings of a variety of fruits and vegetables every day. Diets rich in fruits and vegetables are associated with a lower risk of dozens of diseases, including obesity, cancer, and cardiovascular disease.

A number of studies show that women who include more fruits and vegetables in their diets are not only healthier but also thinner. There's a perfectly logical explanation for this: Fruits, vegetables, and other plant foods tend to fill you up faster than foods that are highly processed.

You probably know from experience that you don't necessarily stop eating just because you've consumed an appropriate number of calories. When it comes to pushing back from the table, feeling full is an important trigger. A growing body of evidence indicates it isn't just the caloric content of the foods you eat that makes you feel full and want to stop eating, it's also the *volume* of food you eat.

Let's face it — almost everyone likes to eat, and nobody wants to feel deprived. Many of us would rather eat more food than less, if at all possible. If Americans didn't like quantity in terms of food, there would be no such thing as king-sized candy bars, super-sized fries, or second helpings. For the record, it's okay to eat a lot of food, as long as you eat a lot of the "right" kinds of foods. Foods that lend themselves to bulk consumption are those relatively low in calories, high in moisture content, and rich in nutrients, such as fruits and vegetables. In contrast, certain foods are not appropriate for eating in bulk. Eating too many of the "wrong" kinds of foods, such as chips, cookies, and candy, can be disastrous for your health and, of course, your weight.

If, for example, you decide to snack on a 2-ounce serving of milk chocolate, you'll consume about 300 calories, 17 grams of fat, and less than a gram of fiber. There's no doubt you'd derive a great deal of pleasure from eating the morsel of chocolate, but no matter how determined you might be to savor it, you would be hard pressed to spend more than 60 seconds eating the entire 2-ounce serving. In addition, you probably won't feel the least bit full after eating such a meager portion, and, as a result, you might be tempted to eat another serving.

If, on the other hand, you decided to treat yourself to some fresh, juicy apples instead, you'd have an entirely different experience. For roughly the same number of calories, you could eat more than a pound of raw apples. You could, in fact, eat four medium-sized unpeeled apples, each measuring approximately 2¾ inches in diameter and weighing in at about 5.5 ounces.

Even after eating all this delicious fruit, you'd still come away with only about 324 calories, less than a gram of fat, and roughly 16 grams of fiber. I'm willing to bet it would take you at least five full minutes to eat those four apples, if you were able to eat them all. It's probably safe to say you would feel very satisfied and full afterward.

Sample the Spectrum

When you were a child, your mom probably encouraged you to eat your greens, and she was definitely on the right track. Green-colored fruits and veggies are packed with vitamins and minerals, and they have dozens of important health benefits. Science has marched on since we were kids, and we now know fruits and vegetables in hues of blue, red, orange, purple, yellow, and white also have a lot to offer. Substances called phytochemicals are responsible for the rich, vibrant colors of various fruits and vegetables. Not only do these natural plant compounds safeguard the health of plants, they also impart a measure of disease protection to the humans who eat them.

The results of hundreds of scientific studies demonstrate the power of phytochemicals in fruits and vegetables to reduce the risk of cancer, heart disease, and dozens of other medical maladies. While the ingredients in many nutritional supplements are helpful, they can't come close to duplicating the protective effects of the naturally occurring phytochemicals found in plant foods. When you sample the full spectrum of color offered by a variety of fruits and vegetables, you're giving yourself the broadest scope of health benefits and disease protection possible.

Greens

Green fruits and vegetables should be a staple of every diet. They're loaded with fiber, minerals, and vitamins, and they're packed with potent antioxidants that protect you from a number of illnesses and promote healthy aging. Greens enhance the growth and maintenance of strong bones and teeth. They're also a good source of folate, a B vitamin that can reduce the risk of heart disease and help prevent certain types of birth defects in unborn babies. Spinach, collards, kale, and broccoli are rich in lutein and zeaxanthin, two antioxidant compounds that help prevent macular degeneration. All the cruciferous vegetables, including cabbage, Brussels sprouts, broccoli, and cauliflower, are especially rich in antioxidant compounds that reduce the risk of cancer.

Reds

When you add deep red and bright pink fruits and vegetables to your daily diet, you're also adding powerful phytochemicals called lycopenes and anthocyanins. Diets rich in these antioxidants can dramatically lower the risk of heart disease and some cancers, boost cognitive function and memory, and improve the health of the urinary tract.

Oranges and Yellows

Orange fruits and veggies are rich in beta-carotene and vitamin C. Both substances are natural antioxidants that enhance the immune system's ability to ward off infections and illnesses, from the common cold to cancer. The B vitamin folate also is found in orange fruits and vegetables, as are carotenoids and other bioflavonoids that promote healthy aging of the eyes and cardiovascular system. Bright yellow fruits and vegetables offer many of the same perks similar to the orange group. They're chock-full of vitamins, minerals, and antioxidants.

Blues and Purples

Phytochemicals called anthocyanins are responsible for the brilliant blue and purple colors of many fruits and vegetables. These compounds protect the body against cancer-causing agents and promote healthy aging. Anthocyanins also have been shown to play an important role in the health of the brain and the urinary tract.

Whites

Although their colors are less vibrant, white, tan, and brown fruits and vegetables contain many vitamins, minerals, and phytochemicals. One such phytochemical, known as allicin, is found in the garlic and onion family. In addition to helping regulate blood pressure and lower cholesterol levels, allicin has been shown to have anti-fungal, anti-bacterial, and anti-viral properties that enhance the body's ability to fight infection. Studies show that phytochemicals called indoles and sulfaroraphanes in cauliflower and other cruciferous vegetables help reduce the risk of cancer and cardiovascular disease.

Got Gas?
It Could Be Lactose Intolerance

You know that vegetables, legumes, and whole grains are vital components of a nutritious, well-balanced diet, but what happens if your digestive tract rebels every time you eat them? You could be suffering from complex -carbohydrate intolerance, a condition that

COLOR-CODING YOUR DIET

GREAT GREENS

Vegetables

avocados	artichokes	arugula	asparagus
green beans	broccoli	broccoflower	Brussels sprouts
green cabbage	celery	cucumbers	endive
leafy greens	lettuce	okra	green onion
green peas	snow peas	sugar snap peas	green peppers
spinach	chayote squash	watercress	zucchini

Fruits

green apples	green grapes	kiwifruit	limes
honeydew melon	green pears		

RESPLENDENT REDS

Vegetables

beets	red onions	red peppers	red potatoes
radicchio	radishes	rhubarb	tomatoes

Fruits

red apples	cherries	cranberries	pink or red grapefruit
red grapes	guava	blood oranges	papaya
red pears	pomegranates	raspberries	strawberries
watermelon			

YUMMY YELLOWS AND ORANGES

Vegetables

yellow beets	carrots	sweet corn	orange peppers
yellow peppers	sweet potatoes	yellow potatoes	pumpkin
rutabagas	butternut squash	yellow summer squash	yellow winter squash
yellow tomatoes			

Fruits

yellow apples	apricots	cantaloupe	yellow figs
grapefruit	golden kiwifruit	lemons	mangoes
nectarines	oranges	papayas	peaches
yellow pears	persimmons	pineapples	tangerines
yellow watermelon			

BENEFICIAL BLUES AND PURPLES

Vegetables

purple asparagus	purple cabbage	purple carrots	eggplant
purple Belgian endive	purple peppers		

Fruits

blackberries	blueberries	black currants	elderberries
purple figs	purple grapes	plums	dried plums
raisins			

WHOLESOME WHITES

Vegetables/Herbs

Jerusalem artichoke	cauliflower	chives	white corn
garlic	jicama	kohlrabi	leeks
mushrooms	onions	parsnips	white potatoes
scallions	shallots	turnips	

Fruits

bananas	dates	white nectarines	white peaches
brown pears			

causes varying degrees of digestive distress whenever foods rich in complex carbohydrates are consumed. The condition can put a serious crimp in your gut, not to mention your social life.

Many nutritious foods from the plant kingdom are rich in complex carbohydrates. A short list includes broccoli, kidney beans, barley, and oat bran, but there are dozens more. As it turns out, humans have a hard time digesting these foods completely, due to a lack of alpha-galactosidase, the digestive enzyme required to break down complex carbohydrates.

In the human small intestine, foods made of complex carbohydrates are only partially digested before they're moved along to the large intestine. Once they arrive, the bacteria that normally inhabit the human gut happily feast upon the remains, creating hydrogen and carbon dioxide gas in the process. This intestinal gas is responsible for the most uncomfortable and socially distressing symptoms of complex-carbohydrate intolerance: cramping, belching, and flatulence. Because of these unpleasant side effects, many women avoid eating some of the most nutritious plant foods. Food-avoidance isn't the best plan of action because the health benefits of a plant-based diet are entirely too good to pass up.

If you think you're suffering from complex-carbohydrate intolerance, you may be right. Still, it's a good idea to discuss your symptoms with your doctor as symptoms of carbohydrate intolerance can mimic those of more serious conditions involving the heart, gastrointestinal tract, or reproductive system. Once your doctor has dismissed the possibility of a more dangerous disorder, there's a simple remedy available for reducing carbohydrate-induced discomfort.

An alpha-galactosidase enzyme preparation, called Beano, is available over the counter in most pharmacies and grocery stores. Taking just one tablet or five drops of the liquid preparation for each half-cup serving of complex-carbohydrate foods you plan to eat will prevent the painful, gaseous consequences. For the enzyme preparation to work, you have to take it right before you eat the food, not during or after your meal.

Although many over-the-counter medicines containing simethicone and activated charcoal can help reduce the symptoms associated with eating plant foods, they don't target the enzyme deficiency at the root of complex-carbohydrate intolerance. Enzyme replacement therapy is the only effective preventive remedy for complex-carbohydrate intolerance, and it can help women with complex-carbohydrate intolerance enjoy all the benefits of a nutritious, plant-based diet — minus the gastrointestinal grief.

Preparation Matters

Most fruits and vegetables are best eaten in natural forms. While some produce requires minimal preparation, including steaming, boiling, or baking, the vast majority of the culinary "improvements" we make to fruits and vegeta-bles aren't really improvements at all. In most cases, they actually detract from their natural goodness and nutritional value.

A baked potato served in its own skin, for example, is rich in fiber, vitamins, and minerals. Unadulterated, it's nutritious, tasty, filling, and satisfying — and rarely eaten by the average American. Far more popular than the "naked" potato is the loaded version of the vegetable. This artery-clogging concoction involves smothering the potato with large quantities of high-fat, cholesterol-laden condiments, including butter, sour cream, cheese, and bacon bits. As if that's not bad enough, we have other means of torturing our potatoes. In the United States, the preferred method of eating a potato is in the form of a French fry — stripped of its nutritious, high-fiber skin, sliced, and soaked and scalded in vats of oil loaded with saturated and trans fats before being slathered in salt.

Even more benign methods of processing fruits and vegetables rob them of nutrients and detract from their value. A whole, unpeeled apple is an excellent source of fiber, vitamins, and minerals. When we peel the apple and press the fruit to make apple juice, we still have lots of vitamins and minerals, but we've now removed the fiber and dramatically increased the concentration of sugar and calories. The best and most nutritious way to eat an apple, or practically any other fruit or vegetable, is with the absolute minimum amount of processing.

Whole Grains

Whole grains offer dozens of health benefits

WHAT'S IN A SERVING?

1 medium size	Whole fruit or vegetable
1/2 cup	Raw, leafy greens
1/2 cup	Peas or beans — cooked, dry, frozen, or canned
1/2 cup	Fresh, frozen, or canned fruit in 100 percent fruit juice
1/2 cup	Fresh, frozen, or canned vegetables
1/4 cup	Dried fruit
3/4 cup (6 ounces)	100 percent fruit or vegetable juice

that you just can't find in most other foods. They're an excellent source of folic acid, a B vitamin that plays a vital role in preventing certain birth defects in unborn children. Diets rich in folic acid also are credited with reducing the risk of heart disease and stroke later in life. Whole grains contain essential vitamins and minerals such as vitamin B-6, vitamin E, and selenium, nutrients that often are lost when whole grains are processed.

Because whole-grain foods are naturally high in fiber, they help ward off a slew of common medical conditions, including diabetes, high cholesterol, gastrointestinal disorders, and heart disease. While fruits and vegetables have long been credited with the ability to reduce the risk of cancer, the cancer-fighting properties of whole-grain foods have been vastly underestimated. For years, fruits and vegetables were known to contain high concentrations of cancer-fighting antioxidants called phenols. Until recently, whole-grain foods were thought to be lacking in these protective ingredients.

Recent research offers sound proof that whole-grain foods are rich in antioxidant phenols, and scientists have demonstrated that the level of anti-cancer activity provided by whole-grain foods is as good as — or better than — the level provided by fruits and vegetables. In the past decade, whole-grain foods have been shown to reduce the risk of certain cancers, including those of the breast and colon.

The key to the cancer-fighting potential of the whole grain lies in its very wholeness. A single grain of whole wheat, for example, is composed of three components: the endosperm, bran, and germ. When wheat is refined during the manufacturing process, the germ and the bran are removed. The germ is rich in antioxidants and is an important source of protein and high-energy carbohydrates while the bran is the main source of fiber. In addition, these two important components contain the majority of the grain's cancer-fighting phytochemicals. Because

TIPS FOR PACKING MORE FRUITS AND VEGETABLES IN YOUR DIET

- Keep cut-up veggies and fruits close at hand for snacking. Purchase them pre-cut or cut them up yourself and keep them front and center in clear containers in the fridge for high visibility and easy accessibility.

- Keep whole, fresh fruit in a bowl on the kitchen counter or table.

- To save time, buy prepared fresh fruits and vegetables, including bagged salads, peeled and washed baby carrots, broccoli and cauliflower florets, and sliced mushrooms.

- When fresh fruit isn't available or convenient, use canned fruit packed in 100 percent fruit juice and frozen fruits without added sugar.

- Use fresh, frozen, or canned vegetables as extenders for chili, meatloaf, spaghetti sauce, and hamburgers. Diced onions, mushrooms, squash, and zucchini make nutritious, flavorful additions to just about any meat dish.

- Top hamburgers with leafy lettuce, ripe tomatoes, and fresh onions, and top pizzas with peppers, onions, broccoli, pineapple chunks, and mushrooms instead of pepperoni or sausage.

- Make fajitas and stir fry with loads of sautéed vegetables, including colorful bell peppers and onions, summer squash, and eggplant.

- When eating out, ask for a side dish of cooked veggies with your dinner instead of French fries, and order delicious strawberries, melons, or raspberries for dessert, instead of cake, pie, or ice cream.

- Fill your plate with fresh fruits and vegetables at restaurant salad bars, but go easy on the cold pasta dishes, creamy salads, and high-fat salad dressings.

- When you're on the go, take dried fruit and nuts along for quick, high-energy snacks.

- At the grocery store, choose a fruit or vegetable of every color, and buy a fruit or vegetable that you've never tried. Be sure to take advantage of prepared items at the salad bar.

- Strive to eat one fruit or vegetable from each color group each day.

each part of the grain contributes different nutrients, the best way to get all the benefits is to eat the whole grain.

To obtain all the goodness offered by whole-grain foods, you have to include them in your diet. Try eating brown rice, barley, whole-grain breads and pasta, and even grains that may be unfamiliar to you, including millet and kasha. Look for breads, cereals, and pastas that list whole wheat or other whole grains as the first item on the list of ingredients. Choose whole-grain breads for making sandwiches and whole-grain crackers for snacks. Try substituting whole-wheat pasta or brown rice for potatoes or white rice.

The most recent dietary guidelines for Americans recommend consuming at least half of all grains in the form of whole grains, or three 1-ounce servings of whole grains daily. That doesn't sound like much, but the average American eats less than an ounce of whole grains daily, and nearly a third of Americans eat none at all.

Dairy Foods

You may not wear a milk mustache as often as you did when you were a kid, but keeping dairy in your diet is just as important now as it was then. Dairy products are an important source of calcium, and while there are other food sources of the mineral, the calcium in dairy is easily absorbed and particularly beneficial. In the United States, dairy products are the most popular source of the mineral, supplying roughly 70 percent of total dietary calcium.

Women require calcium at every stage of life. As a child, you needed it to make strong bones and teeth. In adulthood, the mineral is necessary to preserve existing bone loss and ward off osteoporosis. In addition to its bone-building properties, calcium from dairy sources also is known to help prevent high blood pressure, colon cancer, and obesity. In spite of all the perks provided by dairy products, most folks don't get nearly enough. The typical American adult consumes only about a serving and a half a day while most folks need more along the lines of three servings a day.

Low-fat dairy products are excellent sources of dietary calcium. Each serving has roughly 300 mg of the mineral. Shellfish, soy products, and greens are also good sources. Food manufacturers are making it easier to get more of the mineral by fortifying foods such as orange juice, breakfast cereals, and bread with extra calcium.

Although the National Academy of Sciences recommends daily calcium intakes of 1,200 mg for women over age 50, and 1,000 mg for women ages 19 to 50 and those who are pregnant or nursing, many nutrition experts recommend higher intakes. A daily intake of 1,500 mg for women who are pregnant, nursing, or menopausal may be optimal.

Lactose Intolerance — Be Wary of the Dairy

Milk is often referred to as nature's "perfect food," and while it may be perfect for babies, many adults can't stomach it. Millions of Americans suffer from lactose intolerance, a condition that renders them unable to digest the sugar in milk.

The primary sugar in milk is lactose, a bulky molecule composed of two smaller sugars. Before lactose can pass through the walls of the intestines and be used for energy by the body, the molecule must be split into its smaller constituents. Splitting the milk sugar lactose is a relatively simple process, but it requires a special enzyme called lactase. In folks without lactose intolerance, the enzyme is produced in adequate amounts by the lining of the intestine.

Almost all healthy infants make plenty of the enzyme lactase, but after they're weaned from milk, lactase production naturally begins to slack off. In individuals with lactose intolerance, production of the enzyme ceases altogether. Lactase production is a genetically programmed process and has a lot to do with your heritage. The majority of African Americans, Asian Americans, and Native Americans can't properly digest dairy products because they don't make enough of the lactase enzyme.

In most cases, the enzyme deficiency is permanent and irreversible. If you're lactose intolerant now, you're likely to remain so for the rest of your life, unless you happen to become pregnant. More than 40 percent of lactose intolerant women temporarily regain the ability to digest the milk sugar during pregnancy.

If your body doesn't produce enough lactase to digest the dairy products you consume, much of the milk sugar remains undigested in the small intestine, drawing fluid into the bowel like a sponge. The undigested sugar in 1 cup of

milk can pull up to a cup of water into the gut, resulting in intestinal cramping and diarrhea. The gastrointestinal discomfort may not be the worst of it, at least as far as your social life is concerned. As the normal bacterial inhabitants of your gut devour the undigested lactose sugar, they shamelessly form gas as a by-product. The excess gas in your belly can lead to bloating and give you a killer case of cramps. When that gas finally makes its exit, it can make you very unpopular with the people around you.

The symptoms of lactose intolerance can arise within 15 minutes of eating dairy foods, or they may take several hours to develop. Surprisingly, many people with lactose intolerance aren't aware that they have the condition because they may not associate their intestinal fireworks with the consumption of milk products.

How do you know if you're lactose intolerant? Your doctor has several high-tech, high-priced tests available to help you find out, but the least expensive way to make the diagnosis is simply to adopt a lactose-free diet for a few weeks. If most of your cramping, bloating, gas, and diarrhea disappear, you've probably got the condition.

Even if you don't seem to have the intestinal fortitude for milk, you don't have to give up dairy products altogether. Because lactose intolerance affects people in varying degrees, you may just need to experiment a little to find out exactly how much lactose you can tolerate before your gastrointestinal tract rebels. You'll probably be able to squeeze in a glass of milk or two a day, especially if you drink it with your meals. Consuming dairy products in modest amounts and with other foods helps hold the milk sugar in your stomach longer, increasing the chances that it will be digested.

Most people with lactose intolerance can enjoy aged cheeses such as Swiss and extra-sharp cheddar, which contain only traces of lactose. Because yogurt contains helpful bacteria that have already begun the process of lactose digestion, you'll probably be able to eat it without any problems. Thanks to modern technology, many lactose-reduced dairy products are available in most supermarkets and health food stores. You also can buy over-the-counter lactase enzyme supplements, including Lactaid and Dairy Ease. These products work just like the natural enzyme, so that you're able to enjoy nature's "perfect food" without being perfectly miserable.

Protein

Protein can be obtained from a number of dietary sources, but it is often accompanied by other, less desirable ingredients. As you decide which protein-rich foods to include in your Riding for Life diet, try to choose those that not only satisfy your body's requirement for the nutrient but are also good for your overall health.

Beef, Pork, and Poultry

Meat products are packed with high-quality protein, and they serve as a major source of the nutrient in the typical American diet. Beef, pork, and poultry also provide B vitamins and minerals, including iron. Because iron from red meat is the type most easily used by the body, it is especially beneficial for women with low iron levels or iron-deficiency anemia. On the down side, meat and other animal sources of protein are often high in fat, cholesterol, and calories and should be consumed in moderation.

Poultry products, including chicken and turkey, are generally lower in fat than other meats, but only if they're eaten without the skin. Although skinless dark meat is leaner than some cuts of beef or pork, it has nearly twice as much fat as white meat. Because ground poultry often includes dark meat and skin, it may have as much fat as ground beef. In some cases, it may have even more, so be sure to compare nutrition labels.

Soy

Soy is an excellent source of protein, vitamins, minerals, and heart-healthy polyunsaturated fat. Unlike animal sources of protein, soy products are typically low in saturated fat and cholesterol. Several studies suggest that eating a soy-rich diet (containing 25 grams or more of soy protein per day) may lower blood pressure, total cholesterol levels, and low-density lipoprotein cholesterol (LDL) levels, which in turn can reduce the risk of heart disease.

Soy products have long been praised for their ability to alleviate menopausal symptoms, including hot flashes and night sweats. In theory, it makes sense. Soybeans are rich in phytoestrogens, plant estrogens that can mimic the actions of the human hormone in many body tissues. In recent years, however, many carefully designed scientific studies have failed to demonstrate a relationship between soy consumption and a reduction in menopausal symptoms. In clinical trials in which phytoestrogens from soy were found to alleviate hot flashes and other menopausal symptoms, women generally consumed large amounts of soy protein — up to 50 grams a day, which is the equivalent of a pound and a half of tofu or eight glasses of soy milk. In contrast, the typical American ordinarily consumes only a few grams of soy protein daily.

If soy can mimic the actions of human estrogen, it would make sense that it might trigger the growth of some estrogen-dependent cancers, such as cancer of the breast and uterus. While soy was once praised for its ability to reduce the risk of breast cancer, a handful of recent reports suggest that a concentrated supply of soy proteins may actually stimulate the growth of breast cancer cells. Although soy products may not protect women from breast cancer or even menopausal symptoms, they're still an excellent source of heart-healthy protein and can provide a sound, low-fat alternative to animal products.

Beans

Because they're packed with protein, dried beans and other legumes are considered part of the meat group. Beans are low in fat, cholesterol, and sodium, and loaded with vitamins, minerals, and fiber. They're considered to be the best vegetable source of folate, an important B vitamin that protects the heart. The soluble fiber in beans also offers heart-healthy benefits by lowering cholesterol. One cup of cooked beans provides as much as 15 grams of dietary fiber, more than half the daily recommended intake for women.

Dried beans are those that are dry-packaged in sealed bags, as well as those that come pre-cooked in cans. Pinto, navy, lima, and black beans are considered to be dried beans, but green beans, string beans, and soybeans are not.

Nuts

If you're keeping an eye on your weight, you're probably trying to steer clear of high-calorie snacks, including nuts. While most varieties of nuts can pack a caloric punch, there's no reason they can't be part of a nutritious, well-balanced diet. Because they're protein-rich, nuts are considered to be part of the meat group. Ounce for ounce, nuts supply roughly the same amount of protein as meat.

Most nuts are the seeds or dried fruit from trees. Although peanuts are commonly thought of as nuts, they're actually members of the legume family, which makes them close cousins to peas and beans. Because nuts come from plants, they're naturally cholesterol free. Most varieties are good sources of thiamin, niacin, phosphorus, zinc, and folate, and some are excellent sources of selenium, copper, magnesium, and vitamin E.

True to their reputation, nuts are high in fat, but the fats found in nuts are the friendly types, including monounsaturated and polyunsaturated fats. Unlike the saturated fat in animal products, the unsaturated fats found in nuts won't send your cholesterol levels soaring. In fact, several studies show that eating nuts actually lowers total cholesterol and low-density lipoprotein (LDL) cholesterol levels. Recent research also reveals that people who eat nuts regularly are less likely to be overweight than people who avoid them. Because they're satisfying and filling, most folks tend to eat fewer total calories when they snack on nuts.

Eggs

Eggs are an excellent source of high-quality protein that many women overlook. For years, Americans were encouraged to go easy on the eggs because they're a concentrated source of cholesterol. A large egg contains roughly 213 mg of cholesterol, about two-thirds of the recommended daily intake.

In recent years scientists have discovered that the cholesterol contained in foods doesn't have as much of a negative effect on blood cholesterol as once believed. The most important factors determining whether you have high cholesterol levels are the genes you inherited from your parents and the amount of saturated fat in your diet. If you're reasonably healthy, it's probably safe to say that eating an egg a day won't drive up your cholesterol — or your risk of heart disease.

Even if your cholesterol level is higher than you or your doctor would like, you still don't have to swear off eggs altogether. You just have to approach the yolk of the egg with caution because it contains the entire 213 mg of cholesterol and 5 grams of fat, to boot. The egg white, however, is totally free of fat and cholesterol.

An omelet made with four egg whites offers just 68 calories and no fat, yet it is still packed with 16 grams of protein.

Egg protein is of such high quality that it is often used as the gold standard by which other types of protein are compared. In its entirety, each egg contains around 75 calories, 6 grams of protein, and varying amounts of 13 vitamins and several minerals. The yolk of the egg is one of the few food sources of vitamin D, an ingredient that helps your body use calcium and build strong bones.

Fish

If you're looking for a good way to work more high-quality protein into your diet, eating three servings of baked or grilled fish each week is a good place to start. Fatty fish such as mackerel, lake trout, herring, sardines, albacore tuna, and salmon are especially beneficial, since they're rich in omega-3 fatty acids.

Because human beings aren't capable of producing essential fatty acids, including those of the omega-3 variety, these substances must be obtained from food. Consumption of these compounds benefits the heart by lowering blood pressure, cholesterol, and triglycerides.

Due to industrial pollution, fish may contain trace amounts of the toxin methylmercury. Salmon, sardines, flounder, cod, catfish, canned tuna, and trout tend to have lower levels than larger fish such as swordfish, shark, tilefish, tuna steak, and king mackerel. As methylmercury is tightly bound to proteins in all fish tissues, no method of cooking or cleaning will reduce the amount. With this in mind, a weekly intake of two to four servings of fish is recommended, with special emphasis on varieties known to have the lowest levels of mercury.

Drink To Your Health

When it comes to your health and nutrition, the liquids you drink are just as important as the foods you eat. Recent research suggests that most American adults obtain about a fifth of their daily calories from beverages, many of which are sweetened with sugar. Not only do extra calories and sugar contribute to weight problems, they also increase the chances of developing diabetes.

The Beverage Guidance System, created by Dr. Barry Popkin at the University of North Carolina, classifies beverages on the basis of their contribution to caloric intake, essential nutrients, and beneficial and adverse health effects. In order of most preferred to least preferred, the six classes are noted on this page.

For optimum health, you should strive to meet most of your daily fluid needs with beverages from the lowest levels. Ideally, just 10 percent — and no more than 14 percent — of your daily calories should be obtained from liquids. Some of the beverages you drink can benefit your health while others detract from it. Here's a brief overview of what beverages bring to the table:

Water

While significant dehydration can be deadly, even mild dehydration can negatively impact your physical and mental health. Effects of mild dehydration include fatigue, irritability, and muscle weakness, as well as impaired concentration and memory. Water is the best hydration fluid for your body, bar none.

LEVEL 1
Water

LEVEL 2
Unsweetened coffee and tea

LEVEL 3
Low-fat and non-fat milk and soy beverages

LEVEL 4
Calorie-free sweetened beverages, including diet sodas and other diet drinks.

LEVEL 5
Calorie-containing beverages with some nutrients, including 100% fruit and vegetable juices, sports drinks, and alcoholic beverages.

LEVEL 6
Calorie-containing sweetened beverages, including sodas, fruit drinks, and other beverages sweetened with sugar or high-fructose corn syrup.

Caffeine-Containing Beverages

For most healthy non-pregnant women, moderate caffeine consumption isn't harmful. Moderate caffeine intake is defined as an intake of up to 400 mg per day, which is the equivalent of four cups of coffee, eight cups of tea, or about nine 12-ounce cans of soda. Scientific evidence reveals that intakes of up to 400 mg a day do not increase the risk of heart disease, osteoporosis, or high cholesterol levels in adults. While caffeine acts as a mild diuretic, most folks can consume up to about 500 mg a day without becoming dehydrated or creating a water imbalance in their bodies. A caffeine consumption of more 300 mg a day in pregnant women has been associated with an increased risk of miscarriage and delivery of low birth weight babies.

Coffee

Drinking coffee the American way — brewed and filtered — seems to be perfectly safe, as long as you don't exceed the recommended caffeine intake. Consumption of boiled, unfiltered coffee, on the other hand, appears to elevate total and LDL cholesterol levels, which may contribute to heart disease. Two compounds in coffee, cafestol and kahweol, are thought to be responsible for this effect. Because paper coffee filters trap these agents, filtered coffee doesn't elevate cholesterol levels or increase the risk for heart disease.

Tea

Numerous studies suggest that antioxidants and other compounds in tea enhance the body's immune function and lower the risk for heart disease and certain types of cancers. While black tea and green tea offer a number of health benefits, you may have to drink at least three cups a day to reap them.

Low-Fat and Non-Fat Milk

Milk is an important source of calcium, vitamin D, high-quality protein, and other essential nutrients. While consumption of calcium-rich milk has long been linked to healthy bones and teeth, recent research suggests that drinking milk can lower the risk of high blood pressure, colon cancer, and obesity.

100 Percent Fruit and Vegetable Juices.

Eating whole fruits and vegetables in their natural states is better than drinking them as juices. Vegetable juices typically contain substantial amounts of added sodium, which most women don't need. While fruit juices are nutrient-rich, they're also a concentrated source of sugar and calories. When eaten whole, fruits and vegetables are higher in fiber and typically more satisfying than juices.

Sports Drinks

The minerals and electrolytes in these beverages replenish those that are lost during strenuous training and competition, enhancing the performance and stamina of athletes. But unless you're exercising or working for periods longer than an hour or so, they're not really necessary.

In the short term, water is all your body needs to replace lost fluids, and any minerals and electrolytes lost are easily replenished at the next meal or snack. Because most sports drinks are relatively high in sugar and calories, they're not the best choices for fluid replacement on a regular basis.

Alcoholic Beverages

Moderate consumption of alcohol, defined as a maximum of one drink a day for women, is associated with a reduced risk of heart disease, type II diabetes, and even gallstones. Drinking more on a regular basis can cause problems, including an elevated risk of breast cancer and accidents. No amount of alcohol is considered safe during pregnancy because even modest alcohol consumption is associated with an increased risk of birth defects.

Diet Drinks

The artificial sweeteners used in diet drinks have been deemed safe and nontoxic by the FDA, but that doesn't mean that they're good for you. Several studies suggest that the sweet taste of diet sodas and other diet drinks may promote a preference for other sweet foods and beverages and may ultimately contribute to weight gain rather than weight loss.

Calorie-containing Sodas

There's little doubt that these sugary beverages contribute to obesity and diabetes, and they provide very little in the way of vitamins, minerals, or other beneficial nutrients. They aren't the best choices for replacing body fluids, and they should be consumed in moderation.

Portion Misfortune

If you're a card-carrying member of the clean plate club, now might be a good time to rethink your eating strategy. In the United States, portion sizes are at an all-time high — most have tripled in the past 30 years. When it comes to your health, bigger isn't always better. Recent research has demonstrated that larger portions encourage overeating by as much as 56 percent.

The super-sizing of foods and beverages in U.S. restaurants and fast-food joints is at least partially to blame for the up-sizing of Americans, who typically eat at least three meals a week away from home. Increases in serving sizes over the past two decades are closely matched by the rising trend in obesity. Currently, more than half of American adults and more than a third of American children are overweight or obese, and this extra weight contributes to more than 300,000 preventable deaths each year.

When fast food first debuted in the 1940s, a typical meal consisting of a burger, fries, and a soft drink offered about 450 calories. The same meal today — in super-sized proportions — provides around 1,500 calories. For some folks, this number fulfills an entire day's caloric requirement. While burger joints may have started the trend in portion distortion, they certainly don't have a corner on the market. Serving sizes in all types of restaurants — and even in the average American home — have increased dramatically.

That's not good because the amount of food on your plate has a tremendous influence on the amount that you end up eating. In a survey conducted by the American Institute for Cancer Research, a third of Americans polled said that the more they're served, the more they tend to

PROPER PORTIONS AT A GLANCE

Portion Size	Compare To
3 ounces of meat, poultry, or fish	Deck of cards or cassette tape
1 medium baked potato	Computer mouse
1 cup cooked pasta, rice, yogurt, milk, or vegetables, large fruit, or large potato	Baseball or large fist
1 medium-sized fruit, half-cup ice cream, sorbet, or yogurt; half-cup of pasta or rice; half-cup cooked vegetables; 1 small baked potato	Tennis ball, ice cream scoop, or cupcake wrapper
2 tablespoons peanut butter or salad dressing	Entire thumb (medium to large hand)
1 ounce of meat, poultry, fish, or cheese; 1 fluid ounce	4 small stacked dice, 2 dominos, or an ice cube
1 tablespoon olive oil or chopped nuts	Tip of your thumb to first knuckle or half-dollar

eat. In the same survey, 70 percent of Americans adults said that when they're dining out, they almost always polish off everything on their plates.

It would seem logical that eating too many calories at one meal would lead you to settle for fewer calories at the next one, but this doesn't seem to be the case. Studies show that most people don't compensate for the extra food they consume by cutting calories later in the day. As the calories accumulate, the pounds pile up. While most of us are busy battling dietary bad guys, including fat, cholesterol, and simple carbohydrates, we may be ignoring another critical factor in the nutrition equation: quantity.

When you're serving yourself, controlling the amount of food that ends up on your plate is relatively easy. To avoid overeating at home, always eat from plates and bowls, rather than directly from the box or bag, which makes it harder to keep track of the amount you consume. It's a good idea to use small dishes instead of large ones, so that you don't underestimate the amount of food they contain.

When you're dining out, your best bet may be to base your food consumption on serving sizes recommended by the U.S. Department of Agriculture, rather than the amount dished out to you. No matter how good you feel about choosing the 8-ounce sirloin over the 12-ounce T-bone, it's important to remember that the recommended serving size of steak is actually much smaller. According to the USDA, a standard serving of meat is a mere 3 ounces, about the size of a deck of cards. And while most restaurants pile your plate with more than 3 cups of pasta, the USDA considers an individual serving size to be just about a half-cup.

If you want to eat out and avoid becoming a victim of portion misfortune, it's a good idea to practice a little defensive dining. You can start by ordering a half serving of your favorite entrée. If that's not an option, you can always share your meal with your dinner date or ask your server to put half of your meal in a take-out box before delivering the remainder to your table. It takes a little effort, but keeping extra food off your plate will go a long way toward keeping extra weight off your body.

To remember the size of recommended portions, compare food servings to objects that you can picture easily in your mind. Measuring and weighing food isn't for everyone, especially if you're busy and short on time. (See Proper Portions chart on previous page.)

Horsewoman's Salad

One way to make sure that you get a wide variety of vegetables in various colors each day is to eat a salad at lunch and dinner. The recipe opposite makes approximately 11 cups, but even if you eat the entire salad over the course of a day it's not a big deal, since the whole kit and caboodle offers just 246 calories, 53 grams of carbohydrates, and a trace of fat. When you eat a 2-cup serving at lunch or dinner, you'll be getting about 45 calories, 9 grams of carbohydrates, 1.6 grams of protein, and 3 grams of fiber. Enjoying a salad with lunch and dinner also increases the volume of food you consume, encouraging you to slow the pace of your eating, and adding a number of important vitamins and minerals to your meal. To keep your salad low in fat and calories, eat it plain, or top it with a touch of fat-free dressing.

Sample Menus

On the following pages, you'll find a week's worth of sample menus, each containing roughly 1,500 calories, a number appropriate for a moderately active woman with a desirable body weight of about 136 pounds. Each is balanced with the proper proportions of carbohydrates, proteins, and fats: roughly 188 grams of carbohydrate, 112 grams of protein, 33 grams of fat, and 25 grams of fiber. As you follow the menus, one thing will become immediately obvious — no junk foods are included. You won't find chips, cakes, or candy, nor will you find any high-fat cream sauces or gravies.

Foods featured in the seven-day plan are rather basic, and there are several reasons for this. First, it's challenging enough to include all the foods that you *should* eat without exceeding your caloric limit. Allotting some of your limited calories to junk foods will automatically displace more nutritious items. Second, it's important to reacquaint your taste buds with the

HORSEWOMAN'S SALAD

Vegetable	Amount	Cals	Protein(g)	Fat (g)	Carb (g)	Fiber (g)
Romaine lettuce	1 1/2 cups	15	tr	0	2	2
Spinach, baby raw	2 cups	20	1	tr	5	3
Red cabbage, raw, shredded	1/2 cup	10	tr	tr	2	1
Carrots, raw, shredded	1/2 cup	20	tr	0	4	2
Cauliflower, raw	1/2 cup	13	tr	0	3	1
Celery, raw, diced	1/2 cup	10	tr	tr	3	1
Broccoli, raw, chopped	1/2 cup	12	tr	tr	2	1
Onion, raw, chopped	1/4 cup	15	tr	tr	6	1
Mushrooms, sliced	1/2 cup	9	tr	tr	2	1
Peppers, green, yellow, red, chopped	1 cup	26	tr	tr	6	2
Cucumber, cut up	1 cup	14	1	tr	2	2
Red tomato, chopped	1 cup	35	2	tr	8	2
Radish, red	1 cup	20	1	tr	4	0
Bean sprouts	1/2 cup	27	4	tr	4	0
Totals		**246**	**9**	**trace**	**53**	**19**

simple pleasures of wholesome, natural foods, without relying on high-calorie additions such as sugar, butter, or sauces. When you begin eating a diet that is rich in natural foods, you'll be able to appreciate and enjoy their unique, delicious flavors, just as they are. Finally, when you remove excess fat and sugar from your diet, your body stops craving these ingredients within a couple of weeks. It would seem that the opposite would be true, but there's a great deal of scientific evidence to support the notion that over-consumption of fat and sugar creates a vicious cycle in which your body craves even more fat and sugar. If you don't believe it, you don't have to take my word for it — try it and see for yourself.

RIDING FOR LIFE SAMPLE MENU 1

Breakfast	Amount	Cals	Protein (g)	Fat (g)	Carb (g)	Fiber (g)
Instant oatmeal	1 cup	138	6	2	24	4
Blueberries, fresh	1 cup	93	1	1	20	2
Egg, hard boiled	1 med	77	6	5	1	0
Milk, skim	8 oz	80	8	0	12	0
Snack						
Dannon Light & Fit Nonfat Lemon Chiffon yogurt	8 oz	100	8	0	15	0
Tangerine, fresh	1 med	37	1	tr	9	1
Walnut halves	1/2 oz (7)	109	3	9	4	1
Lunch						
Turkey breast, baked and shredded	3 oz	120	18	3	0	0
Pita pocket, whole wheat	1 sm	94	3	2	16	2
Tomatoes, fresh, diced	1/2 cup	20	1	0	4	1
Green peppers, fresh, diced	1/2 cup	13	0	0	3	1
Italian dressing, reduced calorie	2 tbsp	52	2	4	2	0
Snack						
Kashi Medley cereal	1/2 cup (1 oz)	100	4	1	20	2
Milk, skim	8 oz	80	8	0	12	0
Dinner						
Chicken breast, grilled without skin	4 oz	163	36	4	0	0
Eggplant, grilled	4 slices (7 oz)	38	2	0	4	1
Zucchini, grilled	1 cup	28	2	tr	8	2
Brown rice, steamed	1/2 cup	80	2	1	16	2
La Choy Snow Pea Pods, frozen	1/2 pkg (3 oz)	25	2	2	4	2
Progresso Vegetable Classics Garden Vegetable Soup	1 cup	70	2	1	13	2
Totals		**1,517**	**115**	**35**	**187**	**23**

RIDING FOR LIFE SAMPLE MENU 2

Breakfast	Amount	Cals	Protein (g)	Fat (g)	Carb (g)	Fiber (g)
Instant oatmeal	1 cup	138	6	2	24	4
Yoplait Light yogurt, red raspberry	6 oz	90	5	0	16	0
Melon balls, frozen	1 cup	55	tr	0	14	0
Snack						
Kashi TLC Original 7 Grain crackers	15 (1 oz)	130	3	3	22	2
Cheddar cheese, reduced-fat	1.4 oz	104	13	6	0	0
Lunch						
Perdue Deli Pick-Ups Sliced Smoked Turkey Breast	3 oz	75	13	2	1	0
Land O' Lakes Light American cheese	1 oz	70	7	5	2	0
Whole-wheat bread	2 slices	140	6	2	26	4
Boston lettuce	2 leaves	2	tr	0	tr	tr
Tomato, fresh	1 slice	8	tr	0	tr	tr
Snack						
Broccoli, fresh, raw	1/2 cup	24	2	tr	4	2
Baby carrots, raw	1/2 cup	40	1	0	9	0
Fat-free ranch dressing	2 tbsp	30	1	0	7	0
Dinner						
Pork chop, lean center loin	6 oz	344	50	15	0	0
Van Camp's butter beans, canned	1/2 cup	110	8	1	22	7
Sweet potato, baked with skin	1 (2.5 oz)	84	1	tr	20	2
Horsewoman's salad	2 cups	45	2	tr	9	3
Totals		**1,489**	**118**	**36**	**176**	**24**

RIDING FOR LIFE SAMPLE MENU 3

Breakfast	Amount	Cals	Protein (g)	Fat (g)	Carb (g)	Fiber (g)
Dannon Frusion Peach Passion Fruit Blend Smoothie	1 bottle (8 oz)	270	8	4	51	0
Lightlife Smart Bacon	2 strips	45	6	2	2	0
Snack						
Dry roasted almonds	1/2 oz (12 nuts)	85	3	7	3	2
Fresh apricots	2	34	tr	tr	8	2
Lunch						
Chicken breast, broiled	1/2 (3 oz)	142	27	3	0	0
Alpine Lace Reduced Fat Mozzarella cheese	1 oz	70	8	3	1	0
Sugar snap peas, fresh	1/2 cup	40	5	0	5	2
Horsewoman's salad	2 cups	45	2	0	9	3
Kiwi, fresh	1 medium	40	1	tr	9	3
Strawberries, fresh	1 cup	45	1	tr	10	4
Watermelon, cut up	1/2 cup	25	0	tr	5	1
Snack						
Fat-free cottage cheese	1 cup	220	26	0	10	0
Pineapple, fresh, diced	1/2 cup	38	1	tr	8	1
Dinner						
Whole-wheat spaghetti	1 cup (4.9 oz)	174	7	1	37	6
Ground beef, extra lean	1 1/2 oz	112	12	7	0	0
Prego Traditional Italian sauce	1/2 cup (2.1 oz)	70	1	2	12	1
Parmesan cheese, grated	1 tbsp (5g)	23	2	2	tr	0
Asparagus spears, cooked	1 cup	40	4	0	6	2
Eggplant, cooked	1 cup	28	1	tr	7	3
Totals		**1,546**	**115**	**31**	**183**	**30**

RIDING FOR LIFE SAMPLE MENU 4

Breakfast	Amount	Cals	Protein (g)	Fat (g)	Carb (g)	Fiber (g)
Egg white omelet	2 egg whites	34	8	0	0	0
	1 whole egg	75	6	5	1	0
Colby cheese, low-fat	1 oz	49	9	2	1	0
Morningstar Farms Veggie Breakfast Bacon Strips	1 slice	30	3	1	1	tr
Cinnamon raisin bread	1 slice	80	1	3	13	0
Snack						
Newtons Fat-free Fig cookie	2	90	1	0	22	1
Milk, skim	8 oz	80	8	0	12	0
Lunch						
Perdue Short Cuts Carved Chicken Breast, fajita style	1/4 cup	140	16	7	3	0
La Tortilla Factory Low-carb/Low-fat Whole-wheat Tortilla	1 reg size	60	5	2	12	9
Yellow, red, and green pepper fresh, sliced	1 med each	60	3	tr	9	tr
Onion, chopped, cooked	1/2 cup	47	1	tr	11	0
Old El Paso Fat-free Refried Beans	1/2 cup	100	6	0	18	6
Snack						
Fruit salad:						
Green grapes, fresh	20	72	tr	tr	9	tr
Peach, fresh	1 med	1	tr	tr	10	1
Dinner						
Sirloin steak, broiled	4 oz	241	33	10	0	0
Baked potato with skin	1/2 med	110	5	tr	25	4
Sweet peas, young, cooked	1/2 cup	60	3	1	10	4
Corn on the cob, fresh	1 med ear	83	3	1	19	2
Totals		**1,412**	**111**	**32**	**176**	**27**

RIDING FOR LIFE SAMPLE MENU 5

Breakfast	Amount	Cals	Protein (g)	Fat (g)	Carb (g)	Fiber (g)
Pink grapefruit, fresh	1/2	42	1	tr	9	1
Pepperidge Farm Mini Bagel	2 (2.8 oz)	220	8	2	44	2
Jif Reduced Fat Crunchy peanut butter	2 tbsp	190	8	12	15	2
Snack						
Fresh peach	1 med	44	1	tr	10	1
Genisoy Ultimate Chocolate Fudge Brownie Protein Bar	1 bar (2.2 oz)	230	14	5	33	2
Lunch						
Carl Budding Original Deli Pouch Lean Turkey Breast	1.25 oz (1/2 pkg)	35	6	2	0	0
Whole-wheat bread	2 slices	140	6	2	26	4
Land O' Lakes Light American Cheese	1 oz	70	7	5	2	0
Tomato, fresh sliced	1 med	11	tr	tr	2	tr
Arugula lettuce	1/2 cup	3	tr	0	tr	tr
Snack						
Cantaloupe, fresh	1/4 med	46	tr	0	11	1
Breakstone's Fat-free Cottage Cheese	1/2 cup	90	12	0	8	0
Dinner						
Halibut, baked or grilled sprinkled with lemon juice	1/2 fillet (5.6 oz)	200	40	4	0	0
Black beans, cooked	1/2 cup	137	12	1	20	8
Okra, sliced, cooked	1/2 cup	25	1	tr	6	0
Totals		**1,483**	**116**	**33**	**186**	**21**

RIDING FOR LIFE SAMPLE MENU 6

Breakfast	Amount	Cals	Protein (g)	Fat (g)	Carb (g)	Fiber (g)
Whole Grain Total cereal	3/4 cup	110	2	1	23	3
Milk, skim	8 oz	80	8	0	12	0
Blackberries, fresh	1/2 cup	37	1	tr	9	3
Egg, hard boiled	1 med	75	6	5	0	0
Snack						
Jim's PermaLean Protein Crunch Chocoholic Chocolate Bar	1 bar	170	21	3	10	tr
Lunch						
Star Kist Chunk Light Tuna in water	1 cup (4 oz)	120	26	2	0	0
Mayonnaise, reduced-calorie	1 tbsp	26	0	2	2	0
Sweet pickle relish	1 tbsp	14	tr	tr	3	0
Reduced-fat wheat crackers	8 crackers	130	3	3	24	4
Apple, fresh	1 med	81	tr	tr	21	4
Snack						
Colombo Nonfat Yogurt, plain	8 oz	100	10	0	16	0
Raspberries, fresh	1 cup	61	2	tr	14	8
Dinner						
Hamburger, ground, extra lean, broiled	3 oz	215	22	14	0	0
Hamburger bun, multi-grain	1 (1.5 oz)	100	4	1	17	2
Colby cheese, low-fat	1 oz	49	9	2	0	0
Hunt's Ketchup	1 tbsp	15	0	0	4	0
French's Classic Yellow Mustard	1 tsp	10	0	0	1	0
Tomato, fresh	1 slice	8	tr	0	tr	tr
Lettuce, fresh	1 slice	10	tr	0	1	tr
Onion, fresh	1 slice	10	tr	0	2	0
Vlasic Hamburger Dill Chips	1 oz	5	0	0	1	0
Van Camp's Pork and Beans	1/2 cup	140	6	1	27	7
Totals		**1,566**	**120**	**34**	**187**	**31**

RIDING FOR LIFE SAMPLE MENU 7

Breakfast	Amount	Cals	Protein (g)	Fat (g)	Carb (g)	Fiber (g)
Post Shredded Wheat cereal, spoon size	1 cup	107	3	1	24	3
Milk, skim	8 oz	80	8	0	12	0
Snack						
Dole Fruit Bowl Mandarin oranges	1 pkg	70	0	0	18	3
Lunch						
La Tortilla Factory Low-carb/Low-fat Whole-wheat Tortilla	1 reg	60	5	2	12	9
Chicken breast, broiled and sliced thin	3 oz	142	27	3	0	0
Teriyaki sauce	2 tbsp	60	0	1	13	0
Alpine Lace Reduced-fat Mozzarella cheese	1 oz	70	8	3	1	0
Horsewoman's salad	2 cups	45	2	tr	9	3
Snack						
Progresso Vegetable Classics 99% Fat-free Lentil Soup	1 cup	130	8	2	20	6
Watermelon, fresh, cubed	2 cups	100	1	0	22	1
Dinner						
Atlantic mackerel, baked	4 oz	297	25	18	0	0
Shrimp, boiled, with lemon	3 oz	84	18	6	1	0
Artichoke hearts, cooked	1 cup	136	6	tr	28	0
Sweet potato, baked, with skin	1 (3.5 oz)	118	2	tr	28	3
Totals		**1,499**	**113**	**36**	**188**	**28**

fine-tuning your health

A LITTLE MORE OF THIS, A LITTLE LESS OF THAT

When you're following the Riding for Life Diet — or any other balanced, nutritious eating program, for that matter — you can take comfort in the knowledge that you're consuming adequate amounts of vitamins, minerals, and other nutrients. Most healthy women who regularly eat a variety of wholesome foods are able to satisfy their body's nutritional demands.

You also can feel good about the fact that you're getting your vitamins and minerals from the best possible sources — the packages provided by Mother Nature. A vast body of scientific research supports the notion that the nutrients provided by fruits, vegetables, grains, and other whole foods are far superior to those found in most pills, tablets, and capsules. Whole foods offer excellent nutrition because they don't provide merely a single vitamin or mineral; they contain unique combinations of the micronutrients your body needs, in Nature's proprietary formula. If you get your vitamin C from an orange instead of a pill, for example, you'll also be getting a few bonus ingredients, including calcium, beta carotene, and fiber.

In addition to vitamins, minerals, and fiber, whole foods contain a number of other health-promoting substances that simply cannot be duplicated in the laboratory, including phytochemicals with antioxidant properties. These naturally occurring plant compounds are known to be protective against dozens of debilitating illnesses that become increasingly common with age, including Alzheimer's disease, heart disease, cancer, and diabetes.

With that said, it's not always a simple matter for women to eat the way we know we should. On days that are especially hectic, it can be practically impossible to find time just to eat five servings of fruits and veggies — not to mention all the other good foods our bodies need to stay healthy.

Nutrition Insurance

Because most of us aren't able to eat a perfectly balanced diet every day, taking a daily multivitamin and mineral supplement just makes sense. While these nutritional aids can reinforce a diet that is reasonably balanced and nutritious, they can't work miracles. Even the best and most expensive supplements can't undo the damage caused by regularly eating foods loaded with excess calories, simple sugars, and artery-clogging saturated and trans fats.

If you're looking for a little nutrition insurance in the form of a pill, there are dozens of suitable once-daily vitamin and mineral supplements on the market. Your best bet is to select a formulation that's not only broad in spectrum but also balanced. As you read the labels of various supplements, pay special attention to the "daily value" column on each one. Ideally, the supplement you choose will provide approximately 100 percent of the daily values (DV) of a wide range of vitamins and minerals, rather than 500 percent of one and 20 percent of another. Calcium and magnesium are two exceptions: most calcium- and magnesium-containing "multiples" don't provide 100 percent of the DV for either mineral. If they did, the pills would be gigantic, and we'd have a hard time choking them down. With this in mind, it's a good idea to take a separate calcium supplement, and as you'll find later in this chapter, some women can benefit from an additional magnesium supplement as well.

Although many once-daily multiples supply 100 percent of the DV of important vitamins and minerals, taking doses that provide even more of certain vitamins — especially C and D — and a few minerals can be beneficial for many women. For those with specific health issues and medical risk factors, or for women who simply want to optimize their health, taking a separate vitamin or mineral supplement, herbal preparation, or plant compound in addition to a once-daily multiple might be especially useful. With thousands of nutritional supplements available, it's impossible to take them all. For most active, healthy horsewomen who routinely

eat a nutritious, balanced diet, an excellent starting point is a daily regimen that includes the following nutritional supplements:

> **SUPPLEMENTS**
>
> **1.** A balanced, broad-spectrum multiple vitamin and mineral preparation
>
> **2.** A combination calcium and vitamin D supplement
>
> **3.** A vitamin C supplement
>
> **4.** An omega-3 fatty acid supplement

After learning more about the specific benefits of these and other nutrients, and taking your own health issues and goals into account, you'll be ready to design a daily supplement regimen that works best for you.

Why Take Extra C?

Vitamin C plays a number of important roles in the body — it's essential for the maintenance of healthy tissues and for the proper function of the immune system. In recent years, however, vitamin C has been touted as a nutritional superstar primarily because of its potent antioxidant properties, which allow it to disarm dangerous molecules called free radicals in the brain and body effectively.

The Fury of Free Radicals

While some free radicals are produced in the human body as by-products of normal metabolism, others are created as the result of exposure to a number of internal and external toxins. Major culprits are ultraviolet light, radiation, smog, cigarette smoke, and dietary trans fats. Regardless of their source, free radicals are like tiny Tasmanian devils — they're highly unstable molecules, bursting with excess energy. As they spin crazily through the cells and tissues of our bodies, they leave a trail of destruction.

Free radicals ultimately lose steam by transferring their energy to innocent bystanders — the cells and tissues that they come in contact with. This process, known as oxidation, inevitably leads to damage and deterioration, in much the same way oxidation of metal leads to rusting and oxidation of ripe fruit leads to rotting.

If free radicals find their way into the control centers of our cells, they can injure the cellular genetic material. It's estimated that human DNA receives about 10,000 free radical "hits" daily. If these attacks aren't intercepted by the body's defenses, the DNA may be rendered incapable of programming cells to divide properly or to repair themselves, triggering processes that can lead to abnormal cell growth and cancer.

While free radicals are best known for their instigating role in cancer, they've also been identified as major players in dozens of other serious and life-threatening conditions. When free radicals attack the brain, for example, Alzheimer's disease or other types of dementia can result. In the bloodstream, free radicals promote the formation of cholesterol plaques that can lead to heart attacks and strokes. In the joints, they initiate the degenerative changes of arthritis, and in the skin, they're responsible for creating wrinkles and age spots. Over the years, repeated free radical assaults eventually lead to the breakdown of all body systems. The cumulative result is the aging process and, ultimately, death.

Fortunately, the human body is not entirely defenseless against free radical attacks. Just as antioxidant compounds can protect metal from rusting and antioxidant additives and preservatives can retard food spoilage, a number of antioxidant compounds, including vitamin C, can deactivate dangerous free radicals before they're able to wreak havoc on cells and tissues. In doing so, these antioxidants slow or stop many destructive oxidative processes throughout the body, reducing the risk of cancer and other degenerative diseases. The trick is to keep the body and brain supplied with a steady supply of antioxidants via the diet, so that they are always armed and ready to defend themselves against the inevitable free radical attacks.

Without a doubt, fresh fruits, vegetables, legumes, nuts, and whole grains are the very best sources of free-radical fighting antioxidants, including vitamins, minerals, and phytochemicals. Still, taking extra vitamin C in the form of a daily 250- to 1,000-milligram (mg) supplement will give your body the extra ammunition it needs to fend off repeated free radical attacks.

The vitamin offers a number of additional

benefits. Studies show individuals with higher blood levels of vitamin C have a reduced risk of heart disease than those with lower levels. The nutrient improves the ability of the arteries to dilate in times of stress, promoting proper blood flow to the heart. Taking 500 mg of vitamin C each day can lower blood pressure and cholesterol levels. Vitamin C has been shown to play a role in the reduction of cholesterol deposits along blood vessel walls, making it useful in the prevention of atherosclerosis (hardening of the arteries).

Women with diabetes can benefit from a daily dose of C because it is involved in regulating the release of insulin from the pancreas and helps prevent diabetes-related damage to the eyes, nerves, and kidneys. Vitamin C also has been shown to reduce the formation of gallstones, protect smokers from toxins in cigarette smoke, and improve mental function in elderly adults.

With all its attributes, it's easy to think that if a little vitamin C is good for you, more is better, but taking mega-doses of any vitamin can produce unwelcome side effects. The safe upper limit of vitamin C is commonly recognized as 2,000 mg daily, but for most women, a supplement that offers between 250 mg and 1,000 mg a day is more than adequate.

While taking massive doses of vitamin C doesn't appear to be deadly, it can cause some minor health problems. A daily intake of more than 1,000 mg can lead to kidney stone formation in susceptible individuals, as well as facial flushing, stomach cramps, and diarrhea.

Thanks to their high acid content, chewable vitamin C tablets can erode enamel from the surface of your teeth, so if you chew your C, be sure to wash it down with plenty of water.

FOOD SOURCES: Vitamin C

Even if you take a daily supplement, it's wise to continue to eat a variety of fruits and vegetables that are rich in vitamin C. In addition to the ever-popular citrus fruits, good food sources include strawberries, peppers, cantaloupes, tomatoes, cabbage, and leafy green vegetables. As heat can destroy some vitamins in plant foods, it's best to eat your fruits and veggies fresh and raw whenever you can.

Vitamin D

Although Americans are rarely considered to be malnourished, a growing body of evidence suggests that vitamin D deficiency is becoming increasingly widespread among women of all ages in the United States. It's a serious problem with a rather simple solution: a daily vitamin D supplement.

Vitamin D is necessary for the absorption and transport of calcium into bones. Early in life a deficiency in D can lead to childhood rickets. In adulthood insufficient intake can result in osteoporosis. Although vitamin D is best known for its role in keeping the skeleton strong, it also is vital in maintaining the health of practically every cell and tissue in the body.

Low levels of vitamin D can lead to an array of puzzling symptoms, including unexplained aches and pains in the bones and muscles. In some cases, a deficiency can contribute to more serious health problems, ranging from depression to heart disease. In the body, vitamin D is a key factor in the regulation of normal cell growth and division. Recent research has shown that a deficiency of the vitamin can contribute to the development of a variety of cancers, including cancer of the breast, colon, and ovary. In laboratory studies, on the other hand, vitamin D has been found to block the growth of cancer cells, preventing the out-of-control cell division that makes cancer such a dangerous disease.

As vitamin D is involved in the regulation of the immune system, it's not surprising that a deficiency can trigger the onset of autoimmune disorders, conditions in which the immune system attacks the body. Autoimmune diseases linked to vitamin D deficiency include type I diabetes, rheumatoid arthritis, inflammatory bowel disease, and multiple sclerosis. In animal studies, researchers have found that low levels of vitamin D can worsen the symptoms of autoimmune disorders, while higher levels effectively suppress symptoms.

Recently, scientists discovered that women who take just 400 International Units (IU) of vitamin D daily are roughly 40 percent less likely to develop multiple sclerosis than women who do not take the supplement. In a study of more than 10,000 children, researchers found that youngsters who took the recommended dose of vitamin D during infancy were significantly less likely to develop type I diabetes than those who did not.

Fortunately, your body has a built-in protective mechanism against vitamin D deficiency. Human skin is capable of producing the vitamin when it is exposed to the ultraviolet rays in sunlight. For young, healthy women, just 10 to 15 minutes of sun exposure each day can help ward off a D deficiency. With increasing age, however, skin manufactures the vitamin less efficiently, and as a result, older women typically have significantly lower levels than younger women. Sunscreen, smog, a dark complexion, and clothing interfere with the absorption of the sun's rays, as well as the skin's ability to produce vitamin D at any age.

Currently, the recommended daily intake of vitamin D is rather controversial, at 200 IU for individuals younger than 50; 400 IU for adults 51 to 70 years of age; and 600 IU for those aged 71 and older. Because nearly 70 percent of women over the age of 51 currently are not getting enough vitamin D, and in light of the growing problem of vitamin D deficiency in the United States, many nutrition experts argue that these recommended intakes should be boosted substantially.

Although it's likely that most adult women could benefit from a daily dose of 800 IU, taking more than 1,000 IU a day isn't recommended because vitamin D can accumulate in body fat stores and become toxic in the long term.

FOOD SOURCES: Vitamin D

Although certain foods, including milk, orange juice, and a few grain products are fortified with vitamin D, the amounts they contain are relatively low and notoriously inconsistent. A cup of milk, for example, typically contains just 98 IU. With about 350 IU in each 3-ounce serving, oily fish, including salmon, tuna, and mackerel are among the best food sources of vitamin D. As it can be difficult to meet your body's daily requirement with diet alone, taking a vitamin D supplement is a smart strategy to help maintain and protect your good health.

Calcium

Regardless of your age, it's highly likely that you could use a little extra calcium in the way of a supplement as it's often challenging to get all the calcium you need from your daily diet. This is especially true if you don't regularly consume three or four servings of dairy foods each day. Studies show that nearly two-thirds of American women are not consuming enough calcium for optimum health.

Getting adequate amounts of calcium is important at every stage in a woman's life. In childhood, calcium is responsible for building strong bones and teeth. During adolescence, the body readily absorbs calcium from food sources and packs it into the bones, creating a kind of calcium savings account for the future. It's critically important for teenage girls and young adult women to consume enough of the mineral so that their calcium savings accounts will be large enough to support them for the rest of their lives.

When women reach their mid-30s, their bones achieve maximum size and strength, a condition known as peak bone mass. At this point the body stops building bone, and maintaining existing bone mass becomes crucial. To worsen matters, the absorption of calcium becomes less efficient in women after age 35 and continues to decline with increasing age. If you don't get enough calcium in your 30s, you can expect that your bone mass — and your calcium savings account — will begin to dwindle.

Women typically lose bone mass most rapidly in the fifth decade of life. The process is accelerated during menopause, when estrogen levels plummet. Because the female hormone plays an important role in bone health, women with low estrogen levels have a higher risk of developing osteoporosis and fracturing bones.

Most of us recognize the importance of calcium when it comes to preventing osteoporosis, but calcium has a number of additional health benefits that aren't as well known. As it turns out, women with calcium-rich diets are significantly less likely to develop high blood pressure, colon cancer, and type II diabetes than women who don't get enough of the mineral.

Calcium-rich diets also can help tame the monthly monster known as premenstrual syndrome, or PMS. Studies have shown that PMS sufferers who consume 1,200 mg of calcium daily are less likely to experience symptoms commonly associated with the syndrome, including bloating, irritability, food cravings, and pain.

Even if you've managed to escape the plague of PMS, a calcium supplement can provide another benefit: promoting weight loss. Animal studies have demonstrated that mice consuming high-calcium diets have higher metabolic rates than those consuming low-calcium diets and they're also significantly leaner. High-calcium diets have been shown to promote weight loss and the reduction of abdominal fat in human subjects. The loss of excess weight and abdominal fat is known to reduce the risk of heart disease and type II diabetes.

How does dietary calcium wield its weight-loss magic? Researchers speculate that the mineral works by lowering blood levels of a hormone known as calcitrol. In the body, calcitrol acts on fat cells to slow fat breakdown. When your dietary calcium intake is high, your blood calcitrol levels are low, which means that fat breakdown occurs more readily. In an analysis of more than 7,000 adults involved in the National Health and Nutrition Examination Survey (NHANES III), researchers found that men and women with the highest calcium intake had the lowest body weights, even when calorie consumption was equal.

In spite of all the perks that calcium has to offer, most women don't get nearly enough of the mineral. The typical American adult consumes only about 600 mg a day, while most need more along the lines of 1,000 mg. Nursing mothers and menopausal women should aim for a daily intake of 1,500 mg, which is still well below the safe upper limit of 2,500 mg.

As there is no accurate test to determine if you have a minor calcium deficiency, taking a supplement is the best way to be sure you're getting all the calcium your body needs. It's usually best to take your calcium supplement in divided doses because absorption of the mineral appears to be most effective at doses of 500 mg or less.

With dozens of calcium supplements on the market, it can be hard to know which one to take. Calcium carbonate is an inexpensive source of elemental calcium, but it requires an acidic stomach for optimum absorption, and it must be taken after meals. Calcium carbonate is found in nutritional products including Caltrate and OsCal, as well as in many antacids, including Tums.

Although calcium citrate is more expensive than calcium carbonate, it doesn't require dosing after meals. In addition, it can be absorbed in non-acidic conditions, which makes it ideal for women who are taking acid-suppressing drugs for the treatment of gastroesophageal reflux disease (GERD). Calcium citrate is the ingredient in Citracal capsules and caplets.

FOOD SOURCES: Calcium

In the United States, dairy products are the primary source of dietary calcium, with about 300 mg of calcium per serving. Shellfish, soy foods, and dark leafy green vegetables are also good sources. Food manufacturers are making it easier for us to pack more of the mineral in our daily diets by fortifying certain foods and beverages with extra calcium, including breakfast cereals, breads, and orange juice.

Omega-3 Fatty Acids

Cardiovascular disease is the leading cause of death among American women, so it's wise to arm yourself against it in as many ways as possible. Eating a high-fiber, plant-based diet low in saturated and trans fats is an excellent place to start, and adding a source of omega-3 fatty acids can significantly boost your level of protection.

Even in the best of circumstances, it can be challenging to pack a sufficient supply of the heart-friendly compounds into your daily diet. Because human beings aren't capable of producing essential fatty acids, including those of the omega-3 variety, these substances must be obtained from food or nutritional supplements. Although fatty fish, including mackerel, herring, sardines, and salmon, are considered to be the best sources of omega-3 fatty acids, most Americans don't eat enough fish to meet their daily needs. With this in mind, it's a good idea to boost your intake of omega-3 fatty acids with a daily supplement including fish oil or flaxseed oil.

Omega-3 fatty acids are known to benefit heart health in several ways. For starters, they lower levels of triglycerides in the blood. Triglycerides, which are derived from foods in the diet, are the predominant type of fat in the human body. When you eat a high-calorie meal, your body uses some of those calories to satisfy its immediate energy needs, and the rest are converted to triglycerides so that they can be used for energy later. In normal amounts, triglycerides are essential to good health, but when levels get too high, they can contribute to heart disease.

While omega-3 fatty acids work to lower triglyceride levels, they also protect the heart by exerting an anti-clotting effect on the blood. When consumed on a regular basis, they can help prevent blood clots that lead to heart attacks and strokes. Consumption of omega-3 fatty acids also may benefit the heart by lowering blood pressure and by preventing the occurrence of abnormal heart rhythms, significantly reducing the risk of sudden cardiac death in individuals with heart disease.

Several studies have shown that people whose diets are rich in fish tend to have lower rates of inflammatory and autoimmune disorders. Regular consumption of fish or fish-oil supplements has been shown to play an important role in the prevention of rheumatoid arthritis. In people suffering from the disease, daily fish-oil supplementation for six to nine weeks can significantly reduce morning stiffness and the number of tender, swollen joints. Fish oil also has been found to have beneficial effects in people suffering from Crohn's disease, asthma, depression, psoriasis, and other skin conditions.

In spite of all the health benefits that omega-3 fatty acids have to offer, most women aren't taking full advantage of them. Nutrition experts estimate that 90 percent of Americans don't get enough of these essential fatty acids in their daily diets. The American Heart Association's recommendations for intake of omega-3 fatty acids state that individuals without coronary heart disease should eat at least two servings of fatty fish per week, along with other foods rich in omega-3 fatty acids. People with known coronary heart disease are encouraged to eat at least one meal a day that includes fatty fish or to take a daily fish oil supplement.

The U.S. Food and Drug Association concluded that dosages of up to 3 grams per day of omega-3 fatty acids from marine sources are "generally recognized as safe." When taken as directed, the most common side effect is a lingering fishy aftertaste.

FOOD SOURCES: Omega-3 Fatty Acids

Flaxseed oil, fish oil, and fatty fish, including salmon, mackerel, sardines, herring, and tuna are rich sources of omega-3 fatty acids. Good plant sources include leafy green vegetables, canola oil, and walnuts.

Beyond the Basics

Most women can cover all their nutritional bases by eating a healthy, varied diet and by taking a daily multiple vitamin and mineral supplement, along with extra doses of calcium, vitamins C and D, and a fish-oil supplement. If you have specific health issues and you've found the traditional approaches to prevention or treatment either unsavory or unsatisfactory, one or more of the following nutrients might be right for you.

Selenium

The fact that selenium is one of the hottest-selling nutritional supplements on the market right now is pretty amazing, considering that just decades ago it was believed to be toxic to humans in any amount. Selenium is a mineral that is vital to life; without it, the heart, muscles, liver, and reproductive system cannot function properly.

Selenium is also a powerful antioxidant. It gained popularity as a cancer-fighting nutritional supplement in the 1990s, when the results of a landmark study were published in the Journal of the American Medical Association. Conducted by researchers at the University of Arizona, the study was originally designed to test selenium's ability to ward off the recurrence of skin cancer in more than 1,300 men and women diagnosed with the disease. Half the volunteers were given daily supplements of 200 micrograms of selenium, while the other half received placebo pills.

By the ninth year of the study, the two groups

had developed new skin cancers at roughly the same rate, but some surprising trends had emerged. The volunteers taking the selenium had 63 percent fewer prostate cancers, 58 percent fewer colon cancers, and 45 percent fewer lung cancers than the placebo group. Overall, the group taking the selenium supplements had just about half the risk of dying from cancer and about a third the risk of getting any form of cancer in the first place.

Other studies have had similar results, showing that individuals with higher-than-average blood levels of selenium have lower death rates from cancers of all types. People who live in regions with selenium-rich soil — including Wyoming and the Dakotas — typically have fewer cancers than those living in the eastern United States, where soil selenium levels are lower than elsewhere in the country.

In addition to its cancer-fighting properties, selenium is known to help bolster immune function, especially in the elderly. There's also evidence to suggest that the mineral can improve mood and boost energy levels, as well as enhance mental performance.

It's been estimated that the typical American diet offers about 100 micrograms of selenium a day, but making an accurate measurement can be challenging. The selenium content of plant food varies widely, depending on the mineral content of the soil in which it's grown. Selenium deficiency is thought to be relatively common among Americans, especially elderly adults.

If you decide to take a selenium supplement, it's important not to get carried away — 200 micrograms is the recommended daily dose. In small amounts, selenium might extend your life, but taking too much of the mineral could definitely shorten it. The maximum safe dose is thought to be about 400 micrograms a day.

Taking more than 800 micrograms regularly can cause nausea and diarrhea and taint your breath with a garlicky odor. Over time, high doses of selenium can leave your fingernails fragile and cause your hair to fall out. Long term overdose can lead to liver damage and, even, death.

> **FOOD SOURCES: Selenium**
>
> You can boost your selenium intake by choosing foods that are naturally rich in the mineral. Brazil nuts and tuna are two of the best sources, but selenium can be found in a number of other foods, including chicken, turkey, salmon, lean beef, and whole grains. Brewer's yeast, garlic, and onions are also relatively rich in the mineral.

Magnesium

Depending on your dietary habits, magnesium is a mineral that you might need to supplement above and beyond the amount you're getting from your daily diet and multiple vitamin and mineral pill. Most once-daily multiples provide only about 100 mg of magnesium, an amount much less than the recommended daily intake of 400 mg.

Magnesium plays several important roles in the body. Because it regulates the metabolism of calcium and phosphorus, it's critical to bone health and prevention of osteoporosis. It is also important in maintaining normal heart and muscle function, blood pressure, and the transmission of nerve signals throughout the body. Research suggests that supplemental magnesium can help prevent depression and insomnia and alleviate many of the symptoms of premenstrual syndrome. For the millions of women who suffer from migraine headaches, supplemental magnesium may be a godsend.

Magnesium for Migraines

Scientists aren't entirely sure how magnesium works to alleviate the symptoms of migraines, but they have a few theories. The mineral is known to be involved in the regulation of the brain chemical serotonin, which is a key player in triggering migraine headaches. Scientists also know that in the brain, fluctuating magnesium levels can send blood vessels into spasms, stretching delicate nerve endings and generating pain in the process. In addition to pain, most migraine sufferers endure symptoms of nausea and vomiting, while some experience visuals changes and sensitivity to light and sound.

In studies examining the link between magnesium and migraine headaches, at least half of migraine sufferers have been found to have low blood levels of magnesium. For many of these individuals, daily magnesium supplementation can dramatically reduce the frequency and severity of migraine headaches and their associated symptoms.

While it's possible to have your blood magnesium levels tested, it isn't absolutely necessary. At the recommended doses, magnesium supplements are safe and generally well tolerated by healthy women, with the most common side effect being diarrhea. For individuals with kidney disease and other chronic illnesses, however, magnesium supplements can be unsafe, and for this reason, they should be taken only with a doctor's supervision.

For migraine prevention, a dose of 400 mg of magnesium a day is recommended. If this dose doesn't significantly reduce the frequency and severity of migraine headaches within a month, you can try increasing the daily dose to 600 mg a day.

FOOD SOURCES: Magnesium

Many foods are rich in magnesium, including dark green vegetables, whole grains, beans, bananas, and seafood. As long as you're not allergic to them, it's a good idea to include these foods in your diet as often as possible. For migraine sufferers whose magnesium levels are on the low side, eating a well-balanced diet may not be enough. Taking a daily magnesium supplement can boost blood levels faster and bring relief sooner.

Iron

Not every woman needs to take an iron supplement, but many could stand to pump a little extra into their diets. Iron deficiency is one of the most common nutritional shortcomings among American women, especially those in their childbearing years.

The body of an average woman contains only about 3 to 4 grams of iron — about the mass of a pea — but even in these minute quantities, the mineral is vital to good health. Iron is an essential part of the blood that allows it to transport oxygen throughout the body.

Your oxygen-carrying red blood cells contain a red pigment called hemoglobin, and each hemoglobin molecule contains four atoms of iron. As the red blood cells pass through your lungs, the iron atoms latch onto oxygen molecules and deliver them to tissues throughout your body. On the return trip hemoglobin transports carbon dioxide from your body's cells to your lungs so that it can be expelled.

If the body doesn't have the iron it needs to manufacture hemoglobin properly, the red blood cells can't transport oxygen very efficiently. As the iron shortage worsens, tissues begin to suffer oxygen deprivation. This condition is known as iron-deficiency anemia.

The symptoms of anemia can arise so gradually that many women don't even notice them, but as the condition progresses, everyday activities can lead to shortness of breath, weakness, and extreme fatigue. Dizziness and headaches are often a problem, and some women notice their skin becomes increasingly pale. In cases of severe iron deficiency, anemia can cause a sore tongue and brittle, ridged fingernails. Some women with the condition experience a disturbing craving for dirt, clay, starch, or ice.

There are dozens of causes of iron deficiency anemia, but the condition almost always results from some type of blood loss. In women, menstrual periods are usually the culprit. Women with normal periods can lose a substantial amount of iron each month, and those with heavier bleeding are especially susceptible to anemia. If menstrual bleeding isn't the problem, anemia may be the result of blood loss from the digestive tract. Stomach ulcers and hemorrhoids are often to blame, and regular use of aspirin or aspirin-containing drugs can trigger bleeding from the stomach that can result in iron deficiency anemia.

Women who are pregnant or nursing are at increased risk for iron deficiency anemia. Both conditions increase the body's requirement for iron, and as it's practically impossible to satisfy the higher demand from food sources alone, it's usually necessary to take an iron supplement. Teenage girls have an especially high risk for iron deficiency anemia, and many don't get enough of the mineral to meet their bodies' requirements for proper growth and development.

A simple blood test is all it takes to determine if you have an iron deficiency. If you're diagnosed with anemia, your physician will work with you to determine the underlying cause. In the meantime, you'll probably be prompted to increase your intake of iron-rich foods and to take an iron supplement.

Most doctors recommend taking iron pills three times a day on an empty stomach, but this is easier said than done. Supplemental iron is frequently associated with nausea, stomach upset, cramping, and constipation. Taking iron with food makes it more tolerable, but it also interferes with the uptake of the mineral. Iron is absorbed best from an empty stomach, and acidic conditions improve its absorption even more. Washing iron pills down with a glass of orange juice works wonders — both the acid and the vitamin C content of the juice increase the uptake of the mineral.

While there's no doubt that supplemental iron can produce some unpleasant gastrointestinal effects, the good news is that if you're deficient in the mineral, a supplement can have a dramatic impact on your health. You'll undoubtedly feel more energetic and motivated. You may notice that your moods improve and that you're able to concentrate and think more clearly.

Although the recommended daily intake of iron for women and teenage girls is 15 mg, it's estimated that nearly three-fourths of us aren't getting enough of the mineral to meet this requirement. While a low intake of iron can cause significant health problems, an intake that is too high can be risky as well, especially in postmenopausal women. Excess iron stores in the body can contribute to heart disease and cancer. To be on the safe side, you should check with your doctor before regularly taking a supplement that offers more than 10 mg of iron a day.

FOOD SOURCES: Iron

You can get iron from both plant and animal foods, but the body absorbs the mineral from animal sources about three times better than from plant foods. Lean red meat, poultry, fish, and liver are good animal sources of the mineral. Whole-grain breads, beans, and green vegetables are good plant sources. You can increase the iron content of any food simply by cooking it in a cast iron skillet. While eating iron-rich foods along with citrus fruit or juice can enhance iron uptake, caffeine-containing beverages can reduce your body's ability to absorb the mineral from foods.

Chromium

Now that type II diabetes has become a national epidemic, chromium supplementation is receiving a great deal of attention, not only from the scientific community, but also from the media. Chromium is a mineral essential for life and plays a key role in the prevention of diabetes. For women who eat a nutritious, balanced diet, food sources usually supply chromium in amounts more than adequate for good health. Unfortunately, the typical American diet doesn't provide optimal nutrition. Because it's loaded with simple sugars, it can cause the body to excrete excessive amounts of chromium. Over time, a chromium deficiency can trigger type II diabetes in susceptible individuals.

In the body, chromium is an important co-factor that aids insulin in the regulation of blood-sugar levels. A growing body of scientific research supports the role of chromium, either alone or in combination with the B-vitamin biotin, in improving insulin function and glucose metabolism in people with pre-diabetes and type II diabetes. At a dose of 400 micrograms twice daily, mineral may also provide a significant weight control benefit, which in turn can improve blood-sugar control and reduce the severity of diabetes and its complications.

FOOD SOURCES: Chromium

Chromium is present in small amounts in yeast, whole grains, and seafood.

Other Antioxidants

Lipoic Acid (ALCAR)

When you think about the aging process, what may first come to mind is the typical external signs — graying hair, wrinkled skin, and stooped posture. These visible changes are certainly a big part of the overall picture, but it's important to remember that the aging process also affects us internally. In fact, you can think of the external signs of aging as a reflection — or even an outward manifestation — of the changes occurring inside the body.

Scientists believe that the aging process originates at the cellular level in structures called mitochondria. Mitochondria are tiny organelles that act as miniature power plants for the cells in our bodies. In the presence of oxygen, these power plants convert nutrients in the foods we eat into energy that can be used by the body to fuel its myriad functions.

In youth, the mitochondria are healthy and efficient, and as a result, young people tend to have sharp minds, strong muscles, and lots of energy. With advancing age, however, the mitochondria begin to show signs of wear and tear, and they become less efficient with each passing year. Eventually, they cease to function normally. In the process of converting nutrients to energy, older mitochondria begin emitting free radicals, in much the same way that an old car begins to emit black smoke. These free radicals — produced by the body's own machinery — bombard the cells and tissues, damaging them in the process.

Fortunately, two supplements are capable of tuning up old mitochondria, enabling them to function more efficiently and churn out fewer disease-causing free radicals in the process. One is acetyl L-carnitine, or ALCAR, an amino acid used exclusively by the mitochondria of the body. The other is alpha lipoic acid, one of the most potent antioxidants known.

With age, natural ALCAR levels become progressively lower, contributing to the steady decline in mitochondrial function. An ALCAR supplement can restore the missing nutrient, making older mitochondria more efficient and less likely to create excess free radicals in the process of converting nutrients to energy. An alpha lipoic acid supplement can help stop the leakage of free radicals from old mitochondria. Laboratory studies reveal that on the cellular level, the nutrients improve mitochondrial function. Animal studies show that when old rats are given the two supplements, they begin to behave like younger rodents. Not only are they more active and energetic, but they perform better on tests of learning and memory.

Acetyl L-carnitine is widely available in 250 mg capsules. For best results, most experts recommend taking one tablet three to four times daily. Alpha lipoic acid is typically taken once a day with a meal, at a dose of 200 mg.

Special Supplements

Ginkgo biloba

Although it's relatively new to the United States, ginkgo biloba has been a staple of Eastern medicine for centuries. Individual ginkgo trees have been known to survive for as long as a thousand years, so it's not surprising that Chinese healers believe extracts from the tree can ward off many age-related illnesses and promote longevity in humans.

In Germany, where many medicinal plants and herbs are available only with a doctor's prescription, ginkgo has long been used in the treatment of short-term memory loss, depression, fatigue, headaches, and poor circulation. Recent research suggests that it may be useful in the treatment of tinnitus, a debilitating condition marked by ringing in the ears.

Individuals diagnosed with Alzheimer's disease also may benefit from the supplement. The results of a year-long study revealed that when Alzheimer's patients took 120 mg of ginkgo extract daily, brain function and social behavior improved in nearly a third of the subjects. Scientists speculate that because gingko is a natural anticoagulant, it helps improve blood flow to the brain. As a powerful antioxidant, it also protects the brain from free-radical damage. Both actions can improve mental function in Alzheimer's patients.

Although Chinese healers have traditionally brewed the nuts of the ginkgo tree into a medicinal tea, most ginkgo products currently sold in the United States are manufactured from the tree's fan-shaped leaves. To date, more than 100 chemicals have been identified in ginkgo extract, and it is believed that the mixture, rather than a single agent, is responsible for the extract's wide range of benefits. In most clinical trials, scientists have used products labeled EGb 761. This is the specific formulation approved by Germany's Commission E, an organization recognized as the world's leading authority on plant and herbal medicines. In most cases, the recommended dose is 120 mg to 240 mg daily.

Although ginkgo is generally well tolerated, known side effects include headaches, stomach upset, diarrhea, and skin irritation. Because the supplement can prolong bleeding, it should never be taken with other anti-clotting drugs, including aspirin and Coumadin, and it should be discontinued at least two weeks prior to having surgical or dental procedures.

Glucosamine and Chondroitin Sulfate

Among American women, osteoarthritis is not only a widespread problem, it is also a leading cause of disability. For horsewomen, the condition can be especially devastating as it can dramatically interfere with our ability to ride and care for our mounts. While there are dozens of prescription drugs available to ease the symptoms of arthritis, most do nothing to prevent the progression of the disease. In recent years, numerous studies have shown that two nutritional supplements, known as glucosamine and chondroitin sulfate, not only reduce the pain and stiffness of arthritis but also may slow its progression.

For decades, glucosamine and chondroitin have been prescribed by physicians in Europe and Asia. In the 1970s the supplements became popular among veterinarians in the United States as a treatment for joint ailments in horses and dogs. Since then, glucosamine and chondroitin have worked their way into the medicine cabinets of millions of Americans suffering from arthritis.

Anti-inflammatory drugs, including ibuprofen, naproxen, and aspirin, have long been considered the mainstays of arthritis treatment, and in most cases, these medications are reasonably effective in reducing inflammation and pain. Unfortunately, they can cause a number of unpleasant or intolerable side effects, including stomach upset, allergic reactions, and even life-threatening bleeding problems.

Dozens of clinical trials involving thousands of patients have shown that glucosamine and chondroitin relieve arthritis pain as well as — or even better than — these commonly prescribed drugs but without the associated risks. More importantly, scientific evidence suggests that the supplements might actually slow the destruction of joint cartilage characteristic of the disease.

Glucosamine supplements typically are made from a substance derived from lobsters, crabs, and shrimp, while chondroitin sulfate is often extracted from the cartilage in the windpipes of cattle. Although their exact mechanisms of action still aren't fully understood, laboratory studies suggest that glucosamine and chondroitin work by stimulating cartilage growth and by inhibiting the action of enzymes responsible for cartilage destruction. In addition, both supplements appear to have mild anti-inflammatory effects that can ease discomfort and reduce swelling in affected joints.

A number of scientific studies have demonstrated the supplements' effectiveness in reducing the pain and progression of arthritis, especially in the knee joint. The results of the largest of these studies, the Glucosamine/Chondroitin Arthritis Intervention Trial (GAIT), suggest that when taken together, daily doses of 1,500 mg of glucosamine and 1,200 mg of chondroitin sulfate may significantly reduce knee pain associated with arthritis.

If you decide to take these supplements for relief of arthritis symptoms, don't expect immediate results. Because both are slow-acting agents, they must be taken daily for at least four to eight weeks to produce noticeable effects; and maximum pain relief may not occur until the third month of treatment. Although glucosamine may cause mild skin reactions in susceptible individuals, both supplements are generally well tolerated and have excellent safety profiles.

Ginseng

If the frenzied pace of modern life is zapping your energy levels and stressing you out, you might find relief in an ancient herb called ginseng. For more than 2,000 years, the root of the plant has been an essential part of traditional Chinese medicine. Chinese healers have long believed the plant has special powers to sooth the soul, banish fatigue, and prolong life.

Today, ginseng is used by people around the world as a mood enhancer and as an energy booster. In animal studies, ginseng has been shown to increase sexual activity, and as a result, ginseng supplements are often used to enhance libido. Scientific evidence supports the notion that the herb may serve as an adaptogen, dampening the body's negative reaction to stress. Ginseng also appears to strengthen the body's natural disease-fighting army, the immune system. The herb stimulates the activity of natural killer cells, affording the body some protection against the development of cancer.

Recent research suggests that ginseng can also reduce the risk of heart disease and stroke. Not only is the herb an antioxidant, it also serves as an effective anti-clotting agent. Ginseng promotes proper blood flow through the vessels of the heart and brain and improves circulation throughout the body.

For women with diabetes, or for those at risk for the disease, ginseng may be especially beneficial. Studies have shown that the herb helps lower blood sugar levels in diabetics, not only during periods of fasting but also after meals.

The optimum dose of ginseng is a subject of debate, but the one most frequently recommended is one to two grams of the root daily, taken in the form of tablets, teas, or extracts, with an upper limit of 15 grams a day. Because moderate doses seem to be just as effective as higher doses, you probably don't need to take large amounts of the herb to enjoy its benefits.

In traditional Chinese medicine, ginseng is prescribed only for short periods. Likewise, most Western experts recommend taking ginseng regularly for three weeks or less and then waiting a week or two before using it again.

In general, ginseng is well tolerated as long as it is taken in moderation and according to the manufacturer's directions. Safety concerns center primarily on the herb's ability to interfere with blood clotting, a phenomenon that can lead to prolonged bleeding. If you're planning to have surgery, you should stop taking ginseng at least a week ahead of time. If you're already taking other drugs that reduce the clotting potential of the blood, including Coumadin or aspirin, you should ask your doctor about the safety of simultaneously using any ginseng-containing product.

Ginseng is known to have stimulant properties. While it may give some women a welcome boost of energy, it can lead to nervousness, insomnia, and headaches in others. When taken with other stimulant drugs or agents, the combination can elevate blood pressure and heart rate to a dangerous degree. Because ginseng is thought to have estrogen-like effects, it may cause breast tenderness and postmenopausal bleeding in some women.

Dihydroepiandrosterone (DHEA)

In our youth-crazy culture, many women are refusing to gray gracefully. For those who are determined to fight old age as long as possible, a supplement known as DHEA might be the perfect weapon. Touted as an anti-aging miracle, DHEA is one of the most popular nutritional supplements of all time.

In the body, DHEA is a steroid hormone made from cholesterol in the adrenal glands. Although DHEA levels are high at birth, they drop steadily during the next decade. At puberty, DHEA production rises sharply, reaching an all-time high in the late 20s. In the early thirties, levels begin to decline again, at a rate of about 2 percent per year. By the age of 80, DHEA levels are pitifully low — just 10 percent to 20 percent of what they were in the second decade of life.

Since DHEA peaks during the prime of life and declines with age, it's not too farfetched to think that dwindling DHEA might have a hand in aging, disease, and even death. Although the effects of the hormone have been studied in rodents since 1934, widespread use of DHEA supplements didn't begin until the 1990s, when a highly publicized human trial yielded dramatic results. When researchers gave adult volunteers supplemental DHEA, 84 percent of the women and 67 percent of the men reported higher energy levels, better sleep, and improved moods. Most of the study participants had significant increases in lean body mass and muscle strength.

The encouraging results of this study fueled others, and subsequent claims for DHEA are almost too numerous to count. The supplement has been reported to melt away body fat, improve immune function and sex drive, as well as ward off cancer, heart attacks, and Alzheimer's disease. A number of studies found DHEA to be useful in the treatment of premenstrual syndrome, diabetes, and osteoporosis. Then came the most alluring claim of all — DHEA reverses the aging process.

Some of these claims have merit; others do not. Although scores of scientists have labored tirelessly to unlock the mysteries of DHEA, none have discovered exactly how it works in the body. What they have determined is that DHEA levels are markedly reduced in humans who are suffering from many major illnesses, including diabetes, obesity, high blood pressure, cancer, and heart disease. Preliminary findings suggest that supplemental DHEA may be advantageous in the treatment of these conditions.

DHEA has been shown to prevent diabetes in mice that are genetically programmed to develop the disease. Because the hormone appears to increase the body's sensitivity to insulin, it may offer humans a measure of protection against diabetes. DHEA has been shown to boost the defenses of the immune system, triggering the production of potent anti-tumor and anti-viral agents in the body.

Supplemental DHEA may play a role in the prevention and treatment of obesity. Overfed mice have been shown to gain less weight when they take the hormone. Because DHEA is converted to testosterone in the female liver, it may promote the loss of body fat and increase muscle mass in women. For some women, taking supplemental DHEA brings about a noticeable increase in libido.

In spite of all its potential benefits, DHEA is not without potential side effects. At high doses, it can cause acne and the growth of facial hair. Long-term use of high-dose DHEA may result in liver damage, and some experts fear the practice could trigger hormone-sensitive cancers of the reproductive tract.

If you decide to take a DHEA supplement, it's wise to take no more than the recommended dose of 25 mg to 50 mg a day. If you're using any other hormone medications, or if you have a history of cancer or liver disease, you should check with your doctor before taking the supplement in any amount.

Melatonin

In recent years melatonin has been touted as a cure for whatever ails you, from insomnia and depression to heart disease and cancer. Advocates claim it can boost energy, enhance immune function, improve sex drive, and slow the aging process.

Melatonin is a natural hormone produced and secreted by the pineal gland, a tiny, cone-shaped organ that lies at the base of the brain. Known as the master gland, it helps regulate the function of every other gland in the body.

The pineal gland also controls the body's biological clock, regulating the rhythms of life. In animals, it governs mating, migrating, and hibernating patterns. In humans, its functions are subtler and less thoroughly understood, but it is known to play a major role in the daily sleep-wake cycle, or the circadian rhythm.

The pineal gland communicates with the rest of the body through its hormone messenger, melatonin. In humans, melatonin levels peak during childhood and begin to drop during adolescence around the time of puberty. With age, melatonin levels continue to decline, with the steepest drop occurring around the fifth decade of life. By the age of 60, the pineal gland produces roughly half the amount of melatonin it did at the age of 20. It may be coincidental, but as melatonin levels fall, the body begins to show serious signs of aging. Some experts postulate that supplemental melatonin can dramatically slow the aging process.

Whether melatonin is the real fountain of youth is still a subject of great debate, but most experts agree that a melatonin supplement can have a profound influence on the regulation of the sleep-wake cycle. In humans, melatonin secretion naturally increases as darkness falls and slacks off with exposure to light. Supplemental melatonin has been shown to help reset the internal clock in shift workers and in international travelers who suffer from jet lag, and to promote sleepiness in people with insomnia.

Insomnia and poor quality sleep are commonly associated with advancing age. Although older women often spend more time in bed than their younger counterparts, most spend far less time sleeping. Studies have shown that people who sleep poorly typically have less than half the levels of melatonin of people who sleep well. For many women, taking a melatonin supplement at bedtime can result in a deeper and more restful slumber.

Although supplemental melatonin is regulated as a drug in Canada and Europe, melatonin preparations are available without a prescription in the United States. Most experts agree that synthetic sources of melatonin are far safer than melatonin obtained from animal products. The supplements are available in sustained- or immediate-release lozenges, pills, and capsules, in doses ranging from .5 mg to 10 mg. Because no one knows the "normal" human level and because levels vary widely from person to person, the therapeutic dose of melatonin is still controversial. At any rate, it's probably slightly less than the dose recommended on labels of many commercially available products.

Doses of 1 mg to 3 mg, taken before bedtime, are most frequently recommended for the treatment of insomnia, but you may find that as little as a third of a milligram works well for you. Taking more than 5 mg at once may knock you out at bedtime, but it also can leave you feeling hung over the following morning. Melatonin usually causes drowsiness in about 30 minutes, and its effects tend to last for at least an hour. While short-term side effects include vivid dreams, morning grogginess, and headaches, the long-term side effects remain unknown.

St. John's Wort

Move over Prozac — it looks like Mother Nature has her own brand of anti-depressant. It's a plant medicine known as St. John's wort, and it has been used in the treatment of depression since the days of Hypocrites. Centuries ago folk healers believed the plant's magical powers could send evil spirits packing. To many women, depression can feel like an invasion of evil spirits.

Although depressive symptoms should always be evaluated by a physician, prescription drugs aren't always necessary, or even advisable. In mild cases, St. John's wort has been effectively to improve mood, relieve anxiety, and promote more restful sleep. In a study of 3,000 mildly depressed individuals, St. John's wort improved symptoms in nearly 80 percent of the people who took it.

It's not entirely clear how St. John's wort works, but it appears to behave in a manner similar to the newer synthetic antidepressant drugs, including Prozac, Zoloft, and Paxil, which increase levels of serotonin, a mood-enhancing neurotransmitter in the brain.

Serotonin has a number of important benefits. It promotes a sense of well-being while it improves sleep, increases pain tolerance, and normalizes appetite. People who suffer from depression typically have lower levels of serotonin than people who are usually happy.

Although most people taking St. John's wort experience noticeable improvements in mood in about two weeks, some begin to feel better after taking the supplement for just a few days. Maximum symptom relief is thought to occur within six to eight weeks of beginning treatment.

When taken alone and in therapeutic doses, St. John's wort appears to be safe, and to date, no significant side effects have been reported in humans. Cases of fatal sensitivity to the sun have been reported in sheep grazing on fields of St. John's wort, but those unfortunate sheep consumed 30 to 50 times the recommended dose for humans. Sun sensitivity hasn't been a problem in people.

The most common side effects of St. John's wort are minor, including stomach upset, allergic reactions, or mild fatigue. Unlike many of the synthetic antidepressants, the herb doesn't appear to cause sexual dysfunction — a depressing situation in itself. Overall, St. John's wort has an excellent safety record.

While St. John's wort can be combined with other antidepressant drugs, it should be done with caution and only with a physician's supervision. Patients taking one or more antidepressants that act on serotonin are at risk of developing what is known as serotonin syndrome, a distressing condition in which high serotonin levels lead to confusion, fever, diarrhea, tremor, and muscle spasms.

Depression can be a serious illness, and every treatment program should include the expertise of a physician. Before you begin taking St. John's wort, be sure to talk it over with your doctor.

Functional Foods

Like plant medicines and dietary supplements, some foods have unique health-promoting and disease-preventing attributes that make them especially beneficial for women. Because they can be considered to have both nutritive and pharmaceutical properties, these functional foods are frequently referred to as "nutraceuticals." Once you've identified a few of these super-foods, you easily can work them into your diet.

Probiotics

Probiotics are naturally occurring, friendly bacteria that dwell in the human gut.

These microorganisms have several important benefits in terms of enhancing digestion, normalizing bowel function, improving immunity, and boosting overall health.

Although the human gastrointestinal tract is most commonly associated with the digestion of food and the absorption of dietary nutrients, it has another, equally vital function. The gut is a major component of the body's immune system, and it plays a critical role in defending us from disease-causing germs. Beneficial bacteria in the gastrointestinal tract protect us from colds, stomach bugs, and other infections. Because these good bacteria are constantly being turned over in the body, it's important to replenish them on a regular basis.

One of the easiest ways to boost the population of good bacteria in your gut is to add a source of probiotics to your daily diet. Probiotics can be found in dietary supplements, a cultured dairy product called kefir, and in certain brands of yogurt, including DanActive and Activia, which contain live bacterial cultures.

Studies have shown that adults who regularly consume probiotics preparations suffer significantly fewer infections of the gastrointestinal system and upper respiratory tract. The results of several large clinical trials revealed that both children and adults taking probiotics on a daily basis not only experienced fewer illnesses, but they enjoyed reduced rates of absenteeism from school and work.

If you're allergic to milk products, probiotics pills and powders are excellent choices. If you're merely lactose intolerant, on the other hand, you may be able to consume dairy products containing probiotics without experiencing the slightest bit of gastrointestinal grief because the lactose is pre-digested by the friendly bacteria.

Psyllium

Fiber contains no vitamins, minerals, or calories, but, nonetheless, it's a key component of every woman's diet. Although adult women need about 28 grams of fiber daily to stay healthy, most consume only about 10 to 15 grams a day. Needless to say, there's plenty of room for improvement. While eating a balanced, plant-based diet is one of the best ways to boost fiber consumption, it's not always easy for busy women on the go. If you're in

search of an inexpensive and convenient fiber source, a product called psyllium is well worth considering.

Psyllium fiber is derived from the husk, a shrub-like herb native to parts of Asia and North Africa. In the United States it's sold as a nutritional supplement at supermarkets and health food stores in various forms, including tablets, capsules, water-soluble crystals, and wafers. It is also the primary ingredient in several over-the-counter products, including Metamucil and Fiberall. Although psyllium has long been used to alleviate constipation, this unique source of fiber does more than just promote regularity and good bowel health.

Clinical trials have shown that in combination with a low-fat diet, a daily dose of just 10.2 grams of psyllium can reduce the risk of heart disease by significantly lowering cholesterol levels. Among adults with diabetes, the same dose can dramatically reduce blood sugar levels.

In addition to its positive effects on cholesterol and glucose, psyllium is also beneficial in terms of weight management. The soluble fiber in psyllium and other foods, including oats, peas, and many types of fruit, helps reduce hunger and curtail overeating by contributing to a sensation of fullness. Not only does soluble fiber absorb water like a sponge in the stomach, it also delays gastric emptying. Both actions make you feel fuller for longer.

Adding psyllium to your diet will likely improve your health, but it's best to start with a low dose and gradually increase it. Drastic increases in fiber intake, regardless of the source, can lead to intestinal bloating, cramping, and excessive gas production, which can not only be uncomfortable but also can make you rather unpopular with your friends and family. Drinking plenty of water will reduce the likelihood that you'll experience any of these unpleasant side effects.

If you're in search of a supplement that can lower your blood sugar and cholesterol levels, curb your hunger, or just boost your fiber intake, a daily dose of psyllium may be your best bet.

Chocolate

If you're like most women, you probably find yourself giving into an irrepressible chocolate craving every now and then. As long as you're not trying to eat your weight in M & Ms, you're probably not doing any major damage. As a matter of fact, you might just be enhancing your health. Although it's long been considered a guilty pleasure, chocolate is finally getting the respect it deserves.

In years past, chocolate has been accused of causing everything from hyperactivity to PMS, but there's little scientific evidence to support those claims. When eaten responsibly, certain types of chocolate have a number of benefits.

Contrary to popular teenage myth, chocolate doesn't cause acne, a condition more related to genetics and hormones than to diet. Chocolate doesn't wreak the dental havoc our mothers told us it would, either. It's true that sugary foods can lead to tooth decay if you don't

brush your teeth regularly. But unlike most sweet treats, chocolate contains anti-bacterial substances that slow the destructive action of cavity-causing enzymes and prevent plaque formation, reversing much of the damage caused by sugar.

We like to blame our weight-related woes on chocolate. Hefty amounts of any food can make you fat, but when eaten in moderation, chocolate isn't any more fattening than many other popular snack foods. A 1.5-ounce chocolate bar has around 220 calories and about 5 grams of fat, compared to the 230 calories and 6 grams of fat found in a similar portion of potato chips. Even the fat in chocolate isn't as bad as it could be. More than half of it is in the form of stearic acid, which doesn't drive up blood cholesterol levels.

If you want to derive the greatest number of health benefits per ounce, you should satisfy your sweet tooth with chocolate of the dark variety, which is derived from the cocoa bean. Like fruits, vegetables, and whole grains, cocoa beans are rich in natural antioxidants called flavonoids. A 1-ounce chunk of dark chocolate provides twice as many antioxidants as Americans typically get in a day's supply of fruits and vegetables.

Like green tea and red wine, dark chocolate is considered to be a plant extract, in which flavonoids are condensed and concentrated. Because it takes a large number of cocoa beans to produce a single candy bar, dark chocolate is a particularly flavonoid-rich food. Milk chocolate, on the other hand, contains fewer flavonoids, and white chocolate, which is made from cocoa butter and sugar, has no flavonoids at all.

Because flavonoids are bitter-tasting compounds, dark chocolate isn't as sweet as the other varieties. As a rule, the more flavonoid-rich a particular chocolate bar is, the more bittersweet it will taste, and the greater health benefits it will offer.

A growing body of research supports the role of dark chocolate in the prevention of cancer and heart disease. Studies have shown that eating a daily serving of dark chocolate can reduce blood pressure as much as some prescription drugs. Dark chocolate also has been found to increase insulin sensitivity, improving the ability of insulin to lower blood sugar levels.

As a health food, dark chocolate will probably never achieve the same status as say, broccoli or asparagus, as it's still relatively high in fat and sugar. But thanks to its newly discovered benefits, at least we can eat a little chocolate every now and then without experiencing a lot of guilt.

Nuts

Most women who are watching their weight try to steer clear of high-calorie snacks, including nuts. In spite of their caloric content, nuts can be an important part of a balanced diet. Not only are they delicious and nutritious, but they also offer some very important health benefits.

Most nuts, including walnuts, pecans, almonds, and Brazil nuts, are the seeds or dried fruit from trees. They're naturally cholesterol free and loaded with important vitamins and minerals. Although peanuts are commonly thought of as nuts, they're actually members of the legume family, which includes peas and beans.

True to their reputation, nuts are high in fat. In most varieties, nearly 75 percent of calories come from heart-healthy monounsaturated and polyunsaturated fats. These beneficial fats reduce the stickiness of the blood and interfere with the formation of clots that can lead to heart attacks and strokes.

Nuts are good sources of arginine, an amino acid capable of relaxing blood vessels and lowering blood pressure. The crunchy little nuggets are also rich in plant sterols, compounds that block cholesterol absorption in the gut. Plant sterols were once sold by prescription as cholesterol-lowering drugs, but today they're used as the active ingredients in many cholesterol-lowering margarines and spreads. Eating just eight to 11 walnuts a day has been shown to reduce total and low-density lipoprotein cholesterol (LDL) by an average of 10 percent.

By lowering cholesterol levels and blood pressure, regular nut consumption appears to contribute to a reduced risk of heart disease. A 14-year Harvard study of 86,000 women showed that those who ate 5 ounces of nuts each week cut their risk of heart attack by 35 percent.

Nuts can help you lose weight. The results of a study published in the *International Journal of Obesity* revealed that when overweight volunteers included raw or roasted almonds in their calorie-restricted diets, their weight-loss efforts were dramatically accelerated.

The study included 65 overweight and obese adults who were placed on one of two diets designed to promote weight loss. Although the calorie counts and protein levels of the two diets were equivalent, one included a 3-ounce serving of almonds daily.

After 24 weeks, the two groups showed a striking difference in their weight-loss patterns. The almond-eating group had lost 62 percent more weight and 56 percent more body fat than the nut-free group. The almond eaters also experienced significantly greater reductions in abdominal fat and waist circumference.

Researchers speculate that almonds promote weight loss for at least two reasons. Because they're so filling, they help stave off hunger for hours after they're eaten. Even better, the fiber in almonds binds with dietary fat in the intestine so that it cannot be absorbed by the body.

Cinnamon

While you already may be using cinnamon to add a spark of flavor to your favorite recipes, a sprinkle of cinnamon also can spice up your health. Thanks to its anti-bacterial and anti-fungal actions, cinnamon has long been used in the treatment of minor infections.

Cinnamon also may benefit women with diabetes. Preliminary studies suggest that consuming slightly less than a half-teaspoon a day can produce significant reductions in blood sugar levels. Cinnamon appears to make cells in the body more sensitive to the hormone insulin, which allows them to regulate blood sugar more effectively.

The results of a 2003 study, published in the journal *Diabetes Care*, revealed that diabetics who took capsules containing 1 to 6 grams of cinnamon daily for six weeks experienced a 20 percent reduction in their fasting blood sugar levels. In addition, the volunteers' triglyceride levels fell at least 25 percent, while total cholesterol levels dropped 12 percent to 26 percent.

While it's unlikely that cinnamon will ever replace prescription medications, a healthy diet, or regular exercise, many women can undoubtedly benefit from adding a half-teaspoon of the spice to their daily diets. Sprinkling cinnamon on foods may soften the spike in blood sugar that can occur after eating, a phenomenon that is magnified following consumption of foods rich in simple carbohydrates, especially in women with diabetes. Of course, you're much better off adding cinnamon to foods that are good for you, such as oatmeal, rather than foods that are loaded with sugar.

Using a dash of cinnamon a day appears to be safe for most people although a few sensitive individuals may develop allergies, mouth irritation, and skin rashes after long-term exposure. While it's probably too early to move cinnamon to the medicine cabinet, sliding it to the front of your spice rack might not be a bad idea.

Garlic

Eating garlic can be tough on your social life, but it's actually good for your health. One of garlic's greatest virtues may be its ability to reduce the risk of heart disease. Regular consumption of the stinky little bulb can lower total blood cholesterol and triglyceride levels, while increasing levels of heart-healthy HDL cholesterol.

Garlic also protects your heart by hindering the clotting ability of your blood. Not only does it promote the formation of clot-busting enzymes, but it also diminishes the stickiness of blood cells so that they're less likely to form clots in the first place. Both actions can reduce the risk of having a heart attack.

While the anti-clotting properties of garlic are beneficial to most healthy women, they can be dangerous for those with bleeding disorders. If you're already taking aspirin or other anti-clotting drugs, be sure to talk to your doctor before you start consuming garlic in earnest.

In addition to lowering cholesterol levels, garlic also protects the heart by lowering blood pressure. With age, blood vessels inevitably become stiffer, and this hardening of the arteries often leads to the development of high blood pressure. Regular garlic consumption seems to keep blood vessels more supple and elastic, lowering blood pressure in the process.

The results of some studies suggest that garlic can reduce the risk of many types of cancer. In laboratory animals exposed to cancer-causing agents, those fed garlic-rich diets consistently developed fewer cancers than animals receiving garlic-free rations. While several compounds in garlic are known to have powerful antioxidant properties, there's also evidence to suggest these agents bolster the body's production of specialized cancer-fighting cells known as natural killer cells.

Garlic also is capable of warding off infection by damaging many types of microbial organisms that can invade the body. While its anti-fungal properties make it ideal for preventing and treating minor yeast infections, its antiviral actions can kill some viruses responsible for causing the common cold. Because garlic is known for its broad-spectrum antibiotic activity, many people rely on the herb for the treatment of minor bacterial infections.

Scientists aren't in total agreement about how and why garlic works, but many suspect that a compound called allicin is the main source of its medicinal benefits. Allicin is definitely responsible for the distinctive odor — it's released whenever raw garlic cloves are cut, crushed, or chewed. Because allicin is destroyed by heat, raw garlic is more powerful than cooked garlic, but it's also far more pungent.

Aside from giving you breath that can clear a room, garlic has very few side effects. It's been known to trigger skin rashes in people with allergies to the herb, and some folks can't tolerate any amount of garlic without developing serious stomach upset.

You don't have to spend a fortune on specially processed and packaged garlic pills, oils, and extracts to derive its medicinal benefits. In most cases, fresh garlic cloves are more potent than supplements. And because fresh garlic is usually cheaper, you might have enough money left over for breath mints.

Xylitol

Undoubtedly, the vast majority of us get far more sugar in our diets than our bodies need. Incredibly, the average American consumes about 150 pounds of sugar each year. Most health and nutrition experts — including those affiliated with the U.S. Department of Agriculture — recommend an intake of no more than 10 teaspoons of sugar a day. If you do the math (a pound of sugar contains about 108 teaspoons), you quickly realize that the average American consumes more along the lines of 45 teaspoons of sugar each day. It's no wonder that obesity and diabetes are national epidemics.

To avoid the high-calorie consequences of a sugar-laden diet, many women turn to calorie-free artificial sweeteners. Although they may temporarily avoid some unwanted calories, they may not be avoiding the associated weight gain. In fact, numerous studies have linked consumption of non-caloric artificial sweeteners to weight gain, rather than weight loss. Animal research suggests that calorie-free artificial sweeteners actually stimulate hunger and trigger overeating.

While the reasons for the increased appetite are not fully understood, some experts believe that when non-caloric sweeteners are consumed, the brain responds to the sweet taste in the same way it responds to the sweet taste of pure sugar — it alerts the pancreas to prepare for an incoming caloric load. Although there are no calories in artificial sweeteners, the brain doesn't know this. As a result, it signals the pancreas to begin pumping insulin into the bloodstream.

Insulin's job is to escort sugar molecules from the bloodstream to cells in various tissues throughout the body. Because there are no sugar molecules in artificial sweeteners, the newly released insulin goes to work on sugar that is already in the bloodstream, and, as a result, it can cause blood sugar levels to drop well below normal. Low blood sugar levels, in turn, are a powerful stimulus for hunger.

Because artificial sweeteners can end up causing more harm than good, you're far better off choosing a low-calorie sweetener than a no-calorie sweetener. A natural sugar substitute known as xylitol is an excellent choice, for many reasons.

Discovered in 1891 by a German chemist, the substance became popular in many European countries during World War II, when sugar was in short supply. Since the 1960s, xylitol has been used as an FDA-approved nutritive sweetener in diabetic diets. These days it can be found in a few brands of baked goods and beverages, as well as in chewing gum, mints, and toothpaste.

Xylitol isn't a true sugar but rather a naturally occurring sugar alcohol found in many plants, including some fruits and vegetables. Although it was originally derived from birch trees, corn is now the primary source of commercially produced xylitol. In its pure form, the sweetener is a white crystalline substance that looks, tastes, and measures like sugar. Unlike table sugar, which has 15 calories per teaspoon, xylitol provides just 9.6 calories per teaspoon.

Because the human body metabolizes sugar alcohols in a unique manner, xylitol doesn't produce the rapid, dramatic spikes in blood glucose and insulin levels that commonly occur following the consumption of regular sugar. As a result, eating xylitol-sweetened foods won't leave you tired, hungry, and craving sugar afterward.

While sugar is known to wreak havoc on dental health, xylitol has the opposite effect. The natural sweetener has been shown to prevent tooth decay by inhibiting the growth of *Streptococcus mutans*, the bacteria primarily responsible for causing dental cavities. Over the past two decades a number of studies have shown that when volunteers chew xylitol-sweetened gum three times daily following meals, they develop significantly fewer cavities than those chewing sugar-sweetened gum. Xylitol also has been shown to increase saliva production, help control bad breath, reduce the frequency and severity of mouth sores and ear infections, and improve oral health in individuals with periodontal disease.

Preliminary research suggests that the sugar alcohol also may play a role in the prevention and treatment of osteoporosis. When fed to aging rats, xylitol not only reduced bone loss but actually increased bone mineral density by an average of 10 percent. Scientists speculate that the sweetener may enhance bone health by boosting the body's absorption of calcium. While the optimal dose necessary to promote bone health is still unknown, a daily intake of 6 grams of xylitol has been shown to help prevent dental cavities and improve oral health. For best results, two pieces of gum, each containing 1 gram of xylitol, should be chewed three times a day following meals. In these amounts, xylitol is generally well-tolerated. At doses greater than 30 grams a day, however, the sugar alcohol may have a laxative effect, which many women find to be quite beneficial.

While xylitol is perfectly safe for human adults and children, canines can't properly metabolize the sugar alcohol. If your dog accidentally eats a xylitol-containing food, you'll need to get him to the vet immediately because he may experience a sudden, life-threatening drop in blood sugar levels.

Like regular sugar, xylitol can be purchased in bulk, as well as in single-serving packages. Unlike sugar, xylitol isn't widely available in supermarkets: It's more likely to be found at stores and shops that sell natural foods and nutritional supplements. Xylitol is more expensive than regular table sugar, but if you're looking for a reduced-calorie sweetener that offers a few bonus benefits for your health, it's an excellent investment.

Green Tea

Wouldn't it be great to find a thirst-quenching beverage that not only tastes great but improves your health at the same time? It's a tall order, but a glass of tea might just measure up.

Although tea can be found in dozens of different flavors, there are really just three types: black, green, and oolong. All three are derived from the leaves of the same plant, an evergreen shrub known as *Camellia sinensis*. It's the processing conditions that determine the type of tea the leaves are destined to become. Black tea is produced when the leaves are thoroughly fermented while leaves that are partially fermented become oolong teas. Green teas are produced by skipping the fermentation festivities altogether.

Each of the three teas has a distinct taste, and each has unique health-promoting properties. Green teas are especially rich in polyphenols, compounds with built-in antibacterial and antiviral properties. The polyphenols also serve as powerful antioxidants, neutralizing free radicals that contribute to a number of deadly diseases, including cancer.

As antioxidants go, those in tea seem to be far more potent than the ones found in most fruits and vegetables. They're also about 100 times more effective than vitamin C, and nearly 25 times more effective than vitamin E. The antioxidants in tea aren't the only ingredients that make it such a powerful weapon in the war on cancer. A compound called EGCg (epigallocatechin gallate) appears to squelch an enzyme necessary for the growth of cancer cells. When EGCg was added to cultures of healthy and cancerous mouse cells, researchers found that the agent helped wipe out the cancer cells without harming the healthy ones. EGCg also seems to trigger the production of proteins that can repair DNA damage before it leads to cancer.

A growing body of evidence suggests that drinking tea is also good for your heart. Studies show that it not only widens the coronary arteries, but it also improves blood flow through those vessels. Both actions are beneficial to heart health.

In addition to warding off cancer and heart disease, tea may boost the protective powers of the immune system. Drinking tea increases production of interferon, a substance known to play a key role in protecting the body against infection. In subjects who drank five cups of black tea daily for a month, interferon levels increased five-fold.

As long as it's consumed unsweetened, tea is naturally calorie-free. If you want to slim down, you should drink up: Green tea has been shown to promote weight loss by boosting the metabolism of both fat and calories. If you're just looking for a simple, tasty way to quench your thirst and improve your health, tea is still an excellent option.

Coffee

If you're determined to improve your health and nutrition, you may be saying a fond farewell to a few of your favorite foods and beverages. Fortunately, it's probably not necessary to pull the plug on your morning coffee.

Although coffee has long been vilified, recent research has practically elevated it to the status of a health elixir. Moderate consumption of America's favorite beverage has been shown to yield a number of perks for the brain and body.

Because it's made by brewing beans, there's no denying that coffee is a plant-based beverage. Like other plant foods, including fruits and vegetables, coffee is rich in disease-fighting antioxidants.

While fruits, vegetables, and grains are undoubtedly more nutritious sources of antioxidants, the unfortunate reality is that few Americans eat the recommended amounts of these wholesome foods. In fact, studies have shown that coffee is the largest source of antioxidants in the typical American's diet.

Although many foods, including red beans and blueberries, have far higher antioxidant concentrations than a cup of coffee, most Americans don't eat beans and berries regularly enough to derive their disease-fighting benefits. We do, however, drink plenty of coffee. More than 80 percent of U.S. adults consume coffee at least occasionally, and over half of us drink it every day.

Coffee's greatest claim to fame may lie in its ability to boost brain power. After a jolt of java, individuals tend to perform better on tests that measure concentration, memory, and learning. Coffee may have even greater benefits in the human brain, protecting it from degenerative processes that lead to dementia. Recent studies suggest that habitual coffee drinkers have a lower risk for Parkinson's disease and Alzheimer's than individuals who abstain.

Researchers once suspected that coffee might increase the risk for a variety of cancers, but this theory has been disproved. As it turns out, regular consumption of the brewed beverage appears to afford a measure of cancer protection. Coffee has been shown

to reduce the risk of colorectal cancer by as much as 25 percent. Because coffee hastens the elimination process, cancer-causing toxins in digestive waste material are in contact with the intestinal lining for shorter periods. Coffee also appears to increase the activity of enzymes responsible for the detoxification of carcinogens in the body.

At least one study has demonstrated that coffee drinking can have a protective effect against some types of breast cancer as well. Among women with breast-cancer causing gene mutations, those with high levels of coffee consumption were found to have a reduced risk of developing breast cancer.

Coffee has long been implicated in the development of osteoporosis, but there's never been any convincing scientific evidence to support the theory. Studies examining the effects of moderate coffee consumption on bone loss in postmenopausal women reveal that as long as dietary calcium intake is adequate, drinking one to three cups of coffee a day has no detrimental effect on bone health.

Recent research also refutes the notion that drinking coffee is bad for your heart. In a study funded by the National Institutes of Health, scientists analyzed caffeine consumption among more than 100,000 adults, and found that drinking coffee was not associated with an elevated risk of coronary heart disease.

Coffee may offer a measure of protection against diabetes. In an 18-year-long study of more than 120,000 adults, Harvard scientists concluded that regular coffee consumption was associated with a significantly lower risk of developing type II diabetes.

Coffee can help improve the staying power of exercisers, equestrians, and other athletes — the caffeine boosts endurance by delaying the onset of fatigue. When athletes drink three or four cups of coffee about an hour before they compete, they can outlast their caffeine-free competitors by up to 20 minutes. This effect on athletic performance is real — so real, in fact, that the International Olympic Committee classified caffeine as a "restricted drug." Olympic competitors are allowed to use caffeine, as long as they don't overdo it.

While a cup of coffee offers a number of potential health benefits, there's no advantage to loading it with lots of sugar, cream, and artificial flavorings. The next time you visit your favorite coffee shop, remember that some gourmet varieties contain up to 600 calories and 25 grams of fat. You're far better off drinking your coffee black or with just a touch of low-fat milk. As long as you consume coffee responsibly, you can sit back, relax, and enjoy all the perks it has to offer.

Alcohol

For women who aren't morally opposed to an occasional libation, small amounts of alcohol can be quite therapeutic, especially in terms of cardiovascular health. Interest in alcohol as a heart-protecting agent was piqued after scientists began to investigate a phenomenon known as the "French paradox," which refers to the fact that the French, who habitually consume foods loaded with saturated animal fats, have very low rates of heart disease. Years ago, experts first speculated, and later demonstrated, that the French's penchant for wine is responsible for their extraordinary cardiovascular health.

Since then, moderate alcohol consumption has been found to protect against heart disease in several ways. Not only does it help keep fat in the bloodstream from clinging to artery walls, but it also boosts levels of heart-friendly HDL cholesterol in the body. Alcohol seems to have an anti-clotting effect on the blood, accounting for the reduced risk of stroke seen in conservative drinkers.

Although these findings are relatively new, some doctors have long recognized the benefits of an occasional cocktail or glass of vino to improve appetite and digestion, and to help their patients relax at the end of a hectic day. Still, you'll never hear a physician discuss the benefits of alcohol without uttering the word "moderation" in the same breath.

That can lead to misunderstandings as the definition of moderation can vary significantly depending on who's doing the defining. What seems like moderation to college sorority sisters may seem like extravagant excess to sisters in the Baptist faith.

In light of this discrepancy, officials at many nationally recognized health organizations and government institutions have taken it upon themselves to remove the guesswork from the matter. They've defined "moderation" as one daily drink for women and two daily drinks for men. Since men tend to weigh more, have less body fat, and metabolize alcohol more efficiently than women do, two drinks in the male body tend to have about the same biological effect as one drink in the female body. One drink is considered to be 12 ounces of beer, 5 ounces of wine, or 1.5 ounces of 80-proof liquor.

There's some debate about which type of alcohol affords the greatest protection to the heart. While several studies suggest that wine — especially red wine — is best, most have failed to find any significant difference. Still, some scientists argue that red wine is most beneficial in terms of cardiovascular health because it's loaded with antioxidants, especially resveratrol, a natural anti-fungal agent found in grapes.

It's true that while a drink or two a day may help keep the grim reaper away, any more will serve as a formal invitation to the ghoulish one. Although heavy alcohol consumption is associated with a low risk of death from heart disease, it's probably because other diseases cross the finish line first. People who drink beyond moderation have higher rates of death from cancers of the liver, mouth, and throat, not to mention deaths caused by accidents and injuries.

Women need to weigh carefully the risks and benefits of alcohol consumption. Drinking just one alcoholic beverage a day increases the risk of breast cancer by about 10 percent. Having two drinks a day bumps the risk up to 25 percent.

In some cases, you're better off foregoing the benefits of alcohol and opting for total abstinence. Pregnant women should refrain from drinking altogether until after the blessed event. Recovering alcoholics should refrain from drinking forever. Whenever you're planning to slide behind the wheel, you should steer clear of the stuff as well.

Because more than 100 prescription and nonprescription medications are known to interact unfavorably with even small amounts of alcohol, people who take any type of medicine should find out about potential interactions before drinking. Alcohol can deepen the sedating effects of some drugs, including antihistamines and antidepressants while other drugs can become toxic or completely ineffective when mixed with a drink. If you're taking several medications, you're best bet is to stick with beverages of the nonalcoholic variety.

If you've made it this far in life as a teetotaler, there's probably no good reason to start drinking at this point. But if you're a moderate consumer of alcohol, now you can drink at least one toast to your good health.

fitness

AND THE FEMALE EQUESTRIAN

The Equestrian Athlete

If you're a seasoned equestrian, you know how physically demanding and mentally challenging riding can be. Even if you're a newcomer to the sport, it probably didn't take you long to realize riding is much more than just sitting on a horse. Equestrians are athletes, just like dancers, golfers, and tennis players. Some folks might argue that riding is even more difficult than the vast majority of other sports, and they'd have a good point. Riding effectively requires the athlete to perform her skill while she's astride a moving animal that may easily weigh in excess of 1,000 pounds. To make matters even more challenging, the animal has a mind and a will of its own, in contrast to, say, a golf club or tennis racket. While the rider is coordinating the movements of her own body, she must simultaneously direct the movements of her equine partner.

People who have never ridden a horse — or those who have never ridden in earnest — often have the misconception that riding is easy. You just climb aboard, sit back in the saddle, and let the horse do all the work, right? It's true that skilled equestrians make riding look effort-less, in much the same way that an Olympic gymnast makes a double-back somersault dismount from the balance beam appear as simple and as natural as rolling out of bed in the morning. In many athletic endeavors, including gymnastics and riding, the more accomplished the athlete, the more subtle her effort.

Skilled riders may appear to be virtually motionless in the saddle, but, in reality, dozens of muscles throughout their entire bodies are actively working at any given moment. Excellent muscle control, flexibility, and balance make their movements so precise and so fluid as to be practically imperceptible. Extraneous movements, on the other hand, are practically nonexistent because any action that doesn't help the horse do his job only serves to hinder him.

It's all easier said than done, of course. While you're riding, you're using the muscles of your body to communicate with your horse on a moment-to-moment basis. You're relying on many of these same muscles to keep you safely astride so that you don't end up on the ground. It takes hours of practice to master the ability to do both simultaneously.

Practice and Patience Make Perfect

When you're learning any new skill, especially one as challenging as riding, it's important to be patient with yourself. You may have been born to ride, but that doesn't mean that you were born knowing *how* to ride. Expert riders aren't created overnight, but only after countless hours of practice and years of experience. Because becoming a skilled equestrian takes time, you might as well relax and enjoy the ride — and the learning process.

No matter how simple the overall act of riding may seem, in reality, it consists of the synchronization of hundreds of smaller, individual tasks. A beginner is acutely aware of this phenomenon. As soon as she focuses her attention on maintaining proper leg position at a particular gait, her hands drift up and apart. When she concentrates on repositioning her hands, her head drops. In the early stages of the learning process, it's practically impossible to pay attention to the position of every body part at the same time although our instructors often admonish us to try. Our brains and bodies just aren't designed to learn several tasks at once, and for this reason it is necessary to learn one skill — even if we don't gain complete mastery of it — before attempting to learn another.

Research shows that in the first five to six hours after a motor skill is learned, there is a period of vulnerability during which that skill can easily be unlearned, or forgotten, by attempting to learn a second skill. During that five- to six-hour window, the brain and the central nervous system are busy consolidating a unique pattern of neural pathways that control the performance of the task. These neural pathways form the "motor memory" that will allow the body to perform the task again at a later time.

Once this memory is established, it is transferred from one part of the brain, where it is temporarily held, to other parts of the brain, where it is placed in permanent storage. The good news is that after five or six hours, even without practice, the blueprint for the task is virtually hardwired into the central nervous system. The passage of time serves to cement new skills in our brains. This may explain why we're able to surprise ourselves with significant improvements in a particular aspect of riding even from one day to the next.

Learning any new skill is an intricate and complex process that requires you to use your brain, nerves, and muscles in new ways. It involves chemical and physiological changes in the molecules and cells of the brain and body. Sometimes, even after your brain and nerves have established the correct neural pathway for a particular task, your body isn't fully cooperative. You might be able to perform the task to some degree, but you may not be able to execute it perfectly, or even smoothly. It could be that you don't have sufficient muscle strength or that you lack the necessary flexibility, coordination, or balance. These physical attributes will improve with time and practice.

Make Mistakes — Gain Mastery

The process of *mastering* any new skill requires us to perform the skill in some form or fashion, detect errors in its execution, and then modify our subsequent attempts to reduce or eliminate those errors. Riding instructors help us gain mastery, not only by teaching us the proper techniques but by pointing out our mistakes. Compassionate fault finding is one of the most effective teaching tools they have. Only when we're aware of what it is that we're doing wrong are we able to correct and improve our performance.

This also is why repetition of any newly acquired skill is essential, whether it's riding or performing a particular exercise as part of a fitness program. Repetition allows us to make mistakes continually and modify them. With each attempt we're able to make finer and finer distinctions between the actual performance and the desired performance. With each attempt we inch forward toward perfection.

As the old saying goes, repetition is the mother of skill. Wise teachers have known this to be true since the beginning of time, long before scientists had high-tech brain scans and blood tests to prove it. Repetition of a skill allows an individual to activate the correct neural pathways over and over. The nerves controlling specific muscles fire in a precise sequence, directing the movement of those muscles to execute the task properly. The more often the appropriate neural pathways are activated, the more deeply etched they become in the brain, muscles, and nerves, like a well-trodden trail. Not only are they preserved as mental memories, they're also maintained as muscle memories.

Activating Your Autopilot

The more often you perform a specific task, the more natural and seemingly effortless it becomes. When you first learned to push your horse into a canter from a walk, for example, you probably found that the task required your total attention. You may have found yourself consciously running through a checklist: slight shift in seat, steady contact on the outside rein, lighter contact on the inside rein, inside leg at the girth, outside leg behind the girth, and so on. With each repetition of the task, you relied less and less on your mental checklist. By the time you mastered the skill, you simply had to think "canter," and your body took over. Almost subconsciously, the nerves and muscles of your hands, arms, seat, and legs naturally performed each of the myriad functions necessary to push the horse from a walk into a canter.

This phenomenon can be compared to driving yourself home when your mind is in a state of preoccupation. When you first moved to your current address, you probably had to stay alert to make sure you ended up at the right place. You might have given yourself mental instructions: Turn left here, go to the end of this street and turn right, and so on. But if you've lived at your current address for some time, all you have to do is hop in your car and think "home," and your body goes on autopilot. Before you know it, you find yourself pulling into your driveway.

Whether you're new to the sport of riding, or whether you've been riding for years, you will continue to improve as long as you practice regularly. The more often you ride, the faster you will progress. If you're not able to master a particular skill right away, don't get discouraged! It could be that you just need a few more — or a few dozen more — repetitions until you're able to perform the skill so naturally and effortlessly that your autopilot takes over.

Key Components of Equestrian Fitness

Strength

As you're learning and practicing new riding skills, your brain may respond quickly and competently. Your body, on the other hand, may not be quite as nimble, especially if it's a little out of shape. Your brain and nervous system might be perfectly willing to practice a sitting trot for another five-minute stretch and may happily activate the proper neural pathways. If your body isn't reasonably strong, however, your aching, trembling leg muscles may simply refuse to cooperate. In this situation, your physical condition — or lack thereof — becomes the weak link, or the limiting factor, in your ability to advance as an equestrian.

If you're able to spend as much time riding as you like, you can work on improving your muscular strength while you're in the saddle. The more you ride, the more you'll use the muscles involved in riding, and the stronger and fitter you'll become. If, on the other hand, you're only able to ride a couple of hours a week, you may want to develop your strength and stamina elsewhere so you can make better use of your time in the saddle. This is where a good fitness program comes into play.

Many of the muscles involved in riding are those you're already using regularly. You use your arms, legs, back, hips, and abdomen repeatedly throughout the day to walk and climb stairs, open doors, and carry briefcases, children, and groceries. Riding uses the same muscles, but it often requires you to use them in unfamiliar ways. In the course of an average day, for example, you might use your buttock and inner thigh muscles to cross your legs at least a dozen times. The act of leg-crossing requires a few mild, momentary contractions of these muscles. When you're riding, however, you may find yourself contracting and relaxing the same muscles dozens of times a minute to maintain your position in the saddle. This is a huge effort for muscles that were previously rarely used, and it's the reason that you may have experienced some minor — or even major — discomfort in your inner thighs when you first started riding. While it may take dozens of sessions in the saddle to stretch and strengthen these muscles, you can accomplish the same feats at home by regularly performing a few simple exercises.

Not only will a good fitness program help you strengthen the appropriate muscles, but it will also help you improve your stamina, flexibility, and balance. As a result, you'll become a better rider more quickly.

Stamina

Stamina refers to your ability to sustain a particular type of physical effort over time, and it is dependent upon your degree of cardiovascular fitness: how well and how long your heart, lungs, and blood vessels are able to meet the rigorous demands of your working muscles. If you're just planning to do a little light riding in an arena a couple of times a week, you may be perfectly satisfied with your current level of cardiovascular fitness.

But if your equestrian discipline requires more effort — and most do — you'll want to prepare your body for the challenge. No matter how strong and flexible your muscles are, you won't be able to ride your best without the stamina that comes with good cardiovascular fitness.

Flexibility

Like strength and stamina, flexibility is a critical component of fitness. Tight muscles not only restrict your body's range of motion but also make your movements short, choppy, and imprecise. These types of movements can confuse and irritate a horse. A strong, supple body helps you achieve a deeper and more relaxed seat, better leg position and posture, and more responsive hands. With greater flexibility, you'll be able to use your body to communicate more effectively with your horse. You'll also be far less vulnerable to muscle soreness, spasm, stiffness, and injury.

Balance

Maintaining balance is a complex process, even when you're walking on solid ground, propelling yourself forward with your own two feet. It's infinitely more challenging when you're sitting astride a moving horse. Maintaining your balance while you're riding requires your nerves, muscles, and joints to make split-second adjustments on a moment-to-moment basis so that your center of gravity is always in sync with the moving horse's center of gravity. How well you're able to maintain your balance is a function of how quickly and capably your brain, nerves, and muscles can react to small changes in your body position.

If your horse spooks or shies or if he refuses a jump, your body position will begin to change suddenly and dramatically. Your brain will, no doubt, take notice. It will immediately begin firing off signals, via the nerves, to various muscles throughout your body, with the goal of preventing you from falling. If your muscles are quick enough and strong enough to react in mere milliseconds, you'll be able to make the adjustments necessary to retain your seat. If they're not, you'll end up on the ground, dusting off your seat.

The more you ride, the better your balance will become. You'll learn to read your horse's body language and anticipate his movements. Your brain and body will become adept at detecting subtle changes in your position and will learn to correct them without conscious effort. If you exercise for no other reason than to improve your balance, it's an excellent investment of your time and energy. Good balance is critical to good riding: It's what allows the horse and the rider to move as one.

The Riding for Life Fitness Program

The Riding for Life Fitness Program is designed to help you develop and improve those four key components of equestrian fitness: strength, stamina, flexibility, and balance. No matter what your age or fitness level, it's never too late to begin an exercise program. The principles of learning apply to exercising, just as they apply to riding. If you've never performed a biceps curl or a front squat, you'll have to develop the appropriate neural pathways before you're able to execute these tasks with skill, and then repeat the exercises to gain mastery of them. Just as you need to be patient with yourself while you're learning new riding skills, you need to be patient with yourself as you develop new fitness skills.

Keep in mind that the Riding for Life Fitness Program is only meant to serve as a launching pad. Once you've mastered the basics, you'll be ready to explore other fitness activities. If you've been riding and exercising for a while, you may be so physically fit that the exercises don't pose a challenge to you. If this is the case, congratulations! You're already an accomplished athlete. Still, you won't want to rest for long on your laurels. The human body quickly adapts to physical demands, and to improve your overall level of fitness and your expertise as an equestrian, you continually have to present your body with new challenges.

Just as there's no such thing as the perfect horse, there's no such thing as the perfect rider. Every equestrian has a unique combination of strengths and weaknesses that are part and parcel of the total package. One rider may be incredibly strong, but she may lack the flexibility necessary to achieve a relaxed seat. Another rider may have great balance but lack strength in her legs. The goal is to recognize your weaknesses and make continual, incremental improvements in those areas so that you'll become a better rider.

You don't have to be a world-class athlete to be a good rider, but you'll find that you're able to ride far more comfortably and effectively if you're reasonably physically fit. In addition to enhancing your skills as an equestrian, exercise offers a number of bonus benefits in terms of your overall health and happiness.

Nature's Mood Booster

When you start exercising regularly, you'll notice an increase in your energy and a greater sense of well-being. Exercise promotes the release of potent, mood-altering endorphins. The powerful, positive effects of endorphins are responsible for the "runner's high," a profound sense of euphoria experienced by athletes during periods of intense aerobic exercise. This natural buzz is the direct result of the mood-boosting actions of endorphins on the brain, and the feelings of elation and optimism they create persist long after the exercise session has ended. Many athletes are so addicted to the endorphin rush that comes with exercise that they are almost compulsively driven to achieve it.

There's a perfectly logical explanation for this phenomenon. Endorphins are chemically similar to morphine and heroin. They're so similar, in fact, that they actually bind to the same cellular receptors in the brain and trigger many of the same responses in the body. Like morphine and heroin, these endorphins can be powerfully addictive substances.

Regular physical activity also reverses many of the damaging consequences of chronic stress. Like riding, other forms of exercise allow you to forget about your endless "to do" list for at least a few minutes each day. Treating yourself to a half-hour of exercise gives you a little time to traipse around in your own head and be alone with your thoughts. The endorphins released during exercise counteract the negative effects of stress hormones and have a soothing effect on your brain and body. These biochemicals also help alleviate anxiety and depression, which helps explain why women who exercise regularly are much less likely to suffer emotional disorders than those who are sedentary.

Exercise isn't necessarily a cure for depression, but it definitely helps alleviate many of the symptoms. Dozens of studies have shown that women who are regularly physically active have lower rates of anxiety and depression, and they're better able to cope with life's endless stream of stressors. In women suffering from clinical depression, exercise is known to improve treatment outcomes and enhance recovery significantly.

Exercise Boosts Your Metabolism

As you grow older, there's one thing you can count on — growing wider. All that talk about middle-age spread isn't just an ugly rumor; it's a fact of life. You can blame this unfortunate turn of events on your ever-declining metabolic rate. Your metabolic rate is the energy cost of fueling normal body functions, such as breathing, maintaining your body temperature, and

keeping your heart beating on schedule.

Starting around your 30th birthday, your metabolic rate begins to drop by about 1 percent each year. By the time you're 55, your body may require 200 to 400 fewer calories each day than when you were an adolescent. If you don't fine-tune your eating habits and devote more time to exercise, you can expect to pile on about 3 to 5 pounds each decade after the age of 35.

Scientists once believed that a sluggish metabolism was an inevitable part of growing older, but this theory isn't entirely correct. The most important factor determining your metabolic rate is not your age; it's the amount of lean muscle tissue your body is sporting. Because most women become less active with age, their muscle mass gradually dwindles away. This doesn't have to happen to you. You can dramatically rev up your metabolic rate by adding muscle tissue to your body. While fat tissue is metabolically sluggish, muscle tissue is a metabolic inferno — it burns far more calories to support itself, even at rest. Any type of exercise can increase your muscle mass, but weight training is especially effective. The more muscle tissue you have, the more calories you burn, even when you're asleep. Adding just 2 or 3 pounds of muscle tissue to your frame will help you burn an extra 70 to 100 calories each day — enough to produce a weight loss of 7 to 10 pounds over the course of a year.

The Anti-aging Activity

No matter what your age, it's never too late to start exercising. In fact, the older you are, the more important it is to stay active. In older adults, regular exercise reduces the risk of illness and even death. Physical activity has been shown to increase life expectancy, even among women who don't start exercising regularly until the age of 75.

Without regular physical activity, aging takes a tremendous toll on the female body. Joints lose their mobility and their ability to lubricate themselves, muscles shrink, tendons and ligaments become less flexible, and strength and stamina steadily decline. If women don't take steps to prevent these changes, they can expect to experience a 15 percent drop in muscle strength from the fifth to seventh decades of life, and up to a 30 percent drop per decade after the age of 70.

While the aging female body loses muscle tissue, it also loses bone mass. Nearly a fifth of a woman's lifetime bone loss can occur in the first five years following menopause. In addition to weight-bearing aerobic exercise, such as walking and jogging, weight training helps prevent bone loss that can lead to osteoporosis. Research has shown that when postmenopausal women engage in just two strength-training sessions a week for one year, they can expect their bone mineral density to increase by 1 percent. That may not seem like an earth-shaking benefit, until you consider that if those women had remained sedentary for that year, they could have expected to *lose* about 2 percent of their bone mass. The take-home message is that if you're a postmenopausal woman and you're not actively taking steps to shore up

your skeleton, you're probably experiencing significant bone loss.

Although the changes that affect the inside of your body may be less noticeable than those on the outside, aging also affects the cardiovascular system. Blood-vessel walls harden and the heart muscle grows thicker, resulting in high blood pressure and heart disease. As the lungs become less elastic and less efficient, they lose some of their ability to take in oxygen. By engaging in regular exercise, you can significantly slow the age-related decline of your cardiovascular system.

Exercise won't completely stop the hands of time, but it can offset many of the not-so-wonderful changes that accompany aging. It can dramatically improve your overall health, as well as your joint function and mobility, muscle strength, endurance, and flexibility.

Regular Exercise Reduces the Risk of Chronic Disease

In terms of life-threatening conditions, heart disease is one of the greatest risks women face as they grow older. In the United States it's the leading cause of death among women. Fortunately, exercise can dramatically reduce your chances of developing — and dying from — heart disease. In addition to improving the overall health and fitness of your cardiovascular system, physical activity also improves many conditions known to be independent risk factors for heart disease, including high cholesterol levels, diabetes, obesity, and high blood pressure.

Exercise boosts levels of heart healthy high-density lipoprotein (HDL) cholesterol and reduces levels of harmful low-density lipoprotein cholesterol (LDL) and triglycerides. It helps lower blood sugar and blood pressure and promotes weight loss. Studies show that even moderate exercise can have a huge impact on heart health — walking just two and a half hours each week can lower your risk of developing heart disease by as much as 30 percent.

Physical activity also can reduce your risk of developing many of the most devastating types of cancer, including those of the colon, endometrial lining of the uterus, and breast. For women who are breast cancer survivors, walking just over an hour each week has been shown to prolong survival significantly. Breast cancer survivors who walk three to five hours each week (or engage in similar types of physical activity) are 50 percent less likely to die from the disease compared to sedentary breast cancer survivors.

The protective effect of exercise appears to arise from its ability to reduce levels of hormones that trigger breast cancer, including the female hormones estrogen and progesterone. While moderate activity prolongs breast cancer survival, lack of exercise is associated with weight gain, which is known to increase the risk of developing breast cancer and diminish the chances of survival.

Aerobic Exercise

Aerobic exercise is any extended activity that involves moving the large muscle groups of your body at a pace sufficient to cause increases in your heart rate and breathing. The goal of aerobic exercise is to improve your cardiovascular fitness and, thus, your stamina. Brisk walking, jogging, cycling, swimming, and rowing are all excellent aerobic activities. As you perform any of these tasks, your working muscles require a greater volume of blood and oxygen to sustain the activity. This means that your heart must pump harder and faster, and you must breathe harder and faster. Aerobic exercise strengthens not only the muscles of your arms and legs but also strengthens the heart muscle itself, improving its ability to pump blood throughout the body. It increases the capacity of your lungs to take in oxygen and deliver it more efficiently to body cells and tissues. As your cardiovascular fitness improves,

Adding muscle helps burn calories, which in turn leads to weight loss.

Exercise reduces the risk of developing disease and contributes to longevity.

your heart, blood vessels, and lungs are better able to supply oxygen and fuel to your working body during longer periods of sustained activity.

As you gain cardiovascular fitness, you'll find that you tire less easily whether you're vacuuming the carpet in your living room or mucking stalls at the barn. You'll also be able to ride longer and stronger without succumbing to fatigue.

Target Heart Rate Zone

To make sure you're getting the most from the time you invest in an aerobic workout, it's important to move your body fast enough to elevate your heart rate. How high you strive to raise your heart rate depends primarily on your age. The average adult woman has a resting

heart rate, or pulse, of about 70 to 80 beats per minute. As a general rule, the better your physical condition, the lower your resting heart rate.

Your maximum heart rate can be determined by subtracting your age from 220. If you're 40 years old, for example, you'll subtract 40 from 220, which equals 180. But don't worry; you don't have to get your heart beating to the tune of 180 beats per minute to get a good cardiovascular workout. You just need to step up your pulse to a number that falls between 50 percent and 75 percent of your maximum heart rate. The range of numbers that is 50 percent to 75 percent of your age-adjusted maximum heart rate is known as your target heart rate zone.

If you're 40 years old, your age-adjusted maximum heart rate is 220 minus 40, or 180 beats per minute. Fifty percent of 180 equals 90; and 75 percent of 180 equals 135. If you're serious about getting the most from your aerobic workout, you should exercise energetically enough to elevate your pulse to a point between 90 and 135 beats per minute, and then keep it at this rate for at least 30 minutes. You'll need to repeat this process at least three times a week.

Before you go to the trouble of bumping up your heart rate, you might want to practice taking your pulse at rest a few times. You can usually feel a nice, strong pulsation at your carotid artery, the blood vessel that lies just beside your windpipe in your neck about an inch or so below your jawbone. Be sure not to push on both sides of your neck at once because blocking the flow of blood to your brain might cause you to lose consciousness. This is generally considered to be a bad thing!

If you don't have any luck finding your carotid pulse, you might be able to pick up a good pulse at your radial artery. This blood vessel can be found on the thumb side of your inner wrist, just above the point where the hand bone connects to the arm bone. If your radial pulse remains elusive, you may be able to feel the pulsation of your temporal artery, which lies on the side of your forehead at your temple. Once you've experimented with various pulse points, use the site that allows you to feel the beating of your heart most easily.

If you located your pulse, congratulations! Now all you've got to do is count it. To count your heartbeats, press down lightly on the site you have chosen with the index and middle fingers of one hand. Using a watch with a second hand, count the number of pulsations you feel beneath your fingers for 15 seconds, and then multiply this number by four. This will give you the number of heartbeats per minute, or your heart rate.

It's important to determine your pulse by counting the beats of your heart for 15 seconds and then multiplying the number by four, rather than counting for an entire 60 seconds. Why? Because as soon as you stop exercising to take your pulse, your heart rate begins to drop dramatically, even in the first few moments of rest. The pulse that you count in the first 15 seconds will most accurately reflect your actual heart rate during exercise, and you'll want to give yourself full credit for every single beat of your heart.

Strength Training

Strength training, or weight training, is one of the most beneficial forms of exercise that women can undertake; unfortunately, it is probably the one that is most neglected. Many women don't work out with weights for the simple reason that they've never learned how. While boys are often introduced to the weight room during adolescence to strengthen their muscles for football, baseball, or other traditionally masculine sports, the same opportunity isn't always offered to young female athletes.

Some women shy away from weight training because they fear it will cause them to develop big, bulky muscles. Competitive women body builders wish it were that simple — not only do they spend hours in the gym each day lifting extremely heavy weights, but they also rigor-

Practice taking your pulse a few times.

ously control their diets and take loads of nutritional supplements. Some even resort to taking muscle-enhancing steroids to develop the bulk and brawn they desire.

If you're just planning to work out with weights a few days a week, it's highly unlikely that you'll be able to achieve the same results as a female body builder, whether you want those results or not. As a woman, your natural hormonal makeup simply doesn't support the growth of large muscles under ordinary circumstances. While the male hormone testosterone is responsible for building and strengthening muscles, the female hormone estrogen is designed to help us deposit fat rather than develop massive muscles.

Just because you don't develop big, bulky muscles doesn't mean that working out with weights isn't beneficial. If you can fit just two half-hour weight-training sessions into your weekly schedule, you'll see dramatic results in a short period. Within just a few weeks you'll notice that you're stronger and more energetic. In a couple of months the muscles of your arms, legs, chest, and back will be more toned and defined, and your abdomen will be flatter and firmer. As you learn to target and strengthen individual muscle groups, you'll have a greater sense of body awareness, balance, muscle control, and coordination.

Each of these improvements translates to enormous benefits in terms of riding. Not only will you be able to maintain a more secure and balanced seat with far less effort, you'll be able to use the muscles of your legs and seat to com-

municate more effectively with your horse. With stronger abdominal and back muscles, your balance and posture will improve. Strengthening your chest and arms will allow you to use your hands more fluidly and precisely. As your body grows stronger, you'll tire less easily.

If weight loss is your goal, strength training can help. Like moderate-intensity aerobic workouts, weight-training exercises can burn up to seven to eight calories a minute. In addition to the calories burned during your workout, weight training creates an "after-burn" effect: It causes your body to continue to burn calories at a higher rate for hours after the workout. Studies have shown that after a half-hour weight-lifting session, the metabolic rate remains elevated for up to 15 hours. In contrast, a half-hour session of aerobic exercise leads to increases in the metabolic rate that persist for only about an hour or so.

If you stick with your strength-training program, the weight-loss benefits begin to snowball. Your body composition gradually changes so that your percentage of body fat declines as your percentage of body muscle increases. Pound for pound, muscle tissue burns far more calories than fat. The more muscle tissue you have, the more calories your body burns each day, making weight loss even easier.

While strength training helps you build muscle, it also helps you build bone mass, reducing your risk of osteoporosis. The skeleton responds to an increased workload by laying down extra bone tissue in the relevant areas. When you walk or run, you're building and strengthening the bones in your hips and legs, but not in your wrist, one of the most commonly fractured bones in postmenopausal women. Weight training is one of the most effective ways to increase the mass and strength of all the bones in your body.

Getting Started

If you've never lifted weights, you might want to hire a personal trainer for a session or two to help you learn the basics. Getting the desired results from your strength-training routine requires you to use good form and proper technique. Like a good riding instructor, a good personal trainer can help you identify your areas of weakness and develop a plan for improvement. A few sessions with an expert will go a long way toward boosting your self-confidence in your ability to engage in strength training and your motivation to stick with it.

The key to success — and safety — is to start low and go slow. Regardless of the exercise you're performing, you should choose a weight that you can comfortably lift and lower a minimum of eight times. Each movement should be performed in a slow, deliberate, and controlled manner. If you can't lift the weight without swinging it or contorting your body, it's too heavy for you. Strength training is far more effective when you use a lighter weight and proper technique rather than a heavier weight and improper technique.

If, for example, your goal is to work the biceps muscle of your upper arm, you'll be much better off starting with an 8-pound dumbbell that you can lift primarily with your biceps muscles. If you start with a 15-pound weight, you may end up recruiting the muscles of your chest, back, and forearm to help your biceps lift the weight. Strengthening individual muscles is best achieved by isolating those particular muscles as much as possible so that those muscles are forced to bear the brunt of the work.

This isn't always as easy as it sounds. Your body's natural tendency is to use as many muscles as possible to share the load and to make work easier. Using the proper technique as you perform each strength-training exercise will allow you to target the relevant muscles better and get maximum benefits from your weight-lifting workout.

When you're training with weights, remember that lowering the weight is just as important as lifting it — it's half of the exercise. Concentrate on lowering the weight as slowly, or even more slowly, than you raised it. Suddenly dropping the weight puts gravity to work instead of your muscles and reduces the effectiveness of your workout. Don't forget to keep breathing throughout the exercise, exhaling as you lift the weight and inhaling as you lower it.

As long as you want to continue making improvements in your body shape and muscle strength, you'll need to increase the demands of your workout progressively. Your muscles gradually adapt to lifting weights by becoming stronger and more efficient. When you can comfortably lift the weight you're using in a given exercise for 12 repetitions using the correct technique, it's time to advance to a heavier weight. You should be able to increase the weight you're lifting by 5 percent to 10 percent at your next training session.

As degree of effort and level of intensity are critical factors in attaining maximum benefits, exercising a particular muscle or muscle group to the point of muscular fatigue — but never pain — yields the best results in the shortest time.

Flexibility Training

Even if you fully appreciate the importance of flexibility, you may not give stretching the time or attention it deserves. To reach your full potential as an athlete, both in the saddle and on the ground, flexibility training should be a part of your workout, rather than an add-on or an afterthought.

Stretching should feel good. There's no need to force flexibility — it will come with time and repetition. If stretching hurts in any way, you should stop — continuing to stretch in the presence of pain could lead to injury. It's also safest to avoid bouncing or bobbing during any stretching exercise as these types of ballistic movements can dramatically increase your risk of sustaining a muscle strain or tear.

Warm Up Before You Stretch Out

While stretching is essential for improving flexibility, you should never stretch out before your muscles are warm. Numerous studies have proven that stretching out at the beginning of a workout provides absolutely no protective benefit. In fact, stretching cold muscles is more likely to cause injury than not stretching out at all. To improve your flexibility without risking an injury, you should either warm up before you stretch out or stretch out after you work out.

How Much Is Enough?

How much physical activity do you need to stay healthy? Current guidelines from the American Heart Association and the American College of Sports Medicine suggest accumulating a minimum of 30 minutes of moderate to strenuous aerobic activity on most days of the week to obtain a measurable cardiovascular benefit. The activity should be sufficiently rigorous to allow you to achieve 50 percent to 75 percent of your maximum heart rate. If you do nothing more than take two brisk, 15-minute walks, you'll meet your minimum daily exercise requirement, and your heart, lungs, and blood vessels will thank you.

Whether riding qualifies as an aerobic activity depends on how vigorously you ride. If you're able to elevate your pulse sufficiently to achieve your target heart rate and keep it elevated for a half hour, your riding session meets the criteria for an aerobic exercise. Even if your time in the saddle doesn't qualify as moderately intense aerobic activity, your barn duties might. If you're doing some heavy duty stall cleaning that involves raking, shoveling, and pushing a loaded wheelbarrow, there's a good chance that you're getting a good aerobic workout.

Keep in mind that while a 30-minute session of moderate-intensity exercise performed three days a week might help your heart and lungs, it probably isn't sufficient to produce significant benefits in terms of losing weight or gaining muscle strength and overall stamina. For women who aren't currently active, even brief bouts of light exercise are beneficial. If you're already riding three days a week and you're not as fit as you want to be, you need to step up your level of activity. If your goal is to become a strong, physically fit equestrian athlete, you'll need to push your body even more. A good starting point is a program that includes at least 30 minutes of moderate-intensity aerobic exercise five days a week, at least 15 minutes of flexibility training three days a week, and at least 30 minutes of strength-training two days a week.

Shake It Up, and Avoid the Rut

It's tempting to choose a fitness routine that is easy and convenient rather than one that is new, unfamiliar, or challenging. If the exercises you're doing now are comfortable, chances are they're not doing you much good. It's time to broaden your horizons and try something new.

Varying your workout routine is important for several reasons. For starters, it keeps you from getting bored, which can quickly kill your desire to exercise. Even if you're able to muster up the motivation to put yourself through the exact same paces day after day, at some point you're likely to become so sick of the routine that you stop giving it 100 percent of your attention or effort.

In addition to the mental drawbacks, a few physical limitations are associated with getting in an exercise rut. An athlete who performs the same activity or exercise to the exclusion of others is more prone to specific types of injuries. She's also more likely to overdevelop certain areas of her anatomy, which can lead to imbalances or weaknesses in other areas of her body. Women whose only form of exercise is running, for instance, are likely to have great cardiovascular fitness and extremely strong legs, but their upper bodies may be underdeveloped and weak. The impact of pounding the pavement leaves them vulnerable to foot problems and knee injuries. Women who rely on weight lifting as their sole means of exercise usually have great upper and lower body strength, but if they're not performing some type of aerobic activity, they may lack endurance and stamina.

No single exercise or activity is completely effective in improving every aspect of physical fitness. Because different types of exercise can challenge and transform your body in different ways, it's beneficial to add a little variety to your routine.

Push Your Body, But Don't Punish It

Adding variety to your fitness program is an excellent way to enhance your level of fitness, but it's just as important to increase continually the demands of your workout. The human body adapts very quickly to any type of activity or work, and if you don't challenge yourself to work just a little harder on a regular basis, you'll stop improving. If you're satisfied with your current level of strength, stamina, and overall fitness, there may be little reason for you to change, but if you're still striving to get stronger and fitter, you'll need to increase your workload gradually.

Depending on the activity, you can accomplish this in a number of ways. If you can jog comfortably for 15 minutes, for example, you can increase the physical demands of your workout by simply jogging for a longer period. Or you can continue to jog for 15 minutes, but add a new hill to your route, or you can pick up the pace so that you travel faster and farther. In terms of strength training, you can elevate the intensity of your workout by increasing the amount of weight that you lift during a particular exercise, or you can increase the number of times that you lift the weight in succession.

Progress is good, but increasing the intensity or duration of any activity too quickly is an invitation for injury. To avoid pushing your body too hard too fast, it's a good idea to avoid increasing the demands of any activity by more than 10 percent in any given week. This applies to increases in distance, amount of weight lifted, or duration of exercise. If you're comfortably running 20 miles each week and you're ready to move up, you should add no more than two additional miles to your workout the following week. If you're performing leg presses with 50 pounds and you're ready for a bigger challenge, you should add no more than 5 pounds the following week.

If you're a newcomer to exercise, increasing the duration, distance, or amount of weight lifted during your workouts by a full 10 percent may be too difficult for you to handle comfort-ably. Likewise, if you're already performing at an extremely high level, a 10 percent increase in your workload may be practically impossible. If this is the case, start with an increase of 5 percent, or even 2 percent. In terms of preventing injuries, it's always better to underestimate your capacity to handle more work than it is to overestimate it.

As physically demanding as exercise can be, it should never be painful. During any workout, you're allowed to feel the burn or experience minor aches and occasional twinges. It's perfectly acceptable to moan, groan, and complain about the inconvenience of exercising every now and then, as long as you don't quit. Experiencing pain of any kind, however, is not acceptable. If a particular exercise or activity hurts, the solution is simple — stop doing it. If the pain doesn't go away, you need to discuss it with your doctor.

Remember, the idea is to push your body without punishing it. It's fine to take baby steps, as long as they're leading in the right direction — toward your goal of becoming a stronger, better rider.

Warming Up

Before you dive into any type of workout, whether it involves stretching, riding, jogging, or kickboxing, it's important to take a few minutes to warm up and prepare your body for the task. A good warm-up routine consists of any type of low- to moderate-intensity aerobic exercise, such as walking, jogging, or dancing. If you're preparing to ride, your warm-up routine might consist of grooming, saddling, and lunging your horse. After several minutes of light activity, you'll have elevated your body temperature and warmed your muscles sufficiently to reduce their vulnerability to injury. Now you're ready to either stretch out or move directly into your workout routine.

Muscle fibers, tendons, and ligaments are a lot like rubber bands. When they're cold, they won't stretch very far before they tear or break. Warm body tissues, on the other hand, stretch farther and more easily. There's a logical explanation for this phenomenon. Collagen, the main building block of muscles, tendons, ligaments, and joints, is temperature specific. While it's relatively supple at warm temperatures, it's far stiffer and more brittle at cold temperatures.

If you're planning to work out at the end of the day after you've been sitting stock still at a desk for hours, or if you schedule your workouts first thing in the morning, warming up is even more important. Muscle fibers tend to be thick and inelastic when your body is at rest, but they're pliant and supple after movement. Exercise scientists speculate that during long periods of inactivity, microscopic bonds begin to develop between individual muscle fibers. This explains why you may feel stiff after sitting still for a while, or when you first roll out of bed in the morning. Engaging in a few minutes of low-intensity aerobic activity helps gently disrupt the microscopic bonds that may have formed between muscle fibers during periods of rest or inactivity.

As you elevate your body temperature and gradually increase your pulse and respiratory rate during your warm-up routine, you're also increasing the blood flow to and from your muscles. Greater blood flow not only facilitates the delivery of oxygen and nutrients but also enhances the removal of waste products generated by working tissues. The discs in your back and the cartilage in your joints have a limited blood supply, which makes them more susceptible to injury than other body tissues, especially when they're not properly warmed up. Light, rhythmic motion increases the flow of blood to discs and joints and helps protect them from damage during exercise.

Anatomy of the Female Equestrian

Your miraculous human body has more than 650 muscles, each with a specific purpose and function. You'll be happy to know that it isn't necessary to work each and every one of these muscles intentionally to improve your skills as an equestrian. There are, however, several muscles and groups of muscles that play keys roles in riding, not to mention lunging, leading, grooming, and saddling your horse. The stronger and more flexible these muscles are, the more quickly your skills as an equestrian will advance.

You don't have to have a Ph.D. in human anatomy to exercise effectively, but it is helpful to have a basic understanding of the musculoskeletal system. When you appreciate the general location and function of the muscles you're working, you'll be able to get maximum returns on the time you invest in your workout. Focusing on the muscles you're exercising helps you develop a type of body awareness

that athletes refer to as the "mind-muscle connection." This connection allows you to have
greater control over the muscles you're using,
not only while you're working out but also
when you're riding.

If, for example, you want to communicate
with your horse by applying leg pressure at
the girth, you'll be able to execute the task far
more effectively — not to mention more gracefully — if you've got a well-developed mind-
muscle connection. You'll be able to contract
the appropriate muscles smoothly and subtly,
without entirely disrupting the position of your
leg or foot or your seat. If your horse doesn't
immediately respond to your cue, you can
incrementally increase the pressure applied by
your muscles, without resorting to convulsive,
total-body movements, or even worse, kicking
your poor horse in the ribs. The better you're
able to control your muscles, the better you'll
be able to communicate with your horse.

Arm
Biceps, triceps, and forearm muscles

The muscle at the front of your upper arm is
the *biceps brachii* muscle, which is responsible
for curling the arm toward your chest. The
triceps brachii muscle, on the back of the upper arm, works in opposition to the biceps: It
straightens the arm. Your forearms are made up
of several smaller muscles that further control
the actions of the wrist and hand. The flexor
muscles, on the inside of the forearm, curl the
palm down while the extensor muscles, on the
outside of the forearm, curl the knuckles up.

Chest
Pectoralis muscles

The *pectoralis major* is a large, fan-shaped
muscle that covers much of the front upper
chest on each side of the body. Its main function
is to move the arm across the body. The *pectoralis minor* is a smaller, triangular muscle that lies
just beneath the *pectoralis major*. This muscle
helps move the shoulder blade up and down.

Back
Latissimus dorsi

The *latissimus dorsi* muscles are the largest of the upper body. They are triangular and
extend from beneath the shoulder blades to the
small of the back on both sides. These muscles
pull the shoulders down and to the rear as if
you were rowing a boat or swimming.

Trapezius

The trapezius is a flat, triangular muscle that
covers the back of the neck, shoulders, and
thorax. Its function is to lift the entire shoulder
girdle in a shrugging motion and to draw the
shoulder blades up, down, and to either side.
The trapezius muscle also helps turn the head
and draw it back.

Spinal Erectors
Iliocostalis, spinalis, and longissimus

The spinal erectors are a bundle of muscles
and tendons that lie in the grooves alongside
the spine. Their primary purpose is to extend
the spine or straighten the back and to stabilize
the torso.

Shoulder

Deltoids

The shoulder consists primarily of the thick, triangular deltoid muscle, which forms the rounded area at the top of the upper arm and serves to rotate and lift the arm. The deltoid can be divided into three parts, or heads, each with a different function. The anterior, or front, deltoid lifts the arm to the front, while the medial, or side, deltoid lifts the arm to the side. The posterior, or rear, deltoid lifts the arm to the rear.

Abdomen

Rectus abdominus, transverse abdominus, and external and internal obliques

The muscles that comprise the abdominal wall sit on the front and sides of your torso. These muscles are used simultaneously whenever you bend, twist, or turn at the waist and when you move your arms and legs. Even when you're standing still, the abdominal muscles are working to stabilize your trunk, back, and pelvis, and to hold you upright.

CORE MUSCLES

Core training programs have become incredibly popular over the past decade, and while there's no doubt they can help you become a better athlete, they're not the magic bullet that will solve every fitness challenge. In terms of the human anatomy, the "core" generally refers to the center of the body, which comprises several muscle groups, including those in the abdomen, pelvis, and back. The primary function of these muscles isn't to drive your body forward, but rather to stabilize your body so other muscles can. They provide a solid platform from which your arms and legs can move and work.

A strong, flexible core is critically important to all athletes, and the equestrian is no different. It's what allows you to maintain your posture and your seat while you're riding. When you're in the saddle, the muscles of your core are hard at work, continually realigning your position in response to changes in your horse's speed and direction. In this manner, they're responsible for keeping your body centered over the body of your moving horse. A strong, flexible core allows you to bend, rather than bounce, in response to movement generated by the horse. As a result, you're able to maintain a stable, secure seat at every gait. Because your arms, hands, and legs remain virtually motionless, you're able to use them smoothly and relatively independently of your body.

Although there are dozens of core-strengthening programs available, a comprehensive fitness program, such as the Riding for Life Fitness Program, serves the same purpose. Your core muscles stabilize your body in virtually every exercise that involves movement of your arms and legs, so they're getting a good workout every time you walk, run, or ride. Whenever you're engaged in exercises designed to increase the strength or flexibility of your abdomen, legs, back, or buttocks, you'll be improving the strength and the flexibility of the core muscles as well.

Rectus abdominus

The *rectus abdominus* is the long, flat muscle that runs vertically from the rib cage to the pubic bone. It's the showy muscle that creates the "six pack" effect, but its primary purpose is to bring the rib cage toward the pelvis and flex your spine, which allows you to bend forward at the waist. It is also involved in rotating your trunk or bending it to the side.

External and internal obliques

The external obliques are large, flat muscles that lie on both sides and the front of the abdomen. The internal obliques are smaller muscles that lie beneath the external obliques. Both muscle groups not only help stabilize your trunk but allow you to twist and bend your torso. They also assist the other abdominal muscles when you're drawing your pelvis and rib cage together.

Transverse abdominus

The *transverse abdominus* lies deep beneath the other abdominal muscles and plays a crucial role in stabilizing the back, torso, and pelvis. It also acts as a corset, pulling your abdominal wall inward toward your spine.

Buttocks
Gluteus maximus, gluteus medius, and gluteus minimus

The gluteus muscles are a large, powerful group of muscles that comprise your seat and buttocks. The largest of the three muscles, the *gluteus maximus*, is typically the body's stron-gest muscle, and it covers a large part of the buttock. Its primary role is to move your thigh to the rear. It allows you to straighten your body at the hip when you're walking, running, climbing, and riding, and lifting your body from a sitting position, as you do when you're posting or going over a fence. The *gluteus medius* and *gluteus minimus* are smaller muscles that lie beneath the *gluteus maximus*. These two muscles move your leg to the side, away from your body.

Legs
Inner Thigh: Adductor Muscles
Adductor longus, adductor brevis, adductor magnus, gracilis, and *pectineus*

The adductor muscles are situated along the inner thigh, and they're responsible for moving your leg toward the center line of your body. When the adductor muscles of both legs are used, they draw your legs together. In the vast majority of women, these muscles rarely get a good workout, but they're of critical importance to the equestrian athlete because they're primarily responsible for keeping you in the saddle while you're riding.

Back of Thigh: Hamstrings
Biceps femoris, semitendinosus, semimembranosus

The hamstring muscles make up the mass of the back of the thigh. These muscles work together to help you straighten your body at the hip and bend your leg at the knee. Strong hamstrings are important for mounting, dismounting, posting, and lifting your seat out of the saddle when you're riding.

Front of Thigh: Quadriceps

Rectus femoris, vastus lateralis, vastus medialis, vastus intermedius

The four muscles of the quadriceps make up the large, fleshy mass at the front and sides of your thigh. Working together, these muscles are primarily responsible for straightening your leg at the knee, another action that is extremely important in riding.

Calves

Gastrocnemius and *soleus*

The gastrocnemius muscle sits on the back of the lower leg and forms part of the calf. Beneath it is the thick, flat, soleus muscle. Both muscles are joined to the Achilles tendon, which attaches to the heel bone. The muscles of the calves help support your weight when you're standing and allow you to stand on the balls of your feet and push your body up and forward when you're walking, running, and riding.

Strengthening Exercises

Now that you're familiar with the location and function of the various muscles and muscle groups, you're ready for a few exercises that will strengthen them. Keep in mind that while you're performing some exercises, you'll be able to target specific muscles, but it is virtually impossible to isolate any given muscle to the exclusion of all others because muscles are designed to work together. This phenomenon becomes especially evident when you're performing leg exercises. The muscles of the legs work in unison, and they also get involved in most types of work performed by the gluteus muscles of the buttocks. For this reason, most exercises that are designed to work and strengthen one set of leg muscles, such as the hamstrings, simultaneously work and strengthen the other sets of leg muscles, including the quadriceps and the adductor muscles. As you perform specific exercises, you'll soon discover which muscles are working — they'll let you know!

If you're already going to the barn several days a week, you may not have enough time left in your schedule to go to a gym or an exercise class. The strength-training exercises included in this chapter are simple to do at home, at the barn, or in your office. For most of the exercises, you won't need any equipment, but several require the use of dumbbells. You'll probably be able to start out with 5-pound dumbbells, but you may be more comfortable with dumbbells that weigh 2, 8, or 10 pounds each. You'll also need a sturdy, armless chair or bench, and a ball that is approximately 12 inches in diameter. A kickball works well, but you can use any similarly sized ball that gives a little when you squeeze it.

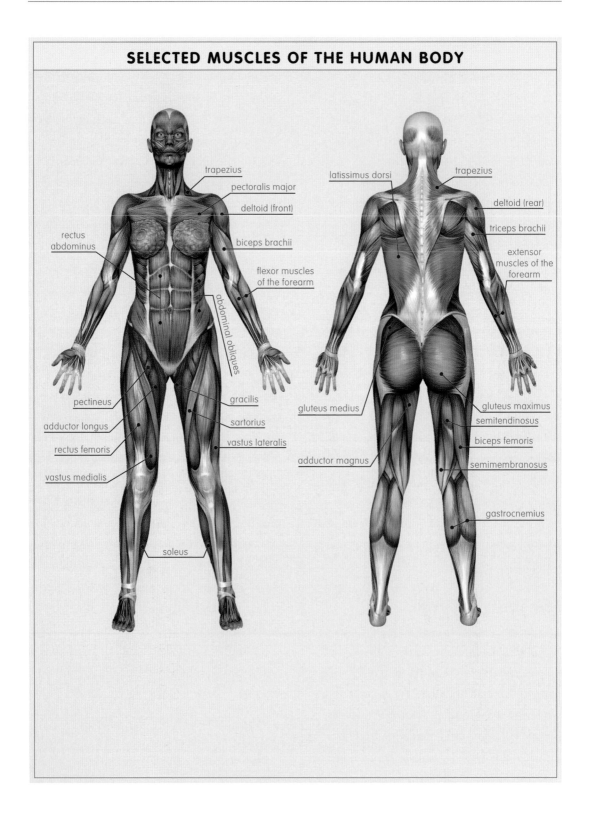

SELECTED MUSCLES OF THE HUMAN BODY

trapezius

pectoralis major

deltoid (front)

rectus abdominus

biceps brachii

flexor muscles of the forearm

abdominal obliques

pectineus

adductor longus

rectus femoris

vastus medialis

gracilis

sartorius

vastus lateralis

soleus

latissimus dorsi

trapezius

deltoid (rear)

triceps brachii

extensor muscles of the forearm

gluteus medius

gluteus maximus

semitendinosus

biceps femoris

adductor magnus

semimembranosus

gastrocnemius

BICEPS

STANDING BICEPS CURL
Strengthens the Biceps

Stand erect with your feet shoulder width apart, toes pointing forward and knees slightly bent. With your arms at your sides, hold a dumbbell in each hand with your palms facing forward. Curl the dumbbells slowly up toward your shoulders, being careful to keep your upper arms still. When the dumbbells are shoulder level, pause for a moment, then slowly lower them back toward the starting position, stopping about three-quarters of the way down to keep the tension in the muscles of your biceps. Throughout the exercise, your elbows will remain at your sides, as still as possible, serving as pivot points for the weights. Repeat the exercise for a set of 8 to 12.

SEATED BICEPS CURL
Strengthens the Biceps

Sitting on a bench or an armless chair, place your left hand on your left thigh. With a dumbbell in your right hand, bend forward slightly from the waist and place your right arm on the inside of your right thigh. In this position, your right elbow should be in contact with the inside of your right thigh and your palm should be facing your left ankle. Slowly lift the dumbbell toward your chest, focusing on contracting the biceps muscle of your right arm. Hold the contraction for a moment before slowly lowering the dumbbell back to the starting position. Always keep your elbow still and firmly pressed against the inside of your left thigh so that it serves as a pivot point for the weight. Repeat the exercise for a set of 8 to 12.

TRICEPS

TRICEPS KICKBACK
Strengthens the Triceps

Stand with a dumbbell in your right hand, knees slightly bent. Bend slightly forward at the waist. For balance, place your left hand on your knee. Bend your right elbow so that your forearm is perpendicular to the floor. Keeping your right elbow still and close to your side, slowly straighten your arm behind you until it is parallel to the floor. Hold the contraction in your triceps muscle for one count; then return the weight to the starting position. Perform 8 to 12 repetitions with your right arm. Repeat the exercise with your left arm.

CHAIR DIP
Strengthens the Triceps

Sitting tall on the edge of a chair, grasp the seat on either side of your buttocks. Bend your knees and place your feet hip width apart on the floor. Slide your buttocks off the chair so that the weight of your body is balanced on your palms and your feet. Slowly bend your elbows and lower your buttocks toward the floor. When your upper arms are parallel to the floor, press your body back up to the starting position. Repeat the exercise 8 to 12 times.

ONE-ARM WRIST CURL
Strengthens the Flexor Muscles of the Forearm

Hold a dumbbell in your right hand, palm up. Sit on a chair and lean forward, placing your right forearm on your right thigh. Bend your right wrist and lower the weight as far as possible toward the floor, opening your fingers slightly to stretch the muscles of the forearm. Keeping your forearm still, close your fingers and curl the weight up toward your body as high as you can. Perform 8 to 12 repetitions; then repeat the exercise with your left forearm.

REVERSE WRIST CURL
Strengthens the Extensor Muscles of the Forearm

Stand erect with your upper arms at your sides, elbows bent and forearms parallel to the ground. Hold a dumbbell in each hand, palms facing the ground. Slowly lift your knuckles toward your body, keeping your forearms still. Return to the starting position, and repeat for a set of 8 to 12.

CHEST

WALL PUSHUP
Strengthens the Pectoralis Muscles of the Chest, Deltoids, and Triceps

Stand facing a wall with your palms against it, shoulder width apart. Pull in your abdominal muscles so that your back is straight. Bend your elbows and slowly lower your chest toward the wall. When your elbows are bent at a 90-degree angle, push your body back away from the wall. Repeat the exercise for a set of 8 to 12.

MODIFIED PUSHUP
Strengthens the Pectoralis Muscles of the Chest, Deltoids, and Triceps

Position yourself face down on the floor with your body resting on your hands and knees. Your hands should be slightly in front of your body and shoulder width apart. Tuck in your abdomen and keep your head up and your upper body in a straight line. Slowly bend your arms and lower your torso; then press your upper body back to the starting position. Repeat for a set of 8 to 12.

DUMBBELL ROW

Strengthens the Trapezius, Spinal Erectors, and *Latissimus Dorsi* Muscles

Grasp a dumbbell in each hand and bend your knees slightly. Bend forward from the waist so that your upper body is at a 45-degree angle to the floor. With your head up and your back straight and still, allow the dumbbells to hang directly below your shoulders. Simultaneously lift both dumbbells to the sides of your rib cage, feeling the muscles at the sides of your upper back contract. Hold the contraction for one count; then slowly lower the weights to the original position. Repeat the exercise for a set of 8 to 12.

DUMBBELL SHRUG
Strengthens the Trapezius

Stand erect with feet shoulder width apart. Hold a dumbbell in each hand, palms facing your outer thighs. Keep your arms at your sides with a slight bend at the elbows. Raise your shoulders up toward your ears as high as possible; then slowly lower the weights back to the starting position. Repeat for a set of 8 to 12.

DUMBBELL DEAD LIFT
Strengthens the Spinal Erectors, Gluteus Muscles, and Hamstrings

Stand erect with your feet shoulder width apart and your knees slightly bent. Hold a dumbbell in each hand, arms hanging down from your shoulders so that your palms are slightly in front of your thighs. Keeping your back slightly arched and your chin up, bend at the waist and lower the dumbbells toward the floor, allowing the weight of the dumbbells to pull you down. Slowly return to the starting position, using your gluteus muscles and hamstrings to pull your body back up. Repeat for a set of 8 to 12.

SUPERWOMAN
Strengthens the Spinal Erectors, Trapezius, and Gluteus Muscles

Lie flat on your stomach with your arms extended straight out in front of you and your legs extended straight out behind you. Keeping your arms and legs straight, simultaneously lift your arms, chest, and legs a few inches off the floor. Hold the contraction for a moment; then return to the starting position. Repeat for a set of 8 to 12.

SHOULDERS

FORWARD ARM RAISE
Strengthens the Front of the Deltoid

Stand with your feet shoulder width apart, arms at your sides, a dumbbell in each hand with palms facing the sides of your thighs. Slowly lift your arms in front of your body until they are at shoulder level, parallel to the floor. As you lift your arms, rotate your hands slightly so that your palms face the floor. Hold the weights at shoulder level for one count; then lower the dumbbells to the starting position. Repeat for a set of 8 to 12.

OVERHEAD LATERAL ARM RAISE
Strengthens the Side of the Deltoid

With a dumbbell in each hand, palms facing up, extend your arms straight out to either side, level with your shoulders. Slowly lift your arms and bring them together over your head, without locking your elbows; then slowly lower the dumbbells back to the starting position. Repeat for a set of 8 to 12.

STANDING LATERAL ARM RAISE
Strengthens the Side and Rear of the Deltoid

Stand with your arms at your sides and a dumbbell in each hand. Keeping your elbows slightly bent and your body still, slowly raise your arms out to your sides until they are level with your shoulders and parallel to the ground. As you lift the dumbbells, slightly tilt the side of your hand downward, as if you're pouring a little water from a bottle. Slowly return the weights to the starting position. Repeat for a set of 8 to 12.

ABDOMEN

CRUNCHES

Strengthens the Abdominal Muscles, especially the *Rectus Abdominus*

Lie on the floor with your back flat on the ground and your heels placed on a chair. Your knees should be bent at a 90-degree angle so that your lower legs are parallel to the ground. Keep your chin up, and cross your arms over your chest. Pressing your lower back against the floor, lift your torso upward by squeezing your abdominal muscles. You don't have to lift your torso much — just until your shoulder blades are off the floor. Hold the abdominal contraction for one count; then slowly lower your upper back to the starting position. Repeat the exercise for a set of 8 to 12.

POWER PLANK
Strengthens the Abdominal Muscles, especially the *Rectus Abdominus*

Lie face down on the floor with your weight supported on your forearms. Slowly lift your torso and legs off the ground so that only your forearms and the balls of your feet are touching the floor. Keeping your back straight and squeezing your abdominal muscles, hold the position for 15 to 30 seconds. Relax and repeat for a set of 8 to 12.

HIP LIFT
Strengthens the Abdominal Muscles, especially the *Rectus Abdominus*

Lie on your back and place your hands flat under your hips, palms against the floor. Extend your legs straight up in the air, keeping your feet together and positioned over your hips. With your head slightly off the floor, squeeze your abdominal muscles as you lift your feet and legs straight up, until your hips are about 4 or 5 inches above your hands. Hold this position for a moment; then relax as you lower your hips back to the starting position. Repeat for a set of 8 to 12.

CHAIR LIFT
Strengthens the Abdominal Muscles, especially the *Rectus Abdominus*

Sitting in a chair, scoot forward to the edge and grasp the seat at either side of your hips. Slowly lift your knees up toward your chest. If necessary, lean back a little in your chair, but don't arch your back. Hold the position for one count; then slowly lower your knees back to the starting position. Repeat for a set of 8 to 12.

SEATED LEG TUCK
Strengthens the Abdominal Muscles, especially the *Rectus Abdominus*

Sit on the floor with your knees bent in front of you and your hands placed slightly behind your hips, palms down. At the starting position, you'll be leaning back slightly, with your upper body at a 45-degree angle to the floor. Round your back and curl your upper body toward your pelvis, simultaneously lifting your knees up toward your head. Hold this position for a moment before returning to the starting position. Repeat for a set of 8 to 12.

FLAT LEG RAISE
Strengthens the Abdominal Muscles, especially the *Rectus Abdominus*

Lie on your back with your hands under your buttocks for support, and extend your legs straight out in front of you so that your feet are just a few inches off the floor. Keeping your legs straight, raise your feet as high as you can, and then slowly lower them, without allowing them to touch the floor. Repeat for a set of 8 to 12.

SIDE LEG RAISE
Strengthens the Abdominal Muscles, especially the Abdominal Obliques and the *Transverse Abdominus*

Lie on your left side, propping your head up on your left elbow. Keep your left leg bent under your right leg for support. With your right leg straight, raise it slowly as high as you can and then lower it again, stopping short of letting your right foot touch the floor. Keep your hips still during this exercise. Perform 8 to 12 repetitions with your right leg; then turn onto your right side and repeat the exercise with your left leg.

SEATED CROSS OVER

Strengthens the Abdominal Muscles, especially the Abdominal Obliques and the *Transverse Abdominus*

Sit up straight in a chair with both feet flat on the floor. Position your arms so that your hands are up and your elbows are bent at a 90-degree angle. Bring your right elbow and left knee toward each other as far as comfortable. Return to the starting position and change sides, with the left elbow to the right knee. Repeat for a set of 8 to 12.

BENT-KNEE SIDE LEG RAISE

Strengthens the Abdominal Muscles, especially the Abdominal Obliques and *Transverse Abdominus*

Lie with your left side on the ground with your body propped up on your left elbow and forearm, keeping your left knee bent. Bend the knee of your right leg and slowly raise your leg as high as you can; then lower it back to the starting position, without allowing your right knee to touch the floor. Repeat for a set of 8 to 12. Change sides and perform the exercise with the left leg.

THIGHS

SEATED BALL SQUEEZE
Strengthens the Adductor Muscle Group of the Inner Thigh

Sit on a chair with your feet flat on the floor and shoulder width apart. Place a 10-inch diameter rubber ball (a kickball or soccer ball will work fine) between your thighs, just above your knees. Squeeze the ball firmly between your thighs, holding the muscle contraction for 5 to 10 seconds. Allow your muscles to relax for 5 to 10 seconds and then repeat for a set of 8 to 12.

BRIDGE WITH BALL SQUEEZE
Strengthens the Adductor Muscle Group of the Inner Thigh and the Gluteus Muscles of the Buttocks

Lie on your back on the floor with your knees bent. Hold the ball between your thighs just above your knees. Lift your buttocks off the floor toward the ceiling, contracting your gluteus muscles and squeezing the ball between your thighs. Hold the position for 8 to 15 seconds, relax, and repeat the exercise for a set of 8 to 12.

THIGHS

FORWARD LUNGE
Strengthens the Quadriceps and Hamstring Muscles of the Thigh and the Gluteus and Spinal Erector Muscles

Holding a dumbbell in each hand, stand upright with your feet together. Keeping your head up and your back straight, take a big step forward with your right leg and bend your knee, allowing your left knee to hover above the floor. The right leg should be far enough forward so that the left leg is almost straight. Push yourself back up to the starting position with a strong, smooth movement, bringing your feet together. Step forward with the left leg and repeat the exercise to complete one repetition. Do 8 to 12 repetitions for one set.

FRONT SQUAT

Strengthens the Quadriceps, Hamstrings, and Adductor Muscles of the Thigh, as well as the Spinal Erectors and Gluteus Muscles

Stand erect with your feet shoulder width apart. Keeping your back straight and your head up, bend your knees and lower yourself until your thighs are slightly lower than parallel to the floor. (Squatting slightly below the parallel point protects the knees.) Push up from your heels and return to the starting position, without locking your knees. Perform this exercise slowly and in a controlled manner, making sure your back remains straight and your knees are over your feet. Repeat for a set of 8 to 12.

SKATER STYLE LATERAL LUNGE

Strengthens the Adductor Muscle Group of the Inner Thigh, as well as the Spinal Erectors, Gluteus, Quadriceps, and Hamstring Muscles

Standing erect with your feet together, take a large step directly out to the right side, bending the right knee and touching your right foot with your left hand. In this position, you should resemble a speed skater, bent at the waist so that your chest touches the thigh of your right leg, with your left leg straight. Keep your back flat and your head up, and keep your right knee directly over your right foot, with your toes pointed forward. Now, push off the right foot and return to the starting position. Repeat the exercise on the opposite side, and alternate legs for a set of 8 to 12.

BUTTOCKS

DONKEY KICK
Strengthens the Gluteus Muscles
and the Spinal Erectors

On the floor, support your weight on your hands and knees. Keeping your right knee bent, lift your right leg high until your foot is nearly over your buttocks with your toes pointed toward the ceiling. Concentrate on squeezing your buttocks as you lift your leg. Return your right leg to the starting position, but don't allow your knee to touch the floor. Perform 8 to 12 repetitions with your right leg; then switch sides and work your left leg.

FLUTTER KICK
Strengthens the Gluteus Muscles of the Buttocks and the Spinal Erectors

Lie on your stomach with your hands under your chin and your abdomen and pelvis flat on the floor. Raise your legs off the floor, and kick your legs and feet as you would if you were swimming, concentrating on contracting the muscles of the buttocks. Continue the flutter kick motion for 30 to 60 seconds.

MODIFIED LUNGE
Strengthens the Quadriceps and Hamstring Muscles of the Thigh and the Gluteus and Spinal Erector Muscles

Stand erect with your feet together. Take a large step forward with your right leg. Bending forward at the waist, place your left hand alongside your right foot. In this position, your chest is lying against your right thigh. Push yourself back up to the starting position, standing erect with your feet together. Repeat the modified lunge, using your left leg. Alternate sides 8 to 12 times for one set.

LYING LEG CURL
Strengthens the Hamstrings, Spinal Erectors, and Gluteus Muscles

Lie face down on the floor with your hands alongside your shoulders, palms down. Keep your left leg on the floor and bend your right knee behind you, toes pointing toward the ceiling. Slowly lift your right foot toward the ceiling, bringing your right thigh 4 or 5 inches off the floor; then lower it almost to the floor. Throughout the exercise, keep your back straight and your knees close together. Perform 8 to 12 leg curls with your right leg; then repeat the exercise with your left leg.

CALVES

STANDING CALF RAISE
Strengthens the Gastrocnemius and Soleus Muscles of the Calves

Stand on a stair or a wooden block with your weight on the balls of your feet and your heels hanging over the edge. Keep your knees slightly bent, and hold onto a wall, rail, or chair for balance. Lower your heels as far as you comfortably can; then push yourself up on your toes as high as you can. Maintain this position for a moment; then lower yourself back to the starting position. Repeat 8 to 12 times for one set.

WALL HUG

Stretches the Biceps, Front of the Deltoid, and the Pectoralis Muscles

Stand facing a wall with your right arm outstretched and parallel to the floor. Place your right arm and your shoulders along the surface of the wall at shoulder level. With the entire length of your right arm and your shoulders remaining snugly against the wall, slowly turn your torso to your left, away from your right arm. Turn until you feel a gentle stretch along the inside of your right arm, shoulder, and chest.

BACK SCRATCH
Stretches the Triceps

In a standing position, raise your right arm straight up over your head. Now, bend your right elbow, placing your right hand on the back of your neck as if you were trying to scratch an itchy spot between your shoulder blades. Use your left hand to grasp your right elbow and slowly pull it toward your left shoulder until you feel a gentle stretch along the muscles of your right triceps. Hold the stretch for 15 to 30 seconds, relax, and repeat with the left arm.

SIDE BEND
Stretches the Triceps, *Latissimus Dorsi*, Spinal Erectors, and Abdominal Obliques

Stand with feet shoulder width apart and raise your right arm so that your upper arm is against your head. Bend your right elbow so that your forearm is draped over the top of your head. Reaching behind your head with your left hand, grasp your right elbow and gently pull it as you bend your entire torso to the left until you feel a stretch along the entire right side of your torso and the back of your right arm. Hold for 15 to 30 seconds, change sides, and repeat the stretch.

CHEST

CHEST STRETCH
Stretches the Pectoralis Muscles and the Front of the Deltoid

Stand erect and grasp your hands behind you. Slowly bend forward at the waist so that your back is nearly parallel to the floor. As you bend forward, gently lift your clasped hands toward the ceiling until you feel a mild stretch in your chest and in the front of your shoulders. Hold the stretch for 15 to 30 seconds.

SHOULDERS

SHOULDER STRETCH
Stretches the Deltoid, Triceps, and Trapezius

Place your right arm across your chest so that it is parallel to the ground. Grasp your upper arm above your right elbow with your left hand and gently pull your right arm toward your chest, keeping your hips and shoulders facing forward. Hold the stretch for 15 to 30 seconds; then repeat with your left arm.

BACK

SEATED BACK SWIVEL
Stretches the Trapezius, Spinal Erectors, and *Latissimus Dorsi* Muscles

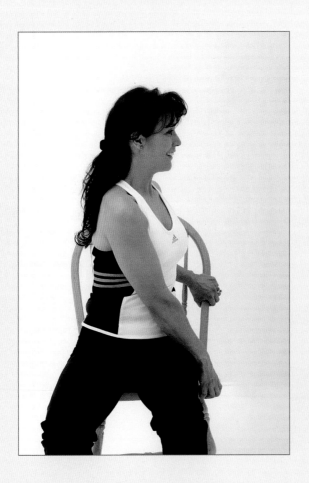

Sit on a chair with your feet flat on the floor and toes facing forward. Slowly turn your upper body to the left, grasping the chair behind you at waist level with your left hand and placing your right hand over your left thigh. You should feel a gentle stretch along the left middle and lower back. Hold this position for 15 to 30 seconds. Release your grip on the chair and slowly turn your body back to the starting position. Turn your body to the right and repeat the stretch.

LATS STRETCH
Stretches the Trapezius, *Latissimus Dorsi*, and Spinal Erectors

Stand an arm's length away from a chair, holding the back with your hands close together. Bow from the waist, pushing your hips slowly away from the chair until you feel a gentle stretch along the muscles of your back. Hold the stretch for 15 to 30 seconds.

SEATED BACK STRETCH

Stretches the Trapezius, Deltoids, *Latissimus Dorsi*, and Spinal Erectors

Sit in a chair with your knees and feet wide apart. Drop your chin and bend forward from the waist so that your torso rests on your thighs and your hands reach out for the floor in front of your feet. You should feel a comfortable stretch along the muscles of your back and shoulders. Hold for 15 to 30 seconds.

ABDOMEN

PRESS UP
Stretches the Abdominal Muscles, especially the *Rectus Abdominus*

Lie face down on the floor with your hands on either side of your shoulders, palms down. Keeping your pelvis on the floor, lift your upper body off the floor with your hands and arms, arching your back and looking up toward the ceiling. Hold the stretch for 15 to 30 seconds.

SIDE BEND
Stretches the Abdominal Obliques and Transverse Abdominal Muscles

Stand upright with your feet slightly greater than shoulder width apart and arms at your sides. Raise your right arm over your head and bend slowly to the left, allowing your left hand to slide down your left thigh. Bend as far to the left as comfortable, feeling the stretch along your right torso. Hold for 15 to 30 seconds, return to starting position, and repeat on the opposite side.

BUTTOCKS

ROTATION STRETCH
Stretches the Gluteus Muscles and the Spinal Erectors

Lie on your back with your right knee drawn toward your chest. Slowly bring your right leg across your body until you feel a gentle stretch in your lower back and upper buttocks. Hold for 15 to 30 seconds; then change leg positions and repeat the stretch.

INNER THIGHS

ADDUCTOR STRETCH
Stretches the Adductor Muscles of the Inner Thigh

Sit on the floor with your legs stretched in front of you, wide apart. Bend your

knees and grasp your ankles with your hands, pulling your heels toward your

groin. As the soles of your feet come together, allow your knees to drop toward

the floor. Gradually lower your chest and abdomen to the floor until you feel a

gentle stretch along the muscles of your inner thighs. Hold for 15 to 30 seconds.

HAMSTRINGS

MODIFIED HURDLER STRETCH
Stretches the Hamstrings and Adductor Muscles of the Inner Thigh

Sit on the floor with your right leg straight out in front of you and the sole of your left foot touching the inside of your right thigh. Allow your left knee to drop to the floor as you lower your chest and abdomen toward your right knee. Move your hands down your right leg as far as comfortably possible, grasping your knee, calf, ankle, or foot. You should feel a gentle stretch along the back and inside of your right leg. Hold for 15 to 30 seconds, relax, and then repeat the stretch on the opposite side.

STANDING HAMSTRING STRETCH
Stretches the Hamstrings, Gluteus Muscles, and Spinal Erectors

From a standing position, extend your right leg in front of you and place your right heel on the seat of a sturdy chair that is slightly higher than knee level. Bending forward at the waist, slowly lower your torso toward your right knee and grasp your leg as far down as possible — at your knee, calf, ankle, or foot — until you feel a gentle stretch in the muscles of your right hamstrings, buttocks, and lower back. Hold for 15 to 30 seconds, relax, and repeat with the other leg.

FORWARD BENDS

Stretches the Spinal Erectors, Gluteus Muscles, and Hamstrings

Stand up straight with your feet together. Bend forward at the waist and grasp the back of your legs with both hands as far down as you comfortably can — at your knees, calves, or ankles. Pull gently with your arms, bringing your head as close as possible to your legs to stretch the muscles of the lower back and hamstrings. Hold the position for 15 to 30 seconds. To get a better stretch on each side, perform the exercise with one foot crossed over the other.

QUADRICEPS

QUAD STRETCH
Stretches the Quadriceps Muscles

While standing straight and holding onto a chair with your right hand for balance, bend your left knee, bringing your foot behind you up to your buttock. Grasp your left ankle with your left hand. Keeping your thigh perpendicular to the floor, gently pull your ankle toward your buttocks until you feel a gentle stretch along the quadriceps muscles of your left leg. Hold the stretch for 15 to 30 seconds. Repeat on other side.

CALVES

CALF STRETCH
Stretches the Gastrocnemius and Soleus Muscles

Stand arms' length away from a wall, facing it. Keeping your arms straight, place your hands on the wall at shoulder height, with your palms flat and your fingertips pointing up. Take a large step back with your left foot, keeping your left leg straight and your right knee bent. With your back erect and your heels on the ground, bend your elbows and allow your upper body to lean into the wall. You should feel a gentle stretch along the muscles of the left calf. Hold the stretch for 15 to 20 seconds; then repeat the stretch with the right leg extended.

a horse in your life
MAKING IT WORK

If you have a dream and are committed to achieving it, you will find a way to make it a reality. A dream backed by unwavering belief cannot be denied or suppressed — it is the power that fuels every success and sacrifice in life.

But before you can ever arrive at your destination, you have to begin by taking the very first step of your journey toward it. The first step is any single action that moves you closer to your dream. Your dream may not unfold exactly according to your plan, or even as soon as you would like. Still, you must always be willing to take even the smallest step toward achieving it. If you're not in a position to buy a horse right now, then owning a horse may not be your first step — it may be your third or fourth or tenth step. Although owning a horse wasn't Brooke's first step, she didn't let it get her down.

"When I was 15," she said, "I was so horse crazy that I couldn't think about anything else. My dad had died when I was 8, and my mother worked two jobs just to keep us off welfare. My mom was so overwhelmed; I knew better than to ask her for a horse."

Brooke got a job cleaning stalls at a horse farm a couple of miles from her house. "I had to ride my bike there and back, but I would have walked through fire to be with those horses," she said.

In exchange for a week's worth of hard work cleaning stalls and grooming horses, the farm owner allowed Brooke to ride every Saturday morning. She's been riding and training horses ever since.

"If my father had lived, I have no doubt that he would have just plopped me on a pony like a little princess, and that might have been the end of it," Brooke said. "I think my love and understanding of horses came from working with them on the ground, rather than in the saddle. Riding was a privilege that had to be earned, so I never took it for granted. I still don't."

While it's easy to see the appeal of diving headfirst into horse ownership, there's a lot to be said for starting low and going slow. Whether you own a horse, you still have to earn your stripes. Becoming a horsewoman requires a significant investment of time and effort and energy. Because it also involves a fair amount of learning and practice, it's not something that happens overnight — it's a process, rather than an event. Becoming a horsewoman requires a type of personal growth that can never be bought — it must always be built from the ground up and from the inside out.

With this in mind, if buying a horse isn't the first step on the journey toward your dream, don't waste a single minute worrying about it. There are many ways to bring horses into your life — the opportunities are limited only by the bounds of your imagination.

Riding Lessons

If you're a newcomer to the world of horses, taking riding lessons is a relatively easy and inexpensive way to get involved. There's no major investment required and no long-term commitment. In most parts of the country, you can find a qualified instructor who is more than willing to share a lifetime of experience and expertise with you, one hour at a time, for as little as $20 to $30 a session.

Some beginners want to skip the riding lessons in favor of a do-it-yourself type of program, but this is rarely a good idea. Learning to ride without the help and guidance of a knowledgeable instructor can be a confusing and frustrating experience — not to mention potentially unsafe — for both you and your horse.

When you're just starting out, regular lessons are a must. You're laying the groundwork upon which the remainder of your growth and progress as a rider will be based, and it is critical to establish a solid foundation. Taking riding lessons with a good instructor is also the fastest way to progress. In a one-hour session, she can teach you more than you could figure out on your own in a month or more.

Every great athlete realizes there is always room for growth and improvement. Olympic athletes, professional tennis players, baseball and basketball stars never get so good that they outgrow their coaches — they realize they will always need experts to help them enhance and refine their skills, and even to maintain those skills. They may change instructors from time to time, but they know better than to try to go it alone. Whether you've ridden only on a handful of occasions or you've logged thousands of hours in the saddle, you need a coach, just like every other athlete.

When should you stop taking lessons? Whenever you're ready to stop advancing as an equestrian. If you're taking lessons and you feel that you're no longer learning or improving, it doesn't necessarily mean that you know everything there is to know, it just means that your current instructor has taken you as far as she can — you've graduated, in effect. It's time to move on to another instructor.

As you become more advanced, you'll have fewer suitable instructors from whom to choose. At some point, you can expect to begin paying more for your lessons, and you may find you have to travel farther from home. Some instructors hold weekend or weeklong clinics for equestrians and their mounts, and these high-intensity learning sessions can be an excellent way to advance in a short time. Even if you only can manage to take one lesson a month or attend a single clinic each year with a top-notch instructor, it's well worth the investment. When you stop learning, you stop improving.

Private or Group Lessons?

Early on, you may have the option of choosing between taking private lessons or group lessons. It's usually best to take private lessons while you're learning the basics of riding and horsemanship because you'll need a lot of individual attention and instruction. Once you've learned to communicate effectively with your mount and maintain your seat, you'll be able to hold your own around other horses and riders, either in semi-private or group lessons. You won't get as much personalized attention, of course, but group lessons are fine for logging hours in the saddle when you're working on developing balance, muscle control, and coordination. As long as your fellow riders and their horses are well-behaved, group lessons can be a lot of fun, and they're usually quite a bit less expensive than private instruction.

Finding an Instructor

The search for a good riding instructor begins in much the same way as a search for any other professional. You can start by looking in the phone book or on the Internet, or by asking your friends, co-workers, and family members whether they know anyone who's taking or teaching lessons. The folks who work at tack shops, feed stores, and veterinarians' offices are excellent sources of information. If you've driven by a horse farm or a stable in your community, don't be shy about calling or stopping in to ask whether someone there is a riding instructor. At the very least, the farm's owner or workers may be able to point you in the right direction. You also can request information from local, regional, or national equestrian clubs and organizations, including Pony Club, American Riding Instructors Association, U.S. Equestrian Federation, 4-H Club, or the American Association for Horsemanship Safety.

The Right Instructor for You

While there's no requirement you fall head over heels in love with your instructor's personality, it is absolutely essential you trust and respect her as a teacher and as an equestrian. It's critical to have complete faith in her ability to develop your skill as a rider in a manner that is safe for you and your mount. The right instructor will put you at ease and help you feel as comfortable and confident in the saddle as possible.

Her style of communication will have a tremendous influence on your ability to learn and advance. If she's prone to yelling and screaming, and this kind of racket makes you tense and anxious, she's probably not the right instructor for you — at least not at first. Learning to ride requires you to open your mind and relax your body, and you won't be able to accomplish either of these feats if your instructor makes you a nervous wreck.

Before you sign up for lessons with any instructor, you'll need to do a little homework. Your first assignment is to determine whether she teaches the style of riding you're interested in learning, and if so, to arrange a brief meeting with her. Ask whether you can make an appointment to speak to her and tour the stable and riding facilities. Simply by walking through her domain, you'll learn a lot about her style and skill as an instructor and as a horsewoman. Her barn doesn't have to be glamorous or high-tech, but it should be clean and free of clutter. The horses should be friendly, healthy, and well groomed. The riding ring should be enclosed by a sturdy rail or a fence, have good footing, and be devoid of potentially dangerous objects.

If you're pleased with the initial evaluation, ask whether you can watch her teach a private and group lesson at your level. This is your chance to find out whether you are likely to be comfortable with her style of teaching and communication. Ideally, the instructor will be genuinely interested in helping her students learn and improve. She'll be fully engaged and involved in teaching and conduct a lesson that not only is well organized but also has some sort of purpose. She'll give clear instructions about how to execute a particular task and then allow the student to try it before giving feedback.

Feedback should be constructive rather than destructive — it should help the rider under-stand exactly what she needs to do to improve her performance. You'll be able to tell from the rider's body language and comments if she's relaxed and enjoying herself or if she appears to be confused or upset. The horse should be as relaxed as the student, with no excessive tail swishing, ear pinning, or head tossing.

If after watching a couple of lessons you're still not sure whether a particular riding in-structor is right for you, you might need a trial run. Ask whether you can pay for a single lesson before signing up for an entire series of classes.

Exchanging Skills

There's no doubt that riding lessons can be expensive, but if you're creative, you may be able to pay for your lessons with your skills and services rather than with your hard-earned cash. Even if your riding instructor doesn't need any extra help around the barn, she may be willing to exchange her expertise as an equestrian for your expertise in another area.

Connie has been teaching riding lessons at her stable near Raleigh, North Carolina, for nearly two decades, and she's never turned her students away because of their inability to pay.

"I don't make a lot of money some months, but I've always got a clean house and plenty of babysitters," she laughed. "I've traded lessons for car washes, catered meals, family portraits, and bookkeeping services."

As long as you're willing to barter, your budget doesn't have to stand in the way of your riding career. There are plenty of ways to finance your equestrian education without spending a lot of money.

Leasing a Horse

Leasing a horse is a great way to get a feel for horse ownership without having to pay the purchase price of the horse or make a long-term commitment. Leasing also can allow you to evaluate a sale horse fully by taking him on a trial basis. If you aren't convinced the horse suits your needs, you can send him back to his owner when the lease expires.

In many cases, a lease arrangement can make it possible for a horsewoman to acquire and ride — at least temporarily — a horse that is far superior to any animal her budget would allow her to purchase. Although lease fees vary significantly from horse to horse, depending on level of training, age, and intended use, they're often in the range of 25 percent to 30 percent of the horse's total value per year. If the horse is worth $15,000, for example, you might expect to pay from $300 to $400 per month to lease him, in addition to paying for his care and upkeep.

As a single mother with two children in college, Elaine from Lexington, Kentucky, didn't have a lot of extra money to invest in a new horse.

"I had been taking riding lessons for several years, and I was really ready for a horse of my own," she said. "I had a couple thousand dollars to spend, but after searching for more than a year, I just couldn't find the horse I was looking for — at least not in my price range. I didn't want a young horse that I had to train; I wanted a well-schooled horse that I could ride to the next level."

Elaine had all but given up her search when her riding instructor called and told her about a gelding in her barn available for lease. His owner had broken her hip in a car accident, and she wasn't going to be able to ride for quite some time.

"When my instructor told me that the horse was Monty, I couldn't believe it. He's beauti-fully trained, and he's had a very successful show career. I could never afford to buy him. In fact, I can barely afford to lease him, but I figured I could either use my $2,000 to buy a horse that I wouldn't be happy with, or I could use it to buy a year with one of the best horses I've ever known."

The Right Horse

Although Monty practically fell into Elaine's lap, finding an appropriate horse to lease isn't always quite so easy. The process is similar to finding a horse for sale. You can start by asking the horse people you know: your riding instructor and fellow riders, vets and farriers, and the folks at the tack and feed stores in your community.

If you're willing to ship a horse from farther away, you can check with breeders and trainers within a certain geographical area. Dozens of Web sites list hundreds of horses available for lease from virtually every state and even from other countries. If you don't find the horse you're looking for, you can always advertise in your local newspaper, in journals and magazines published by breed associations and equestrian organizations, or on horse-related Web sites.

When you find a suitable candidate to lease, it's important to take all the same precautions you would if you were going to buy the horse. One of the most important steps you can take is to have the horse examined by a qualified equine veterinarian. If the horse has any health problems or structural weaknesses that might prevent him from performing in the intended manner, you need to know about them before you agree to support him for the next year. You'll also want to determine and document the current health and condition of the horse before you take him home, should questions arise in the future. Having the horse vet checked prior to leasing will protect you from being held accountable and financially liable for any pre-existing conditions.

In addition to a vet check you'll want to take the horse for a test drive. If at all possible, you should ride the horse on several occasions, in the same manner and under the same type of conditions you intend to ride him after you've leased him, whether it's jumping, trail riding, or barrel racing. It is always a good idea to bring along your riding instructor or another trusted expert to help you assess the horse and to offer an opinion about whether you and the horse are well-suited for each other and make a good team.

The Lease Agreement

The ideal lease agreement is beneficial to all involved parties: the horse owner, the lessee, and the horse. In most lease arrangements, the lessee assumes full care of the horse and pays the owner a specified monthly fee. In exchange, the lessee is allowed to ride and enjoy the horse within pre-defined limits. The owner benefits by having a little extra cash and a little less work to do. The lessee gets to enjoy all the pleasures of owning a horse without having to pay the purchase price. The horse is happy

because he's got a new rider and caretaker who will lavish him with lots of love and attention.

In most lease arrangements the lessee assumes all the financial responsibilities associated with the horse, including the cost of board, feed, veterinary and farrier care, and transportation. The lessee also is required to maintain the horse in optimum physical condition for the intended use and to report any problem, illness, or injury to the owner in a timely manner. Typically, the lessee must agree to carry comprehensive liability insurance to cover all intended uses of the horse.

No matter how careful you are, a lease arrangement always carries the potential for trouble. Even among the most accomplished and successful equestrians in the world, it's hard to find any two who are in complete agreement about the best practices involved in riding, feeding, and conditioning horses. If your methods are very different from those of the horse's owner, it could become a source of conflict. There's also the possibility that the horse could become sick or injured while he's in your care.

You can avoid a lot of hassle and heartache by communicating openly and honestly with the horse owner on the front end. Tell her about your riding skills and your experience caring for horses. Let her know exactly how you plan to use the horse. The horse's owner, in turn, should be open and honest with you. She should willingly share information about the horse's health, special needs, and habits or vices. She should let you know ahead of time if she requires or disapproves of certain practices. She may, for example, insist the horse be brought into the barn whenever the temperature falls below freezing, or she may not allow the horse to be ridden outside an enclosed area. If, after an informal discussion, the two of you see eye to eye, it's time to seal the deal with a formal agreement.

The Written Contract

Unless the entire lease agreement is put in writing and signed by both parties, you'll have nothing to fall back on should a dispute arise down the road. As you know, oral agreements and handshakes don't always hold up in court. It's always wise to hire a qualified and experienced attorney to prepare a contract that is fair and reasonable to both parties. The contract should be as comprehensive and as specific as possible, but at the very least, it should answer the following questions:

- What is the monthly lease fee, and on what day of the month is payment due?
- What are the starting and ending dates of the contract?
- Who will carry insurance on the horse, and what type of insurance is required?
- What is the value of the horse?
- What are the owner's rights regarding visitation and use of the horse?
- Who will be allowed to ride the horse?
- What is the intended use of the horse?
- Will the lessee be allowed to transport the horse to horse shows, trail rides, or other events?

- In case of an accident or injury, who is responsible for payment of veterinary bills?
- What happens if the horse becomes lame or ill and cannot be ridden?
- If the horse requires surgery or must be humanely euthanized, is the lessee authorized to make the decision?
- What are the expectations regarding feeding, stabling, fencing, and grazing?
- What are the expectations regarding veterinary treatment and farrier work?
- Should the horse be offered for sale by the owner during the term of the lease, and should a legitimate offer be made by a third party, will the lessee have the right to match the offer and assume ownership of the horse before the other offer is considered?
- What is the current health status of the horse? (Attach a copy of the veterinarian's record of examination.)

When you're going over the written agreement, be sure to read it carefully and completely, and ask about anything that you don't understand. Any questions that are answered should be documented on the contract, so that it will be clear the next time you read it.

Even if you start with excellent communication, the best of intentions, and a well-crafted contract, it's always possible that the arrangement may not work out as you planned. For this reason, your contract should cover all the circumstances under which either party can terminate the agreement and how the termination should be handled. It might be a good idea to build a probationary period into the contract, in which either party can withdraw from the agreement during a specified period.

The Share-lease

If you like the idea of leasing a horse rather than buying one, but you're still not ready to assume complete financial and physical responsibility for a horse, you can always try to work out a share-lease arrangement. This type of arrangement may allow an owner and a lessee to share responsibility and use of a horse or it may allow two individuals to jointly lease a horse from its owner. In any case, the monthly fee is typically lower than that of a full lease. You can expect to spend less by splitting the cost of the horse's board and care, but you'll also have less time with the horse than you would if you assumed a full lease. Depending on the nature of your agreement, you may be responsible for the horse's care three or four days a week, and on those days you'll be able to ride and enjoy the horse as well.

Although this type of lease agreement can work well, it also can sour pretty quickly, especially if the expectations and requirements of each party aren't spelled out clearly in advance. In many ways, sharing a horse is like sharing custody of a child. If you and your lease partner have major differences of opinion in terms of how the horse should be fed, conditioned, or trained, you can expect to encounter some areas of disagreement. In your written contract, be sure to address these areas of potential conflict and others, including how to handle horse shows, trail rides, and vaca-

tions, when one rider may want to spend more or less time with the horse.

Before you decide to enter into any type of lease agreement, be sure to weigh the potential risks and benefits carefully. Consider not only what you have to gain from this type of arrangement but also what you stand to lose. As with every major decision you make in life, it's always wise to expect the best while you prepare for the worst.

Adopt a Horse

Given the number of little girls and grown women who long to have horses of their own, it's hard to imagine any horse would be without a loving home. Sadly, thousands of unwanted horses wind up in this situation. Each year approximately 90,000 horses are slaughtered for their meat in the United States alone, and thousands more American horses are shipped to slaughterhouses in Canada and Mexico. Their carcasses are delivered to countries where horsemeat is considered a delicacy rather than an atrocity, including France, Belgium, and Japan.

As horse lovers, most of us would like to believe that the animals sent to slaughterhouses are only those that are very old and very sick. We'd also like to believe they are always humanely euthanized. Tragically, neither is the case. Any horse — including one that is young, healthy, well schooled, and full of life and love — can find himself at a slaughter facility. He just has to be at the wrong sale at the wrong time and end up with a final bid that works out to be less than a dollar a pound. "Kill buyers" for slaughterhouses lurk at horse sales and auctions around the country, and they're always on the lookout for low-priced horseflesh. Many horse lovers are actively fighting this practice, and legislation has been introduced in Congress to ban horse slaughter in this country. In the meantime, compassionate individuals and benevolent organizations across the country are saving thousands of unwanted horses from slaughter by taking them in at equine retirement farms, rescue organizations, and rehabilitation and retraining facilities. Many of these horses are available for adoption, and one of them might be a perfect match for you.

If you decide to adopt a horse from a rescue or rehabilitation facility, you may be asked to furnish proof that you can provide it adequate food, shelter, and care. Most organizations are happy to send you a list of owner requirements at your request. If you don't know of a rescue facility in your area, a quick Internet search will help you find one in your state or region. You also can find lists of equine rescue and rehabilitation organizations at www.equinerescue.info/links, www.savehorses.com, and www.horseworlddata.com.

Nearly a decade ago, Amy Long adopted TJ, a Thoroughbred gelding whose racing career had ended abruptly after he fractured a sesamoid bone. Realizing the horse would likely end up at a slaughterhouse if he were sold at auction, his owners decided to euthanize TJ if they couldn't find a good home for him. Amy came to his rescue.

Although the veterinarian gave the horse only a 50 percent chance of recovery, Amy was determined to nurse her new charge back to health. After a year of rest and rehabilitation, X-rays revealed that TJ's fracture had healed, and the vet pronounced the gelding fit for light duty.

"Rehabilitating TJ was one of the most rewarding experiences of my life," Amy said. "I was uplifted with every little bit of progress he made during his recovery. I knew there were lots of horses like TJ, and I wanted to do something to help them, too."

Amy shared her dream of starting a horse rescue operation with her best friend, a widow who owned 25 acres of wooded land. Amy's friend gave her more than just moral support — she offered to house the facility on her property. Within a matter of weeks, the two women had enlisted the help of a few neighbors, and the creation of Kaleidoscope Horse Rescue in Mount View, Arkansas, was well underway. For the next year Amy and her friends worked almost nonstop to prepare a suitable home for their future residents.

"After we cleared the land, we had to build fences and pens and paddocks," Amy said. "We got a lot of information from the local humane society, and we filed for non-profit status with the Internal Revenue Service. We also started a 4-H program. A year later we had everything ready, but we still didn't have any horses."

When Amy took her 4-H group on a field trip to a horse sale, she found her first rescue candidate: an emaciated buckskin filly that appeared to be on the brink of death.

"She was so weak and sick that she couldn't even support her own weight," Amy said. "She was leaning against a wall with her nose touching the ground. I thought the mare was probably in her 30s, but when I lifted her lip, I was dumbfounded to see that she was only a 2-year-old. The kids in my 4-H group begged me to save her."

When the filly stumbled into the ring, Amy bid on her. The only other bidder was a buyer from a Texas slaughterhouse. When the hammer fell, Amy had bought the horse for $150.

"She was so weak that it took four people to lift her into the horse trailer," Amy said. "The kids named her Hope because they knew we were her last hope."

Although the filly was a draft horse cross, she was so malnourished that she weighed only about 480 pounds. Amy's veterinarian diagnosed Hope with a sinus infection and pneumonia. Ringworm and rain rot ravaged about 35 percent of her body, and she was suffering from a severe case of thrush in all four feet. She was infested with worms, lice, ticks, and ear mites. The vet wasn't optimistic that the filly would survive.

As the first resident at Kaleidoscope Horse Rescue, Hope got plenty of love and attention. For two weeks, Amy, her fellow rescue workers, and the 4-H members took turns sleeping in a tent beside the filly so that they could keep an eye on her around the clock.

"Today," Amy said proudly, "Hope is 17.1 hands tall and weighs 1,700 pounds. She's one of the sweetest and most loving horses I've ever known."

Operating a horse rescue facility isn't easy — it's both physically and emotionally challenging.

"Not all of the horses survive," Amy said. "As difficult as it is, we have to put some of them down when they're too sick or injured to recover. I tell myself that at least they were loved before they left us and that they won't have to suffer any more."

Since opening its doors, Kaleidoscope Horse Rescue has been a haven for dozens of mistreated, malnourished, and unwanted horses. Most have been rehabilitated and placed in loving homes.

"The horses that we're able to save make it all worthwhile," Amy said. "It's a wonderful feeling when we can nurse them back to health and place them with loving owners."

Volunteer

Operating a rescue facility — or even adopting a rescued horse — requires an enormous commitment of time, labor, and love, and these options aren't right for everyone. If you've got a big heart and a little extra time, you can always volunteer. Most equine rescue and rehabilitation operations can always use an extra pair of hands. You also can help the members of a local horse club or breed association host its next horse show or clinic, or volunteer to work with horses and kids in Pony Club or 4-H groups. If there's a therapeutic riding center in your community, there's a good chance it needs volunteers who can assist handicapped riders and also help care for the horses.

Working with Horses

If you're determined to be around horses, you might want to consider working full time or part time at a riding stable or a breeding farm. Even if you're not a seasoned horsewoman, it's entirely possible to find someone who is willing to teach you what you need to know, as long as you're willing to learn and work hard while you're at it. No matter your age or your level of experience, it's never too late to start working with horses.

Robin is living proof. She grew up around horses in Bristol, Tennessee, and she developed a passion for riding at an early age. As a young girl, she accompanied her aunt, who refurbished saddles and bridles for a living, to horse sales and shows throughout Tennessee and Virginia.

"While my aunt was working, I would roam around the sale barns and show grounds," Robin said. "Most of the horse owners were good to me. They'd take the time to answer my questions and teach me what they could. The best part was just being around the horses."

Robin's carefree childhood jaunts ended when she got married at age 15. She gave birth to her first child when she was just 17 years old, and before her 20th birthday, she had her hands full with a husband and two young children.

"You know how that goes," she laughed. "Having babies put an end to my involvement with horses. I always knew that one day I'd find my way back, but my first responsibility was to take care of my kids."

When her children started school, Robin got a full-time job in a bookbinding factory.

"I put the gold trim on Bibles," she explained. "It was a rough job that involved sanding, routing, and a lot of heavy lifting, and I was one of the first women the company allowed to perform that kind of work. I didn't always love what I was doing, but I was grateful for my job. The pay was good, and the money helped me raise my children."

For the next 13 years, Robin often worked seven days a week for six months at a stretch. It was a demanding schedule that left her with little time to pursue her interest in horses, and it also took a tremendous toll on her relationship with her husband.

"It cost me my marriage," she said. "Sometimes, things just don't work out the way you planned."

In spite of the change in plans, Robin never lost sight of her dream to make horses a part of her life. Her chance to realize that dream came about in a most unexpected way, when she was 47 years old.

"I got laid off when my job got sent to Brazil," she explained. "There was no way I was going to work in another factory — I decided that I was going to do what I wanted for once in my life. My kids were grown and doing well on their own, and they didn't need me as much as they used to. I figured it was finally my turn to do what I had always dreamed of doing."

Living on her savings and a modest sever-ance pay, Robin didn't have a lot of extra money to buy and board a horse of her own or even to take riding lessons.

"I made up my mind that I was going to get a job on a horse farm, one way or another. I didn't know everything I needed to, but I fig-ured I could learn," she said. "I've always been strong, and I knew I could do the work."

Robin searched the phone book and the Inter-net, and she started calling local horse farms until she found an Arabian horse-breeding op-eration that was hiring. The job involved clean-ing stalls, turning out horses, helping breed and foal out mares, halter-breaking weanlings, and working with yearlings and 2-year-olds.

"I got an interview and a new job working with horses on the same day," she remem-bered. "I told the owners that I had a lot to learn, but they really didn't seem to mind. They said they'd be glad to teach me."

Although Robin's current salary is signifi-cantly lower than her previous one, she doesn't miss the extra income. "I feel like I've come full circle in life, doing what I've dreamed of doing since I was a little girl," she said. "I absolutely love it, and I plan to work with horses for the rest of my life. Money just can't buy the kind of happiness you get from doing what you really love to do."

Apprenticeship

If you can't find a paying job working with horses, you may be able to find one that doesn't pay. Serving as an apprentice is un-doubtedly one of the hardest ways to earn your stripes as a horsewoman, but it's also likely to be one of the most rewarding and educational experiences of your life — it's the ultimate equestrian boot camp.

As an apprentice, you won't be afforded all the courtesies and niceties that you would be if you were a paying student taking riding les-sons. You'll be expected to work long hours, possibly from sunup to sundown, and you'll be expected to give a 110 percent effort while you're at it.

In return, you can easily pack a few years' worth of experience into a few short months. You'll also leave your apprenticeship program with a crystal clear understanding of whether a life with horses is right for you.

Although there are many established ap-prentice programs at farms, ranches, and horse breeding operations around the country, there's no reason you can't design your own. You can swap labor for learning with a number of equestrian professionals, including veterinar-ians, farriers, breeders, horse trainers, or riding instructors. All you have to do is find an expe-rienced horse person who is willing to teach you and give you some hands-on experience in exchange for the sweat of your brow. If you're lucky, you may even get a small stipend out of the deal, but don't count on it.

Lindsey, a 22-year-old accounting student at the University of Virginia, spent her past three summer vacations as an apprentice at a large horse training facility. During the months of June and July, she worked 10-hour days, six days a week, feeding and grooming horses and mucking stalls. She turned horses out, tacked them up, and cooled them down. It was hard work, but as a cash-strapped college student, she realized it was the only way she could continue to advance her riding skills while she was attending college.

"I knew I was going to buy a horse as soon as I graduated and got a job as an accountant," Lindsey said, "but I didn't want to get out of shape or lose my touch in the meantime. I guess I could have gotten a real job with a salary in the summer months, but it's not like I would have made a fortune, and I would have ended up spending everything I earned paying for rent and riding lessons, anyway. As an apprentice, I got free room and board, a hundred dollars a month spending money, and three riding lessons a week."

Becky decided to work as an apprentice for different reasons. After 31 years of nursing, she was more than ready for a career change. Her dream was to buy a few broodmares and start a small breeding operation on her farm near Dallas, Texas. Although she had owned and ridden American Saddlebreds for most of her adult life, they had all been mature geldings.

"My husband and I had a nice barn and plenty of land, but we knew absolutely nothing about taking care of pregnant mares or handling foals," Becky said. "We had a lot to learn, and we had no idea where to start."

While Becky was still figuring out how to advance her equine education, she began her search for a broodmare.

"I found two really nice mares at a farm in Illinois, and I couldn't decide between them," she said. "I told the owner that I would buy them both if he would let me spend the month of March at his barn and allow me to help foal out the mares when the time came. I fully expected him to say no, but he took me up on it."

At age 52, Becky began her five-week apprenticeship during the breeding and foaling season, the busiest time of the year.

"Twelve mares foaled while I was at the farm," she said. "I don't think I've ever worked harder or slept less. It was a very intense crash course in broodmare and foal management, but I got a great education. It gave me the knowledge and confidence I needed to come home and start my own little breeding operation."

Riding Vacations

Becoming a skilled equestrian doesn't have to be all work and no play — you can combine learning with fun by taking a riding vacation. If you've always wanted to experience life as a cowgirl, a number of dude ranches will be happy to help you bring your dream to life. As a guest at a working cattle ranch that doubles as a resort, you can expect to ride trails to your heart's content and try your hand at roping steers and branding calves. You might even have the opportunity to participate in a cattle drive, complete with cowboys, chuck wagons, and campfires.

If life on the open range doesn't sound appealing, how about hacking through the Scottish Highlands on horseback, splashing along a beach in Greece, or foxhunting in France? You might enjoy saddling up with a group of like-minded horse lovers for a themed riding adventure, whether it's a mother-daughter excursion or a ride for singles only. You also can take a more educational vacation, during which you might spend a week with a top riding instructor in your chosen equestrian discipline, whether it's reining, show jumping, carriage driving, or dressage. While it's possible to plan your own riding vacation from scratch, it may be easier to buy a ready-made equestrian vacation package of your choice from one of several agencies that specialize in "adventure travel."

Before you make your final decision, be sure that you fully understand the requirements and realities of your vacation. If it involves riding over rough terrain in the blazing sun for several days at a stretch, is your skill as an equestrian and your level of fitness adequate? If it involves camping out overnight, can you survive without running water and your curling iron? Don't forget to consider any physical and emotional factors that might come into play. If you're allergic to dust, a cattle drive across the dry, open plains could incapacitate you, and if you're afraid of heights, a trek along a steep mountain goat trail could scar you for life. The more you know ahead of time, the more likely you are to choose the riding vacation that will be the safest and most enjoyable for you.

Find a Mentor

Regardless of the path you take to become an accomplished horsewoman, you'll get there faster by following in the footsteps of someone who has gone before you. It's very rare to find a successful horsewoman who made it entirely on her own without someone else giving her a leg up and showing her the ropes. One of the best things you can do to advance your knowledge, understanding, and skill as a horsewoman is to find a mentor.

Although your riding instructor also may serve as your mentor, she's by no means your only option, and she may not even be the best one for you. Whether she's a suitable mentor for you depends primarily on your goals as a horsewoman. While your riding instructor is undoubtedly well qualified to teach you the basics of horsemanship and riding, she may not be able to teach you how to breed a mare, show a yearling at halter, or condition a horse for an endurance event. If you can't find an instructor with expertise in your specific area of interest, choosing a mentor may be the next best thing.

Seven years ago, Susan's goal as an aspiring horsewoman was to train reining horses.

"I was taking dressage lessons from an excellent instructor in Atlanta at the time," she said, "but I wasn't going to be happy until I learned all I could about reining."

Susan was delighted to learn that a woman who had won several reining championships lived just about 30 miles from her home in Roswell, Georgia. She was just as dismayed when she found out that the reining champ, whose name was Christine, didn't teach lessons or work with students in any capacity.

"I even tried to apply for a job at her farm," Susan said, "but her husband told me that Christine only had four horses and that she did all the work herself."

Susan finally got the courage to ask Christine if she could simply watch her work her horses.

"I drove out to her farm on a Saturday morning, and when I got there, she was in the ring working a horse," Susan said. "She didn't seem very happy to see me, but she was too involved with the horse to tell me to get lost. I stood in one spot for over an hour, not only because I was fascinated, but also to prove that I could watch and learn without making a nuisance of myself."

At the end of the training session, Susan introduced herself and asked if she could come back the following Saturday.

"I told her how much I admired her, and that I was desperate to learn what she knew," Susan said. "She didn't say much, but she did agree to let me come back the next weekend."

Over the following months Christine gradually began to warm up to Susan.

"Christine stuttered, and she was very self-conscious about it," Susan said. "Once she got comfortable around me, she started teaching me. Christine never let anyone — including me — ride her horses, but she went with me to pick out my first reining horse, and she helped me develop a training program and a game plan for his career. She ended up being the best teacher I've ever had."

If you ask any accomplished equestrian or successful horsewoman how she got where she is today, she'll likely give you a short list of critical success factors: passion, persistence, and hard work. Then she'll tell you about her relationship with at least one key person who made all the difference in the world — her mentor. This is the person who first educated and inspired her and later challenged and championed her. A good mentor will share your dream with you and continue to visualize it even when you lose sight of it. When you feel discouraged, your mentor will pick you up, dust you off, and encourage you to try again. She'll believe in you even when you aren't able to believe in yourself.

You can learn a lot from books, CDs, and magazine articles, but nothing can replace the kind of learning that occurs face to face, heart to heart. Horsemanship involves equal parts knowledge and nuance: The skills and secrets involved have been handed down from one horse person to the next for generations.

Mentors play a critical role in every profession. As a young physician, I was never without a small army of mentors at every stage of my education and training. Even after reading stacks of medical texts and journals and attending hundreds of lectures, I never could have learned to practice medicine effectively if someone hadn't taken the time to teach me in a one-on-one setting. By shadowing one experienced physician at a time, I learned to appreciate the peculiar swell of an enlarged liver or abnormal breast lump and to recognize the unique rumble of a potentially lethal heart murmur. The same is true with horsemanship.

You can read as much as you like, but until you are on the receiving end of a person-to-person transfer of knowledge and understanding, you will never reach your full potential.

The Mentor

Finding a mentor may seem like a great idea, but it may not be as easy as you think, especially if the pool of knowledgeable, skilled equestrians in your community seems more like a puddle. Even if you live in an area bustling with seasoned horsewomen, you'll still need to find one who not only is a good fit for you but also one who is willing to work with you.

There are several ways to go about choosing a mentor. In a perfect world you would find the person who is already living your dream. She would welcome you into her life with open arms and spend as much time as necessary to mold and shape you into the horsewoman you aspire to be, expecting very little in return. Unfortunately, you're very unlikely to find this perfect mentor, primarily because she doesn't exist. Still, it is possible to find a horsewoman who is doing what you'd like to be doing. If the two of you are compatible and if she is willing and able to spend a little time with you, she's likely to be an excellent candidate.

If you can't find anyone in your immediate vicinity that you'd like to emulate, you can take a different route. Start by determining the purpose of your relationship with a mentor. Ask yourself what you hope to gain. Greater skill as a rider? Knowledge about a particular aspect of equine management, such as nutrition or breeding? Access to the show ring? Take a moment to write a list of the horse-related skills and knowledge you already have. Next, write a list of the skills and knowledge you would like to acquire.

If you're determined to learn how to breed mares and deliver foals, a horse trainer with a barn full of show geldings probably won't be the best mentor for you. Likewise, if you want to learn how to turn out a show horse to perfection, you wouldn't want to choose a broodmare manager as your primary mentor. If you just want to learn the basics of horsemanship, on the other hand, either the horse trainer or the broodmare manager — or both — would be excellent mentor candidates. Having more than one mentor is an excellent way to obtain a variety of skills and a wealth of knowledge.

Once you've identified at least one potential mentor, start by arranging a meeting with her. Let her know you'll be brief because you realize that she's busy and you respect her time. Before you meet with her, make sure you know exactly what you're proposing. If she's never been a mentor before, she may have no idea what it entails. It's up to you to fill in the blanks, and it's important to be as specific as you can as you define the nature of your proposed relationship.

Let her know right off the bat that you're not asking for a free ride (or free riding lessons) and huge chunks of her time but rather that you'd like to shadow her and assist her as she goes about her work for short periods when it is convenient to her schedule. Let her know that you're interested in watching, listening, and learning. Success is more likely if you present yourself as a relatively low-maintenance individual with a reasonably thick skin and an open mind.

Once you've established the fact that you're not going to disrupt her life or her career, you can move on to your objectives. You certainly don't want to issue any demands, but you should let her know exactly what you hope to learn or accomplish. Your mentor may be more than willing to help you, but she won't be able if she doesn't understand your goals. Furthermore, if you don't share your goals with her, she may imagine the worst. You may want nothing more than to watch her introduce a horse to the bridle, while she may have visions of you begging to ride her Grand Prix champion.

Once you've made her aware of your hopes and dreams, it's your turn to tell her what you have to offer in return. You may not be able to spend long hours mucking stalls at her barn, and that's okay. Being a protégé is not the same thing as being an apprentice, and being a mentor is not the same thing as being a slave driver. Being a mentor implies that she'll be willing to share her knowledge and expertise with someone coming up the ranks behind her, mostly as a service, without making a lot of demands in return. Still, it's nice for you to list the ways in which you might be able to contribute.

If your chosen mentor is very successful at her job, she may already have a team of professionals at her beck and call. If she doesn't need any more helpers, you may wonder what you could possibly bring to the relationship. Don't sell yourself short. You have passion and a hunger for knowledge, the same qualities that got your mentor where she is today. Even better, if you admire and respect her, you can help her see herself and her work in a new light, and you can breathe new life into a routine that might have become stale. Having a protégé can be fun and rewarding. It's incredibly fulfilling to pass knowledge along to someone who is hungry for it and to know that you're having a positive influence on another person's life.

Once you've established the nature of the mentor-protégé relationship and you've clarified your basic expectations, you can agree on a schedule. She may welcome you to visit the barn whenever the notion strikes you, but if she doesn't, it's wise to find out exactly when and how often you can come so that you won't disrupt her schedule.

If you approach a potential mentor and she's not receptive to your idea, try not to take it personally. It may have nothing at all to do with you. She may feel that she doesn't have the time or the patience to work with a protégé, or she may lack the confidence to act as a teacher. Because she knows herself best, you'll have to take her word for it. Whatever the reason, don't let it keep you from moving on to your second choice and trying again.

Giving Back

One of the oldest mantras of clinical medicine is, "see one, do one, teach one." As a young doctor in training, I was required to watch seasoned physicians perform a particular medical procedure a number of times before I was allowed to perform it myself. After proving to my mentors that I had gained mastery of the procedure, I was expected to turn around and teach it to a physician coming up the ranks behind me. Virtually every clinical skill I acquired in the course of my medical training was based on the "see one, do one, teach one" philosophy.

Although I didn't realize it as I was growing up and learning to ride, the skills that I acquired as an equestrian were based on the same principle. As long as there are women and horses, there will be a need for experienced horsewomen who are willing to pass along the knowledge and nuances of horsemanship. Once you've had the opportunity to "see one" and "do one," it becomes your responsibility — and your privilege — to "teach one." It's your turn to be the mentor.

teamwork

MAKES THE DREAM WORK

If you've loved horses for as long as you can remember, having one of your own may be the realization of a lifelong goal. As a child, and even as an adult, you may have spent countless hours dreaming about the "perfect" horse, but in reality there's just no such thing. Fortunately, you don't need a flawless horse to be happy and successful as an equestrian — all you need is a good horse that fits you well.

Riding is a team sport, pairing horse and human. Neither is more critical than the other. As with any other team sport, successful riding depends on a number of factors, including mutual respect, cooperation, and compatibility. While you're building your own two-member team, remember that no matter how new you are to riding, you're not starting from scratch. Half of your team is already established, and that half is you. Your physical and mental characteristics dictate the physical and mental characteristics of the ideal teammate.

As you work through the process of choosing and buying a horse, you'll need to consider dozens of factors. Ultimately, you should always come back to the most important consideration: whether the horse is a good fit for you. No matter how "perfect" a horse may seem, he's not the right one if he's the wrong teammate for you.

To ensure you end up buying the right horse, it's wise to do your homework and plan your purchase carefully and as far in advance as possible. When you approach the process in logical steps, you're more likely to be happy with the result. Satisfaction comes from knowing not only exactly what you want but also exactly what you need and then searching until you find it. You should never allow yourself to settle for an unsafe or unsuitable horse.

Your experience with your first horse will impact your desire — and perhaps even your ability — to continue riding. A safe, pleasurable experience will deepen your love of horses and enhance your skills as an equestrian, but a bad experience may cause you to quit before you reap the rewards of horse ownership.

The decision to buy a horse is a big one, and like all major decisions, it should be made with a great deal of thought, consideration, and planning. Because owning a horse will change your life in ways you might never have imagined, you should approach the process as carefully and as cautiously as you might if you were deciding to buy a house, start a new career, or get married.

In the school of hard knocks, most of us have learned reality far differs from expectations.

If you're a wife and a mother, you've learned that marriage doesn't even remotely resemble dating and motherhood is vastly different from baby-sitting or being an aunt or a godparent. It's only natural to focus on the most exciting and glamorous aspects of any project we undertake — that's what drives us to succeed. It's also natural to turn a blind eye to those aspects that promise to be less than wonderful.

If owning a home was once your dream, for example, you undoubtedly focused on the countless positive attributes of home ownership, ranging from decorating your new kitchen to relaxing with friends and family in your spacious, well-appointed living room. You probably didn't spend much time fantasizing about the harsher realities of homesteading, including risking life and limb to clean the gutters or hiring a plumber to fix a perpetually backed-up toilet. By the same token, owning a horse is far more complex and complicated than taking riding lessons or even caring for someone else's horse.

Regardless of your financial status, horse ownership involves a significant cash outlay. In addition to the initial purchase price of your horse, you'll also be shelling out a substantial amount of your hard-earned cash to cover the cost of boarding and feeding your horse. Your horse will likely require a veterinarian's services at least once or twice a year and a farrier's attention every four to six weeks. Any experienced horse owner will tell you dozens of ways in which a horse can help you spend your money.

While horse ownership requires a major financial commitment, there are also the commitments of time, energy, and emotion to consider. Your horse will end up becoming an important part of your family — and an integral part of your life. Even if you don't bat an eye at the purchase price, and even if the monthly expenses don't strain your budget, you'll still need to schedule enough time with your horse.

If you're responsible for every aspect of your horse's care, you can probably count on spending at least an hour a day feeding, watering, and grooming your horse. If you plan on riding, mucking stalls, or giving your horse some turnout time, you're looking at spending two or three hours at the barn. You'll regularly need to replenish feed, hay, bedding, and various supplies. If you're not going to have these items delivered, you'll need to pick them up, so don't forget to consider the time involved in maintaining a well-stocked stable. If you're planning on boarding your horse at a barn that's not within easy walking distance of your house, you've also got to account for travel time.

Taking responsibility for your horse's daily upkeep can be a rich and rewarding experience, but it may cut into your riding time. If your primary goal is to care for your horse and to enjoy his companionship, this isn't a major problem. If, however, you're on a tight deadline to achieve a specific level of training, or if your goal is to compete in specific events or equestrian classes, assuming full care of your horse may not be your best option.

If you're planning to board your horse at a

facility that provides full care, you won't need to spend quite so much time at the barn. Your role may be limited simply to riding and enjoying your horse. The trade-off for this type of full-service care is, of course, a higher monthly boarding bill.

Like all other relationships, the one you develop with your horse will be fraught with emotions, both good and bad. These emotions are often intensified if your schedule and your life are already full. If you buy a horse that you grow to love and cherish, you'll likely suffer a great deal of guilt if you're so busy that you aren't able to spend enough time with him or ride him regularly. If you end up with a horse that you're not entirely crazy about, you'll probably start to feel resentful about the amount of time that you're obligated to spend with him, and, eventually, you may have a hard time dragging yourself to the barn.

Regardless of your feelings toward your horse, you'll be bound to him by a sense of responsibility for as long as you own him. At one time or another you may face trading your nice, warm bed for a freezing barn in the dead of winter. Or you may find yourself fighting flies and fatigue as you ride or care for your horse in the sweltering summer heat. The horse that is right for you is the one that will inspire you to make these sacrifices willingly.

If the realities of horse ownership don't deter you in the least, and if you're convinced beyond a shadow of a doubt that owning a horse is your destiny, then hold on, because you're about to embark on an adventure that will be one of the most exciting and rewarding experiences of your life.

The Ideal Teammate

Whether you realize it, you have certain expectations — and maybe even a fantasy or two — about the horse you will call your own. You already know a few things about this horse. You may know, for example, that he's a gentle gelding that is kind, quiet, and willing to work. This is an excellent place to start, but at some point you'll need to begin filling in the blanks. What breed is your future teammate? How old is he? What level of training has he achieved? Is he a show horse or a pleasure horse? The more you know about the horse ahead of time, the simpler your search will be, and the less likely you'll be to get sidetracked by horses that aren't right for you.

Because it's easy to get carried away by your emotions, it's important to guard yourself against impulse buying ahead of time. Before you start your search, it's wise to sit down and write a detailed description of the ideal teammate. Using your written description, make a list of all the qualities your horse must have. Next, make a list of the qualities you'd like your horse to have but you could live without or you'd be willing to compromise for a more essential quality. The more specific you are, the more likely you are to find the right horse.

Take Your Time

In your search for the ideal teammate, it's perfectly acceptable to be picky and to take your time. There's no shortage of horses for sale, so there's no need to rush and settle for an unsatisfactory mount. It's not uncommon for sellers to inform you that there are "several interested parties" and "this horse will go fast." It may be true. On the other hand, it could be that the seller is being a good salesperson, trying to create a sense of urgency and an "act now, before it's too late" mentality in you, the potential buyer. If you're prepared for this kind of pressure ahead of time, you'll be less likely to succumb to it.

While finding a horse that is the perfect match for you can be time consuming and even downright tedious on occasion, it's far less tedious than owning a horse that is wrong for you. As the saying goes, chance favors the prepared mind. There's no way to foresee every challenge you and your horse will face in the short term, much less in the long term, but the chances of a favorable outcome are much greater if you're well prepared.

If you're patient and diligent in your search, chances are excellent you'll find the right horse. Sometimes it's very easy to cross a horse off your list. If he has a dangerous habit such as kicking or bolting, or if you feel that he's just too small for you, it's easy enough to walk away. At other times you may not be able to put your finger on the problem quite so easily. You may not understand why you're not enthusiastic about a particular horse that seems like a suitable candidate. It could be there's just no chemistry. If something doesn't feel right about a particular horse — even if you're not sure

exactly what it is — trust your instincts and keep looking.

Purpose of the Horse

Before embarking on your search for a horse, you need to understand fully your motives for doing so. Why do you want a horse? The answer may seem obvious to you, but you need to be able to verbalize a response to this question, not only for yourself, but also for others. You must be capable of clearly communicating your reasons for owning a horse so that sellers, breeders, trainers, veterinarians, and even your friends can help you find the right one. What are your goals? What purpose will your horse serve? Do you want to compete in horse shows, endurance rides, or other equestrian events, or do you want to trail ride? Is your primary goal to enjoy the companionship of a horse without competing or, even, riding?

Your Panel of Experts

Once you've defined why you want a horse, it's a good idea to assemble a panel of knowledgeable horse people whom you'll be able to consult prior to making your final decision. This group of professionals should be headed by your riding instructor and the equine veterinarian who will be caring for your horse. It's also a good idea to include a horse trainer and the farrier you intend to hire. When you've narrowed your list of horses to a few finalists, you'll want to critique each horse with the members of your panel before making your final decision. Each of these experts can provide valuable insights, information, and advice that will go a long way toward ensuring the horse you buy is the best possible teammate for you.

Your riding instructor, for example, knows your strengths and weaknesses as an equestrian and can help you determine whether the horse in question will be a good match. The ideal horse will have strengths that complement your weaknesses and vice versa. If you tend to be a timid rider, you don't want a horse that spooks every time the wind blows. If you've got arthritis in your knees and have a little trouble climbing into the saddle, you don't want a horse that dances around in circles while being mounted. Your riding instructor can spot these kinds of mismatches early on and can help you determine whether they can be corrected easily, and if not, whether you can live with them.

A skilled and experienced horse trainer can offer a qualified opinion about the horse's potential to reach a particular level of training, or to compete in specific disciplines, based on the horse's attitude and conformation. Ideally, the horse you buy will be doing what you want him to do already, but if he's not, how can you tell if he's mentally and physically capable? There's no way to know for sure, of course, but a good horse trainer's educated guess may be the next best thing.

After performing a pre-purchase examination, an equine veterinarian can evaluate the horse's health and soundness. It's helpful to know whether the horse has any conditions that will prevent him from fulfilling your goals. Like-

wise, a good farrier's opinion is worth having. Along with the horse trainer and the vet, the farrier can provide you with a great deal of useful information after evaluating the horse's feet, legs, and gaits. The farrier also can determine how the horse behaves while his feet are being handled. For instance, if you knew ahead of time the horse you're considering buying requires a tranquilizer to have his back feet shod would you still buy him?

Ultimately, the final decision about whether to buy the horse is yours alone, but you'll be more likely to make the right decision with the input of qualified professionals.

Breed

The activities you plan to enjoy with your horse will, to a large degree, influence or even determine the breed of horse you end up buying. To spare yourself a few minor hassles — or even a major heartache — ask to see the horse's certificate of registration early on, and make sure the owner's name on the document matches the name of the person you're dealing with, either directly or indirectly, through a trainer or a sales agent.

If competing in breed-specific shows isn't your goal, you can be far more flexible in your search for a suitable teammate. While certain breeds are better suited to certain jobs, horses of many breeds are remarkably versatile and can perform well in a variety of different equestrian disciplines, including dressage, Western pleasure, English, hunt seat, and trail riding.

With that said, you'll probably be happiest

and most successful if you select a breed that has a proven track record in your chosen discipline. If you plan to ride Western, your best bet is to choose a mount of stock horse descent, such as a Quarter Horse, American Paint Horse, Palomino, or Appaloosa. If you're interested in competing in dressage, you'll probably be better satisfied with a horse of warmblood origin, such as a Hanoverian or an Oldenburg. If owning a horse with a smooth ride is your primary goal, you may lean toward a Paso Fino, a Tennessee Walking Horse, or a Missouri Fox Trotter. While American Saddlebreds and Morgans are known for their versatility, they're often used exclusively as show horses. Arabians are not only excellent show horses but also competent trail horses and very competitive endurance mounts.

Although there are dozens of popular breeds of horses from which to choose, you'll undoubtedly find yourself drawn more to some than others. You can learn a great deal about various breeds by reading books on the subject, checking out the Web sites and publications of breed associations and registries, attending horse shows, and visiting area breeders. The more knowledgeable you are about the various breeds, the easier it will be to choose the one best suited for your purposes.

Cost

Depending on its conformation, pedigree, level of training, show record, and dozens of other factors, a horse can range in price from several hundred to several million dollars. The good news is you'll undoubtedly be able to find a horse that meets your needs at an affordable price. The tradeoff is time and effort. The less money you have to spend, the harder you'll have to search to find the right horse. Before you begin your horse hunt, it's important to determine how much you're able and willing to invest. Then buy the best horse that you can afford. The purchase price of the horse you end up buying will likely be far overshadowed by the cost of his upkeep in the years to come. As the old saying goes, it costs just as much to keep a bad horse as a good one.

Age and Training of the Horse

No matter how long you've been riding, the age and the level of training of the horse you're thinking of buying are key considerations. While a young, green horse may be perfect for a skilled equestrian, the same horse might prove too challenging for a novice. If you're a beginner, your best bet is to search for a mature, mild-mannered, and well-schooled mount. Even with regular riding and schooling, a well-trained horse isn't created overnight or even within a year's time.

Among inexperienced equestrians, it's a common misconception that buying a younger horse is preferable to buying an older one. Many beginners think if they buy a weanling or a yearling and raise it themselves, they'll share a stronger emotional bond with the horse than they would if they acquired him when he was older. Some fearless beginners are determined to train their own mounts while others believe that buying a youngster is less expensive than buying a well-trained horse in his prime. Finally, many novices worry that if they buy a mature horse, the animal will succumb to the frailties of old age before they've had a chance for a return on their investment.

An experienced horsewoman will shake her head at any of these examples of beginner's logic and provide you with dozens of reasons why none of them are sound. While you're still perfecting your riding skills, it's critically important to have a mature, well-trained mount beneath you. If you're an inexperienced rider, choosing a young, green horse can have disastrous consequences. At worst, you could sustain a serious injury. At best, your ability to advance as an equestrian undoubtedly will be curtailed.

Training a young horse is as much art as it is science, and it takes years of experience with dozens — or even hundreds — of horses to become good. Buying a young, untrained horse may seem cheaper in the short run, but it's likely to be far more costly in the long run. It's relatively easy to find an older horse with years of training and experience for a reasonable price. If you buy a young horse and pay for those years of training along the way, you can easily end up doubling or tripling the purchase price of the horse.

An older horse may not seem like a good long-term investment until you consider several issues. First, if you buy a mature horse that is healthy and sound, and if you take good care of him, chances are excellent he will remain

a good mount until well into his twenties. It's also important to remember that as long as you continue riding and learning, your skills as an equestrian will improve. In the span of a couple of years, you won't be the same rider you are today, and you probably will "outgrow" your first horse, regardless of his age. With this in mind, it makes sense to buy a mature, capable horse you can begin to enjoy immediately, so you can continue to develop your confidence and competence as an equestrian.

Ideally, the horse you buy will be doing what you want your horse to do. If you're a beginner looking for a trail horse, the right horse already is carrying his current owner on regular trail rides. Not only will he be calm and confident by nature, but he'll be accustomed to stepping over fallen trees, walking quietly alongside other horses, and wading through small creeks.

On the other hand, it doesn't always make sense to spend a lot of extra money buying a horse so advanced in his training that you're not able to ride him effectively. A well-trained horse is like a complex machine — its optimal performance is almost entirely dependent upon the operator. If you randomly push buttons and pull levers, you may get some unexpected results. The same is true of the exceptionally well-trained horse. He's likely to be highly sensitive and responsive to the slightest changes in pressure and position of the rider's seat, legs, and hands. If you're still perfecting your seat and learning the proper use of leg aids, you may end up "pushing buttons" without meaning to. Because the horse doesn't understand what is being asked of him, he may become confused and frustrated. Eventually, he'll learn to ignore your unintentional signals, and as a result, his sensitivity and skill will decline.

No horse is permanently trained — training is always a work in progress. For a horse to maintain mastery of a specific skill, he must practice and perform that skill regularly. While it's tempting for the beginning rider to believe she'll quickly advance to match the horse's level of training, the opposite is usually true. In most cases, the skills of a highly trained horse fall to match those of his novice rider.

Gender of the Horse

After agonizing over far more complex considerations, deciding on your horse's gender will be relatively simple because choices are limited. Most horses available for purchase are mares and geldings, although it's entirely possible to buy a stallion or a neutered mare.

Any experienced horsewoman within a hundred mile radius will tell you — emphatically — that your first horse should not be a stallion. Under the influence of testosterone, stallions are instinctively driven to breed mares. As a result, their behavior can be unpredictable, aggressive, and, at times, downright dangerous.

In the presence of any mare, and especially a mare in heat, a stallion's primary goal is to win her affections. At the very least, he'll want to get involved in some heavy petting, even if it's a one-sided affair. Under these circumstances, it takes a highly skilled and experienced horsewoman to command the respect — and even

the full attention — of a stallion. In some cases, it may even require a little brute strength.

Riding a stallion effectively can be challenging, but boarding him can be even more problematic. Owners of many boarding facilities don't accept stallions at their stables as they require special handling and must be kept apart from other horses. If you manage to find a suitable home for a stallion, you'll likely end up paying more for his care and accommodations.

As a rule, mares tend to be far less aggressive than stallions, but as they're still at the mercy of their reproductive hormones, their behavior can be less predictable than that of geldings. Some mares become especially temperamental and distracted when they're in heat, which generally occurs once a month, except in the winter. Because their monthly mood swings can interfere with their ability to concentrate and perform to their full potential, some trainers and riders take measures to keep their mares from cycling. It's not an uncommon practice with mares to administer drugs that will prevent them from ovulating during the show season. Although it's far less common to spay mares surgically, it is certainly possible.

If you're searching for a well-mannered, predictable horse, you'll probably be happiest with a gelding. Minus the influence of reproductive hormones, geldings are generally far more consistent in their behavior than mares or stallions. Because a gelding isn't as easily distracted by the promise of romance, he's usually quite happy to co-exist on strictly platonic terms with other horses. Even better, he's more likely to devote his full attention to you and the work you have in mind for him.

Size

To a large degree, the size and shape of your own body will influence the size and conformation of the horse you choose. Matching the body type of the horse with that of the rider is important. The horse and rider need to be physically compatible to make a good team.

While the height of the horse might be your first consideration, it's also important to pay attention to the length of his legs and the shape of his body and his barrel. Ideally, the horse's height and barrel size will be such that when you're properly seated, you can easily apply pressure with your lower legs to the horse's sides, both at the girth and behind it.

If you're tall and have a large frame and long legs, you probably won't be able to ride your best on a shallow-bodied, narrow-barreled horse, as your upper body may dwarf the horse and your feet may dangle below his belly. If you're a short woman, you'll have more trouble mounting a 17-hand giant, and once you're in the saddle, you may feel like you're on a pedestal. Even a 14-hand pony with an extra-wide barrel may be too big for you to ride comfortably and confidently, especially if your legs reach only halfway down the horses' sides.

With that said, plenty of petite women manage to ride tall, big-barreled horses successfully, and it's not impossible for large-framed women to do very well astride smaller horses. What's most important is that you and the horse are safe and comfortable as a team, and you're able to use your legs, seat, and hands to control and communicate effectively with your horse while you're riding.

If you're not planning on competing in the show ring, how you feel on the horse is far more important than how you look. You should feel secure, comfortable, and confident, especially while you're learning. If you're going to be showing, on the other hand, you'll have to consider the aesthetics of your team, and you'll want to make sure that you and your horse are appropriately matched and properly balanced in size and other physical characteristics.

If you're a little heavier than you'd like to be, you may wonder if your weight is too great for a particular horse to carry. In general, heavy riders should look for wide-bodied or stocky horses that are not only sound but are also in good physical condition. In general, horses with good legs and feet; short, strong backs; and deep bodies are most suitable for heavy riders. Regardless of the horse's build, you may have to ride him lightly at first if he's out of shape. As his strength, stamina, and level of conditioning improve, you gradually can increase the duration and intensity of your rides.

Color

Some experienced horsewomen will tell you that you should strive to be as color-blind as possible when you're buying a horse, as there's no such thing as a good horse of a bad color. While this is generally true, a horse's color can make a difference in a few instances. If, for example, you want to buy and show a horse that belongs to a particular color breed, including a Palomino or a buckskin, color is of major importance. Even within some breeds, certain colors and markings are discriminated against in the show ring. An exceptionally wide blaze or a bald face may be a desirable attribute for a Clydesdale, for instance, but it may be considered unattractive or even unacceptable on an American Saddlebred. If you're serious about showing your horse, it's a good idea to know about these preferences and prejudices prior to making your purchase.

If you find the right teammate, and his color and markings are acceptable for his breed, you should think long and hard about passing him up simply because his coat is gray instead of chestnut or chestnut instead of bay. The more determined you are to have a horse of a particular color, the greater your risk of ending up with a horse that's less suitable for you in other ways, including level of training and disposition.

Nature and Disposition

Like people, horses have unique personalities formed and influenced by a number of factors, including genetics and past experiences, both good and bad. Never buy a horse with the belief that you will be able to change his personality. Although it may be possible, it's just not all that likely. If a horse is, grumpy by nature, chances are excellent he will remain grumpy no matter how kind or patient you are. If a horse is high strung and nervous now, he'll prob-

ably continue to be high strung and nervous. A horse's personality, nature, and disposition are deeply ingrained, and it is not always possible to change these characteristics under ordinary — or even extraordinary — circumstances.

The horse's body language will tell you a lot about his personality, his attitude toward people, and his willingness to work. When you approach him in his stall or paddock, does he seem happy to see you? If he turns toward you with his ears forward, it's a good sign. If he ignores you, or even worse, if he puts his ears back and walks or runs away from you, you can bet that he's not all that interested in — or happy about — seeing you. When you lead him, does he respect you and your personal space or does he try to walk all over you? Does he stand quietly and accept the bit readily while being saddled and bridled?

It is true that with enough love, patience, and proper training, even a sour, resistant horse can be transformed into a pleasant, willing mount, but this is the exception rather than the rule. Owning a horse is challenging enough, even under the best of circumstances. If you start out with a problem horse, there's a good possibility that horse ownership will be so challenging that it's no longer enjoyable.

There's no doubt that adverse circumstances can produce temporary or transient changes in a horse's attitude and behavior. If a horse is uncomfortable or stressed, either mentally or physically, he may behave very differently than he would in a more secure setting. There's no way to know for sure without removing the horse from his environment. If the current owner will allow you to take the horse for a trial period, it may be worth the effort. If this isn't a possibility, it's probably best to assume the horse's personality isn't going to change much, if any.

For beginning riders, it's important to choose a pleasant, patient, and relatively quiet horse. He should be willing to work and tolerant of your honest mistakes. A horse that is mean, flighty, or fearful may have perfectly good reasons for being so, but that doesn't make him any less unsuitable or unsafe for a novice rider.

Where To Buy

If you have your heart set on a particular breed, it may make sense for you to begin your search with a breeder, and you can get a list of breeders in your area from national, state, and local breed associations. Most established breeders are knowledgeable, and they're more than willing to work with novices and newcomers. Don't hesitate to take advantage of their years of experience and learn all you can from them.

As a rule you can count on reputable breeders to take good care of their stock. In most cases horses raised on successful breeding farms have had excellent nutrition and regular farrier work since birth. They're also likely to be up to date in their vaccinations, deworming regimens, and routine veterinary check-ups.

Since breeders have a reputation to uphold, they'll typically work hard to help you find a safe and suitable horse, and they may offer some type of guarantee that the horses they sell are sound and healthy. Even better, some breeders will allow you to take a horse on a trial basis to make sure the two of you are compatible as a team.

Private Sales

Buying a horse from his current owner can be an excellent way to end up with the horse of your dreams. It's not unusual to find a seller who is parting with a much-loved, well-schooled horse out of necessity. The current owner may be a teenager going off to college or a rider who is ready to move up to a more challenging mount. A seller who genuinely loves her horse is highly motivated to make sure the horse will be a good match for the new owner. You can expect this type of owner to be very honest about the horse's attributes and shortcomings, and you'll probably find she'll allow you to visit and ride the horse a number of times before you make your final decision.

You can find horses for sale by private owners at riding barns and boarding stables, in the classified section of newspapers, on bulletin boards at tack and feed stores, and on the Internet. Don't forget to check with veterinarians and farriers as they're often the first to know when an owner is planning to sell a horse.

Horse Auctions

When you purchase a horse at public sale, you should plan on taking the horse you buy at face value. It's not impossible to get a good horse at auction, but it can be difficult, and it's always risky business. As you may not get to meet the horse's current owner, it's often hard to learn much about the horse's history. When the bidding begins, you'll be required to make a quick decision based on a very limited amount of information, and once the hammer falls, there's no turning back. If you don't want to take this kind of chance, you're better off looking for your dream horse elsewhere.

The Pre-purchase Exam

If you've ever bought a used car, you may have taken it to a reliable mechanic for a thorough once-over before you signed the check or the contract that made it your own. If you didn't, you may have wished later you had. For a specified fee, a qualified mechanic will kick the tires and take a look under the hood to evaluate a car's state of automotive health. While you may not have any reason to doubt the salesman's glowing appraisal of the vehicle in question, it just makes good sense to get an unbiased opinion from a qualified third party. It's even better to get an opinion from someone with your best interests at heart, whether it's your own trusted mechanic or a friend or family member with a thorough understanding of the inner workings of automobiles.

The pre-purchase examination of a horse is similar to that of a car, at least in theory. It is performed by a qualified equine veterinarian who is working for you, the buyer. Its purpose is to determine the health and soundness of the horse you're considering buying so that you can make a fully informed decision before parting with your hard-earned cash. The pre-purchase exam is a top-to-tail inspection of the horse that includes an evaluation of the horse's structural soundness, eyes, mouth, respiratory system, skin, joints, legs, and hooves, both at rest and at work or under saddle, if appropriate. The examination will vary slightly from one veterinarian to the next, and it will be modified to fit the age, breed, and gender of the horse, as well as the type of work he'll be expected to perform.

Even if you're considering buying a horse that will be more of a pet than a performance horse, or even if a horse owner or breeder offers to give you a horse at no cost and with no strings attached, it's wise to invest in a pre-purchase exam. What if you buy a $500 horse only to discover that he needs a $1,000 worth of medicine to clear up a smoldering infection? Knowing this may not change your decision to buy or accept the horse, but at least you'll have a better idea of what lies ahead of you. Armed with the appropriate knowledge, you'll be able to adjust your plans — and your budget — accordingly. In addition to saving you money, the pre-purchase examination can end up saving you a great deal of time, energy, and frustration.

Choosing the Right Veterinarian

Although it's not always practical or even possible, it's best to hire an equine veterinarian who is experienced in diagnosing and treating horses involved in the relevant equestrian discipline. If you're considering buying a racehorse, you wouldn't want to hire a veterinarian whose practice is limited to draft horses. Racing predisposes horses to certain types of injury and unsoundness, and it is important that your vet be aware of these. Likewise, horses of certain breeds are vulnerable to particular diseases, and it's the veterinarian's job not only to know about these diseases but also to recognize them.

History of the Horse

Prior to the examination, all health records pertaining to the horse you're considering buying should be made available to you, the prospective buyer, as well as to the examining veterinarian. This will allow you and the vet to identify any potential areas of concern ahead of time and to address them during the exam. The records should document the horse's veterinary medical and surgical history, complete with breeding, immunization, and deworming schedules.

The owner should willingly disclose any history of colic, previous surgeries, episodes of lameness, or other illnesses or injuries experienced by the horse. It's also helpful for both you and your vet to have access to records pertaining to the horse's training, performance, and show career as those records will allow you to understand the kinds of stresses the horse has been subjected to.

Putting the Prospect Through His Paces

Whenever possible, the veterinarian should observe the horse being ridden in the manner you intend to ride him. If you plan to jump the horse, the vet should watch the horse work over fences. If you plan to compete in barrel-racing events, the vet should watch the horse run barrels. This may seem like overkill, but it often allows the vet to spot a problem not immediately obvious on physical inspection.

The Cost of the Exam

When compared to the purchase price and ongoing costs associated with horse ownership, the expense of the pre-purchase examination is a mere drop in the bucket. It's also a very small price to pay if it prevents you from buying a horse that is sick, unsound, or unsuitable for your intended purposes. The cost of a pre-purchase examination, which typically falls in the range of $250 to $500, is money well spent for the peace of mind it can offer.

The Perfect Horse

While there's no such thing as a horse that is perfect in every respect, it is entirely possible to find a horse that is right for you. When you're considering buying a particular horse, it's helpful to keep a running list of the horse's attributes and faults. Some faults may not matter to you. If you're not planning to show your horse, you may not mind that he's got a bit of a Roman nose as it won't interfere with his ability to serve as a suitable mount for trail riding. If, on the other hand, the horse has a leg problem that predisposes him to lameness, he's not likely to be a good trail horse, and you'll need to cross him off the list. When you've learned as much about the horse as you can, you can weigh the horse's strengths against his weaknesses and make a rational decision about whether the horse will be a good teammate. In the end, the final decision is up to you. You have to determine which faults you can live with and which are unacceptable for your purposes.

Rein In Your Emotions

The more you love horses, the more you'll have to guard against making a purchase based solely on your emotions. Remember, the goal is to find and buy a horse that is right for you, right now. The horse you end up with may not be the most beautiful horse, and it may not be the horse with the best training or the best pedigree, but all things considered, it should be the best possible teammate for you.

As you go about your search, you'll undoubtedly come across a horse or two that strikes your fancy for all the wrong reasons, and you may be tempted to buy it based solely on your feelings rather than cold, hard facts. You might encounter a horse so incredibly beautiful you're tempted to overlook his bad manners or a horse that has such a sweet and endearing personality you're willing to ignore his conformation flaws and his lack of soundness. You may even come across a horse or two you feel compelled to rescue from less than perfect circumstances.

If you have a history of making decisions with your heart rather than your head, you'll definitely want to enlist the help of an objec-

tive, experienced horse person who can help you walk away — or even drag you away — from the wrong horse. It's also a good idea to decide on a mandatory "cooling off" period ahead of time so you don't make a regrettable decision in the heat of the moment. Before you sign a contract or a check, give yourself at least 24 hours to step back from the situation, think things through, and address any doubts that may surface in the interim.

Boarding Your Horse

Long before you purchase your horse, you'll need to decide where your horse will live. If you own a barn and fenced land, you may plan to bring your horse home, but if you're not a landowner, you'll need to choose a suitable boarding facility. Where your horse lives will have a huge impact on his health and happiness, and it also will have a major influence on your ability to have a safe, enjoyable, and rewarding experience as a horse owner.

The Stay-at-home Horse

Caring for your horse on your own property may seem to be more convenient and slightly less costly than boarding him elsewhere, but this isn't always the case. The expenses associated with the upkeep of a barn and land — not to mention a horse — can be enormous, and the demands on your time can be far greater than you might initially suspect.

Cost and convenience aside, assuming full responsibility for the care of your horse on your own property can have a number of additional drawbacks. For starters, it can get pretty lonely, for both you and your horse. As herd animals, most horses are happiest in the company of other horses. Unlike your horse, you may find that you're perfectly content in the absence of other humans, at least for a few hours at a time. Still, when you're riding and caring for your horse in relative isolation, you'll miss out on having a readily accessible support group to offer information, advice, and assistance.

As the owner and manager of a one-horse operation, you may find you have a little more difficulty persuading a veterinarian or farrier to travel to your farm. If they agree, you can probably expect them to charge a little extra for making a trip to attend to a single horse.

When you're caring for your horse on your own property, you'll assume several new roles. In addition to being a rider, you'll also be the farm manager, groom, stablehand, and maintenance worker. You'll be in charge of scheduling visits with the veterinarian and farrier, as well as overseeing the purchase, delivery, and storage of feed, hay, bedding, and other necessary equipment and supplies. As a result, you're likely to have far less time for riding than you would if you boarded your horse at a full-service stable.

Boarding Your Horse

In many ways, selecting a suitable boarding stable for your horse is like choosing a day-care center for your child. In other ways, it's more like selecting a gym or a social club for yourself. No matter where your search takes you,

your first concern should be for the safety of you and your horse. The facility should have an enclosed riding ring or arena with good footing and a level, well-drained surface. The stables and fences should be constructed of sturdy materials that don't pose a danger to horses or humans. The barn, paddocks, and pastures should be free of farm implements or other objects that could cause injury.

Not only should stalls be clean, dry, and bedded with a suitable material, they also should be properly lighted and ventilated. Feed and hay should be properly stored to prevent mold, infestation, and contamination. The staff should be dependable, knowledgeable, and capable, and they should show a genuine interest in providing the best possible care for your horse.

If you're fortunate enough to find more than one boarding facility that provides all of these essentials at an affordable price, you'll have the luxury of considering other, less critical factors, including the atmosphere and the ambience of the place. Every barn and stable has a unique culture, and it won't take long for you to know if it's one that will make you feel welcome and comfortable. Is there a spirit of camaraderie among the boarders, or is it every rider for herself? Are the other boarders reasonably courteous and well behaved, or does there seem to be an inordinate amount of cursing and stomping and storming around? It's always nice to mix and mingle with other boarders who are not only pleasant but also share similar equestrian interests so that you can ride and work together when you feel like company. As you'll undoubtedly be spending a great deal of time at the barn, you'll want to make sure it provides a relaxed, stress-free environment for you and your horse.

Daily and Monthly Expenses

Buying a horse can be expensive, but owning a horse can put an even bigger strain on your finances. When it's all said and done, the initial purchase price of your horse may be far overshadowed by the ongoing daily and monthly costs associated with horse ownership. In most cases, you can expect feed and board to account for your greatest outlay of cash, but these expenses vary tremendously, depending on where the horse is housed. If you're able to keep your horse on your own property, you won't be burdened with a monthly boarding bill, but you'll still be faced with plenty of other expenses. Barns and fences will require routine maintenance and mending, and fields will need fertilizing and mowing. No matter where your horse calls home, he's got to eat. If he's kept outdoors in a paddock or pasture, your feed bill may be lower in the summer, but he'll likely need grain and hay in the winter months.

Total feed and board costs charged by boarding stables can range from a couple hundred dollars to more than a thousand dollars per month, depending on accommodations, servic-

es, and location. Additional monthly expenses include those associated with veterinary and farrier services, grooming supplies and products, tack and equipment, and possibly insurance to cover the life or health of your horse.

If you're planning to show your horse, you'll need to consider the cost of competing. You may not have to buy a truck and trailer if you and your horse can hitch a ride to the shows, but you'll still have to chip in to cover the cost of transportation. Entry fees may be as little as $10 a class or as much as several hundred dollars. If you're planning on stabling your horse at the showground, you'll have to pay the stall fee. Because bedding isn't included, you'll either have to take your own or purchase straw or shavings once you arrive on the show grounds. Depending on the class and the show, you may have to buy special show attire for yourself and special tack for your horse. Both can be quite costly.

Even before you begin your search for the perfect horse, you should plan a monthly budget. To avoid miscalculating, it's best to find out the actual costs of the products and services you'll need. Although it takes a little extra time, it's well worth the effort of contacting the boarding stable, veterinarian, farrier, and feed store to determine their actual prices in advance. Knowing your expenses ahead of time can help you avoid frustration and excessive financial pressure in the future.

SAMPLE BUDGET

ALTHOUGH HORSE-RELATED EXPENSES CAN VARY TREMENDOUSLY, this sample budget will give you a better idea about the range of costs you'll likely incur in purchasing and owning a horse.

PURCHASING EXPENSES	High ($)	Low ($)
Purchase price of the horse	7,500	1,500
Pre-purchase exam	500	250
Transportation of the horse to his new home	300	25
($.25 per mile to $.75 per mile)		
Total purchasing expenses	**$8,300**	**$1,775**

EQUIPMENT COSTS	High ($)	Low ($)
Stable Equipment		
Feed bin	75	20
Water bucket	50	20
Manure fork	60	20
Rake	60	20
Shovel	60	20
Broom	50	10
Wheelbarrow or stable cart	350	50
Grooming tools and supplies	300	30
First-aid items	300	50
Total stable equipment cost	**$1,305**	**$240**
Tack		
Saddle and saddle pad	2,500	250

Bridle and bit	250	50
Halter	50	15
Lead rope	30	10
Stable blanket	300	75
Miscellaneous tack	250	50
Total tack cost	**$3,380**	**$450**

MONTHLY EXPENSES	High ($)	Low ($)
Monthly board	500	200
Grain, if not included in board ($1.50 to $3 per day)	90	45
Hay, if not included in board ($2 to $4 per day)	120	60
Bedding, if not included in board ($.50 to $2 per day)	60	15
Nutritional supplements	100	10
Vaccines ($50 to $200 per year)	16	4
Deworming ($75 to $300 per year)	25	6
Miscellaneous veterinary services ($75 to $750 per year)	63	6
Farrier services ($20 to $35 every 4-8 weeks for trimming and $40 to $150 every 4-8 weeks for shoeing)	150	10
Riding lessons ($20 to $50 per hour, one to two hours per week)	400	80
Horse training	500	100
Total monthly expenses	**$2,024**	**$536**

PRE-PURCHASE BUDGET WORKSHEET

AFTER CHECKING THE PRICES OF PRODUCTS, EQUIPMENT, AND SERVICES in your area, you'll be ready to fill out the worksheet below. When you're finished, you'll have a realistic idea about the costs associated with owning a horse.

PURCHASING EXPENSES	Enter Dollar Amount
Purchase of the horse	$
Pre-purchase exam	$
Transportation of the horse to his new home	$
Subtotal	**$**

MONTHLY EXPENSES	
Monthly board	$
Grain (if not included in board)	$
Hay (if not included in board)	$
Bedding (if not included in board)	$
Nutritional supplements	$
Vaccines	$
Deworming	$
Miscellaneous veterinary services	$
Farrier services	$
Riding lessons	$
Horse training	$
Subtotal	**$**

EQUIPMENT COSTS

Enter Dollar Amount

Stable Equipment

Feed bin	$
Water buckets	$
Manure fork	$
Rake	$
Shovel	$
Broom	$
Wheelbarrow or stable cart	$
Grooming tools and supplies	$
First-aid items	$

Tack

Saddle and saddle pad	$
Bridle	$
Halter	$
Lead rope	$
Stable blanket	$
Miscellaneous tack	$
Subtotal	**$**

TOTAL EXPENSES

Purchasing expenses	$
Monthly expenses	$
Equipment costs	$
Total	**$**

where there's a will, there's a way

OVERCOMING OBSTACLES

If you've always wanted a horse in your life and don't have one, have you ever thought about why? Or if you're involved with horses but not to the extent you'd like, what's standing in your way? Why aren't you living your dream? There's probably a perfectly logical reason — maybe even several. But ordinary logic doesn't necessarily apply to our dreams. Dreams are governed by far more powerful phenomena, including desire, determination, and drive.

While writing this book, I had the privilege of meeting and interviewing horsewomen from all over the country. Some were aspiring equestrians with a deep longing to bring horses into their lives and still searching for a way to make it happen. Some were established horsewomen who had made horses a significant part of their busy lives. Finally, some were completely entrenched — these were the full-time trainers, riding instructors, breeders, judges, and equestrian competitors who had built their careers and their lives around horses.

In my conversations with these individuals, I found the vast majority had, at one time or another, encountered seemingly insurmountable obstacles on their journeys to becoming horsewomen or to becoming better or more committed horsewomen. Some just didn't have the money to invest in a horse and all the necessary accoutrements. Other women had worked hard and enjoyed financial success in their careers but were left with little free time to enjoy the fruits of their labor. Some were mothers with full-time jobs, already stretched thin by the demands of working and raising children. For many women, lack of support from spouses, significant others, or family members was a stumbling block. Finally, most of the women I interviewed had experienced some degree of self-doubt along the way. They simply weren't sure they had what it took — either mentally or physically — to accomplish their dreams, even if all the obstacles standing before them miraculously disappeared.

In my conversations with these women, I also learned one major difference between aspiring horsewomen and highly accomplished horsewomen. It wasn't that the accomplished horsewomen had faced fewer obstacles along the way, but rather they had successfully found ways to overcome them. As you might expect, there was no one-size-fits-all answer; each woman searched and sometimes struggled to find the solution that worked best for her at a particular time in her life.

Not every solution was perfect or even a

permanent one. Without exception, compromises and sacrifices had to be made. In some instances, the tradeoffs were minor: Spending more time at the barn meant giving up sleeping late on the weekends and learning to live with a less-than-immaculate house. Buying a new saddle meant making do with last year's wardrobe; purchasing a horse trailer meant putting off buying a new vehicle. In other cases the sacrifices were more substantial: turning down a job promotion because it involved travel or responsibilities that resulted in too much time away from the barn or losing touch with a friend who didn't share a love of horses.

Although sacrifices are inevitable, they are offset by the tremendous rewards of pursuing a passion and accomplishing a dream. Becoming involved with horses opens a whole new world filled with new friends, greater challenges, and important self-discoveries. It's a world where self-confidence grows and self-esteem flourishes.

I asked Lisa, a 25-year-old chemical engineer from Aiken, South Carolina, about her goals and dreams as an equestrian.

"My dream is to buy a show jumper in the next year and start competing," she said without missing a beat. "I've already found the horse I want. His name is Cavalcade — Cal for short. He's this big, beautiful, Thoroughbred gelding, and he's in my price range. I've jumped him several times, and we were made for each other."

I was curious about why Lisa hadn't already bought the gelding, especially as he was made for her and price wasn't a problem. I asked her what was standing in the way.

"Well, I already have a mare, Maggie, and I really don't need two horses," she explained. "I don't think I would be happy trying to take good care of both of them. I spend a lot of time at work, and I don't have time to give two horses the attention they need."

"What's the solution?" I asked. "What would have to happen for you to overcome this obstacle?"

"Well, I'd have to sell Maggie, and that's a little scary to me," she admitted. "She was my first horse, and I want her to be loved and well-cared for."

I sympathized with Lisa. I know parting with a beloved horse is difficult. At the same time, it's obvious Lisa's mare isn't capable of helping her achieve her dream; in fact, she's keeping Lisa from attaining it.

"What would it take for you to overcome this obstacle in a way that is acceptable to you?" I prodded.

"I'd have to sell Maggie to the right person," she said. "Her new owner would have to take really good care of her and love her as much as I do."

Now we were getting somewhere. "Do you think there's any possibility that you could find a new owner who fits this description?"

Lisa nodded. "I do. She's a great horse, and she would be perfect for a child or a beginner."

Lisa agreed it was highly unlikely the right new owner — or even the wrong one, for that matter — would spontaneously appear, cash

DEFINING YOUR DREAM

BEFORE YOU CAN ACCOMPLISH ANY DREAM IN LIFE, YOU HAVE TO DEFINE IT. You have to know what you want. Do you want a horse of your own? Or a better horse? Do you dream of becoming a more skilled equestrian, a full-time horse trainer, a successful horse breeder, or an Olympic competitor? Take a few minutes to define your dream by writing it in the space below. Remind yourself you're capable of great things, so there's no need to hold back!

What's standing in your way?

Now that you have a better vision of your dream, take another minute or two to identify what's preventing you from achieving it. Is it a jam-packed schedule and a lack of time? Is it a shortage of money, confidence, or support? List the primary obstacles you face:

1. _____

2. _____

3. _____

Now, ask yourself what needs to happen to overcome each obstacle. Do you need to rearrange your schedule or come up with some extra money? Do you need to convince a family member to support you? Write your answers below:

What's standing in your way?

What has to happen for you to overcome this obstacle?

Obstacles:

1. _____

2. _____

3. _____

Solutions:

1. _____

2. _____

3. _____

Now, let's take a look at your "solutions" list. What three actions could you take in the immediate future — I'm talking about hours, days, or weeks here — that would contribute to the solution?

Solutions:

1. a. _____

   b. _____

   c. _____

2. a. _____

   b. _____

   c. _____

3. a. _____

   b. _____

   c. _____

Actions:

1. a. _____

   b. _____

   c. _____

2. a. _____

   b. _____

   c. _____

3. a. _____

   b. _____

   c. _____

in hand, begging to buy Maggie. It would take some initiative and effort on Lisa's behalf. I asked her to list three actions she could take in the immediate future to help her overcome her obstacle and move her closer to her dream of buying Cal. Here's what she wrote:

1. Make a flier advertising Maggie and post it at the barn, feed store, tack store, and vet's office

2. Put an ad in the local paper

3. Call local vets, farriers, and riding instructors to find out whether they know of anyone in the market for a gentle, well-schooled mare

Lisa was still a little apprehensive about the possibility of Maggie ending up in the wrong hands, but she realized she could always say no to a potential buyer who didn't seem a good fit. Lisa also understood she needed to do *something* if she wanted to become Cal's new owner. By taking action, she increased her chances of overcoming this obstacle and moving closer to her dream.

Understanding Your Priorities in Life

Lisa's dream of buying and showing a jumper involved a substantial sacrifice: giving up her mare, Maggie. There's a very good chance that as you realize your dream, you'll have to make sacrifices. Will the satisfaction that comes from achieving your goals justify the sacrifice that must be made? No one can answer this question but you. While there's no way to be completely sure in advance, you'll undoubtedly be happiest when your decision matches your priorities in life.

Understanding and Updating Your Priorities

It would be nice if we didn't have so many difficult choices in life, but there's really no way around it. We each have a very finite set of resources. We have a limited amount of time: There are only so many hours in every day, and only so many days in every week, month, year, and lifetime. We have a limited amount of money to spend and a limited amount of energy to devote to various activities and endeavors. As a result, we're forced to make tough decisions and complicated choices about how to allocate our precious resources. In a perfect world, it would all boil down to our priorities. We would spend the greatest amount of time, money, and energy on the people, pastimes, and passions most important to us — whoever and whatever is nearest and dearest to our hearts.

The reality is we get caught up in minutiae and minor crises of everyday life and often lose sight of our priorities. We may find ourselves investing time and energy in activities that aren't really all that important to us or even good for us. As we grow and mature, our priorities inevitably change. What seemed a matter of life and death 10 years ago may not even interest us in the slightest today.

Because some priorities change and because we lose sight of others, it's helpful to re-examine our priorities and update them from time to time. It's important to make sure you're investing your time and energy — the stuff of your life — in meaningful and fulfilling ways. Living inconsistently with your priorities is a tremendous source of stress, frustration, and unhappiness.

MY LIFE PRIORITIES

1. _____

2. _____

3. _____

4. _____

5. _____

6. _____

7. _____

8. _____

9. _____

10. _____

If, for example, spending time with your children is a top priority, you'll undoubtedly feel incredibly stressed and unhappy if your job requires you to be away from them for days on end. If staying physically fit is important to you, yet your schedule is so full that you rarely have time to exercise, you'll probably experience a great deal of frustration. When your actions and activities aren't aligned with your priorities, you feel out of kilter. Sadly, some women carry on with their lives, day after day, month after month, living in ways inconsistent with their priorities. They may realize they're miserable in their present circumstances, but they may not fully understand why.

To be true to yourself and to maximize your happiness, satisfaction, and fulfillment, it's important to align your life with your priorities. But first you have to identify and acknowledge them. For many women, top priorities include family, friends, spirituality, physical health, career, financial growth, and recreation and leisure. These are just examples — there's no such thing as a wrong answer. If something is important to you and you feel it is well worth the investment of your time, money, effort, and energy, then it qualifies as a priority. Take a few minutes to write down your priorities. List at least five, but no more than 10, in the worksheet.

How Does Your Garden Grow?

Your life priorities are like gardens — each

needs a certain amount of regular care and attention to germinate, grow, and bear fruit. Specific tasks must be performed on a daily, weekly, monthly, and yearly basis to keep these gardens thriving.

When it comes to tending the garden that is your physical health, for example, daily tasks may include brushing your teeth, drinking eight glasses of water, getting seven to eight hours of sleep, and eating a nutritious, balanced diet. You may make a point of exercising several times a week, visiting your dentist every six months or so, and scheduling a complete physical exam once a year. Neglecting any of these daily, weekly, or yearly activities may save you a little time in the short run, but you'll undoubtedly have to pay the piper in the long run. If you deprive yourself of an hour or two of sleep each weeknight, you'll have to repay your sleep debt on the weekend. If you stop brushing your teeth daily, you'll probably end up spending more time in the dentist's office.

Most women find their lives are far smoother and less stressful if they make the effort and take the time to tend their gardens regularly, rather than on a crisis-management basis. If you neglect them, even for short periods, they'll dry up or become choked with weeds. If you continue to withhold your attention, they'll eventually die altogether.

The amount of time and attention your gardens require isn't constant; it changes according to the season. Preparing your garden is labor intensive and time consuming. You have to turn the soil, hoe the rows, and plant the seeds. While you're waiting for the seeds to germinate, there may be little effort required of you, but you'll be busy again during the growing season and even busier when it comes time to gather your harvest.

The gardens of your life will be in different stages at different times. While you're reaping the fruits of your labor in your health garden, for example, you may be waiting for the seeds to germinate in your career garden and adding fertilizer to your friendship garden. A garden that has practically maintained itself for years may suddenly undergo a change that requires your immediate attention — an aging parent who needs your assistance, a new project at work, or a friend experiencing a crisis.

When it comes to making decisions about the allocation of your precious, finite resources — especially your time and energy — it's helpful to determine which gardens these resources are sustaining. Are you investing most of your time, effort, and energy in the people, pastimes, and passions you have identified as most important to you? It's easy enough to find out. All you have to do is take a look at your typical weekly schedule. Of the 168 hours in every week, how many hours are you spending in ways that are meaningful and fulfilling and that bring you closer to your goals?

I asked this question of Rachel, a part-time medical billing clerk, mother of two, and aspiring horsewoman from Cambridge, Ohio. Before she could answer, she first had to identify her priorities, or gardens, in life. Here's what Rachel's list looked like:

RACHEL'S LIFE PRIORITIES

Family

Spirituality and religion

Career

Friends

Community service and charity

Leisure, recreation, and hobbies

Physical health

Next, I asked Rachel to list the activities she performs regularly and to determine how they contribute to each area of her life she deems most important. Here's what she wrote:

Family: Spend one to two hours each day after school with my daughters (sometimes driving them back and forth to soccer and piano lessons), try to schedule a "date night" twice a month with my husband, family vacations to the beach each summer, family ski trips a couple of weekends each winter.

Spirituality and religion: Pray and read devotionals on a daily basis, attend worship services two hours a week with my husband and daughters.

Career: Work 20 hours a week, attend monthly meetings and planning sessions with my boss, attend training programs once or twice a year.

Friends: Visit Linda (my next-door neighbor) several times a week, call Pam at least once a week and try to get together once or twice a month, meet Elizabeth at the barn once a week for riding lessons.

Community Service and Charity: Take meals to elderly shut-ins once a month with my women's group from church; volunteer at my daughters' school, reading to the class and going on field trips once or twice a month; tithe monthly.

Leisure, Recreation, Hobbies: Take the girls skating, shopping, or to a movie once a month; take riding lessons once a week; read a few chapters of a good book every week; watch television most evenings with the girls and my husband; go snow skiing a couple times a year.

Physical Health: Jog on the treadmill for 20 minutes three or four days a week, watch what I eat every day, ride bikes with my girls on the weekends, see my gynecologist for a check-up once a year.

Reading Rachel's list of life priorities, it's obvious that many of her daily and weekly activities nurture more than one garden — there's some crossover. For example, Rachel spends time with Elizabeth as a way of nurturing their friendship, but once a week she and Elizabeth take riding lessons together, which also allows Rachel to invest in her physical health, leisure, and recreation. When Rachel volunteers to read to her daughters' classes at school, she's not only honoring her commitment to her children, she's fulfilling her need to serve her community. Any activity that nurtures at least one garden in your life is likely a good investment of your resources, and if it simultaneously nurtures two or more gardens, so much the better.

I asked Rachel if there was a garden that she felt she was neglecting or if there was one that she hadn't yet started. She said that one day she'd like to travel, but it wasn't a major priority at this point. Rachel admitted she wanted to spend more time riding, and, eventually, she'd like to compete in horse shows.

"What I'd really like to do," she said, "is move 'horses' out of the leisure garden of my life into a garden of its own. I want to have my own horse and ride four or five days a week instead of just one. That's what I'm working toward."

I asked her why she hadn't done it yet.

"I just don't have the time right now," she explained. "I try to work it into my schedule, but something else always comes up."

As Rachel and I discussed her schedule from the previous week, it was obvious she spent most of her time and energy in the major gardens of her life — family, friends, spirituality, and career. She was surprised to find that on most days of the week, she spent about three hours watching television, an activity that she didn't plan, and one that she didn't feel contributed much to her overall happiness or sense of fulfillment.

"Watching television is definitely not one of my life priorities," she insisted. "If I planned my days a little better, I could spend some of that time at the barn riding."

Breaking Barriers

Lack of Time

If you told me that there's simply no way you can squeeze another activity into your busy life, whether it's taking a single riding lesson once a week or spending an extra hour at the barn every day to prepare yourself and your horse for an upcoming competition, I wouldn't doubt you for a minute. When I contemplate the demands and constraints of my own schedule and those of my female friends, co-workers, and patients, I wonder how we manage to do it all. Most of us are already working hard to stay on top of our incredibly busy lives, which often come complete with high-pressure careers, close relationships with friends and family, active children, and aging parents. It's easy to feel as if we're being pulled in a dozen different directions, and it's perfectly understandable that any non-essential activities or hobbies would take a backseat to matters that seem far more urgent.

Taking Care of the Caretaker

Sometimes when women say, "I don't have time to ride," what they really mean is, "I don't take time to ride, because I don't make time for myself." Many women spend so much of their time helping and caring for others that at the end of the day, there's none left to take care of themselves.

It's important to realize taking time for yourself isn't a matter of being selfish — it's a matter of survival. Women who continue to shortchange themselves day after day, year after year often end up losing touch with who they are and what they need to be happy and fulfilled. They begin to feel empty, and when they do, they have very little left to give the people around them.

If you're not carving out a little time for yourself every day, or at least a couple of times a week, you really need to rethink your strategy. Just as there's no shortage of people who are more than willing to help you spend your money, there are plenty of people who will help you spend your time in ways not always in your best interest. Because your time is so precious, and because how you spend it is a huge determinant of your happiness, it's very important to guard it carefully and invest it wisely. It's noble and generous to use some of it to help others accomplish their goals and objectives, but it's critical to save a little time for yourself so that you can realize your own potential and achieve your own dreams.

If horses are your passion, and you've made up your mind that one way or another you're going to pursue it, the rest is pretty straight-forward. All you have to do is find a few holes in your schedule. No matter how busy you are right now, there's an excellent chance that you can find — or make — a couple of hours a week to call your own.

Where Does the Time Go?

The first step is to take inventory. You've got 24 hours in each day, and 168 hours in each week. Where is all that time going? If you've got a full-time job, most of your time is likely spent working and sleeping. Let's say that you work 40 hours a week, and you spend another 12 hours showering, dressing, and commuting to work. That's a total of 52 hours a week. Hopefully, you're getting about $7\frac{1}{2}$ hours of sleep each night and an average of 30 minutes of exercise each day. If you're lucky, you're spending at least an hour a day eating your meals sitting down in a relatively relaxed manner. That's another 63 hours accounted for.

Now, you've got 53 hours remaining in your week. If you have school-age children, you may spend about three hours a day with them. Laundry, pet care, meal preparation, and other household chores can easily consume an hour a day, and if you attend religious services, you may spend about two hours each week in your house of worship. Just to be safe, let's say that other commitments consume another hour a day. That's an additional 37 hours a week accounted for.

When it's all said and done, you may have just 16 glorious hours a week at your disposal. What will you do with these golden hours of opportunity? The easiest thing is to collapse on the couch, turn on the television, turn off your brain, and take a well-deserved rest. That's what the vast majority of Americans do. By the age of 70, most will have spent more than a decade of their lives in front of the television. With such a grueling schedule, no one would begrudge you a little mindless tube time. But is this really what you want your free time to be about? Is this what you want your life to be about? Sitting on the sideline watching other people live their dreams? Of course not. You've got the leading role in your very own reality show called *My Life*, and this is not a dress rehearsal — the tape is rolling.

You've got some important dreams to accomplish before calling it a wrap, and because you don't have a lot of time to waste, you might as well get busy!

The Greatest Time Management Tools of All

Like most busy women, I'm always on the lookout for ways to improve my efficiency and muscle more free time into each day. I've read a number of excellent time-management books and articles, and I've even attended a seminar or two on the topic. While I've picked up some very useful tools and tips, I laugh like a hyena whenever some extra-helpful expert suggests women learn to do more in less time. Why just brush your teeth when you could be scrubbing your teeth with one hand and your toilet bowl with the other? Heaven forbid you should use your commute to and from work to relax and clear your mind when you could be learning a second language on CD, balancing your check-book on your laptop, or spouting off your mile-long to-do list into a miniature tape recorder.

This kind of "do more in less time" philosophy fails to take into account that the vast majority of women are already champion multi-taskers. Not only did we invent the concept of multi-tasking, we perfected it and then pushed it to pathological extremes. When it comes to doing a dozen different things at once, women rule! The last thing we need is someone to teach us how to do more in less time. What we really need to learn is simply how to do less. When we stop trying to do everything, we can spend more time doing what is most important to us.

Learning to Say No

Sometimes, doing less involves saying no to others. Although the word "no" is one of the simplest utterances in the English language, it's one of the hardest for many women to say. It's also one of the greatest time-management tools we have. Only when you master the ability to say this one-syllable word — and *mean* it — will you be able to take full control of your time and your life. Saying no to acquaintances, co-workers, and friends when they ask you to spend your time in a way that doesn't jibe with your life priorities doesn't make you a bad person. It simply means you have a healthy degree of self-respect and that you recognize the value of one of your most precious commodities — your time.

When You Can't Do It All, Delegate

Another time-management tool that is often neglected by women is delegating. You may feel that if you want something done right, you have to do it yourself, and in all likelihood this is absolutely true. But sometimes good enough is good enough, and perfection is overkill. If your husband offers to take care of the laundry so you'll have an hour to go riding, does it really matter that the dishtowels aren't folded at 90-degree angles? Probably not. In the grand scheme of things, you'll probably derive far more satisfaction from riding than you would by staying home and creating origami from your laundry.

If you can't delegate a few of your responsibilities to your able-bodied family members, is it possible that you could hire someone to lighten your load? If you can afford the expense of hiring someone to clean your house, mow your lawn, or watch your children even once or twice a month, you might find that the price you pay is well worth the extra time and freedom it buys you. It might be just enough time and freedom to allow you to move closer to your dreams.

Lack of Financial Resources

If you feel that you can't afford to get involved with horses, are you absolutely, positively sure? Have you checked the cost of riding lessons in your area? Have you taken a hard look at your budget? Is it possible that you can reallocate some of your financial resources from something that's less important to you than being involved with horses?

If it turns out there is absolutely, positively no money left over for equestrian pursuits at the end of the month, that doesn't necessarily mean that there's no way for you to achieve your dream. It just means you'll have to do it without a lot of cash. Hopefully, the options discussed in Chapter 8 gave you some good ideas and convinced you that with a little ingenuity and hard work, you can find a way to bring horses into your life even if you don't have a lot of extra money.

Lack of Family Support

Sometimes, women find it hard to get involved with horses because their spouses, parents, significant others, or children don't fully support their plans. Your family may not want to share you with a horse, and when you think about it, it's perfectly understandable. If they've had you all to themselves for years,

why would they want to start sharing you now? It can be difficult to upset the balance that has been "working" for some time, but you've got to consider who it's really been working for.

Like many women, Kimberly, a homemaker from San Rafael, California, kept her passion for horses on the back burner for most of her adult life so she could devote her time and energy to raising her children and helping her husband achieve his career goals.

"I grew up on a farm with horses, and I think I had the best childhood imaginable," Kimberly said. "We didn't have a lot of money, but Dad always made sure I got to ride in a couple of local horse shows every summer, and he would take me trail riding on the weekends whenever he could. It made him happy and proud that I loved horses as much as he did."

Kimberly started college with the dream of becoming an equine vet, but she got sidetracked along the way.

"I fell head over heels in love with Michael in my junior year, and that was that," she said. "We got married and started our family."

While her husband worked long hours as a financial planner, Kimberly stayed home with their three children.

"I realized that I was probably never going to become a horse vet, and I accepted that," she said, "but I never gave up my dream of having a horse and riding again — not even for a second. Whenever I would try to talk to Michael about it, he wouldn't take me seriously. When our children were little, he'd tell me that we couldn't afford to feed three kids *and* a horse.

Then when the kids got older and they were involved in soccer and dance and baseball, he'd say that I didn't have time to go gallivanting off to some barn."

Kimberly said that Michael was a wonderful husband in every other way and that he was a loving, devoted father. For the most part their marriage was a happy one. While her children were young, they were Kimberly's first priority, and as a result, she never pushed the horse issue with Michael. When all her children were in college, however, the situation changed.

"Once the kids had all left home and I had all the free time in the world, Michael had the nerve to tell me I was too old to ride. That was the very last straw. I just lost it," Kimberly grinned sheepishly. "I told him that I was going to start riding again and that he had better just stand back and get out of my way. I'll never forget how stunned he looked. He said that he had no idea that horses were so important to me and that if he had known that I was really serious, he would have done things differently a long time ago."

Within a month of what Kimberly refers to as Michael's "great awakening," she was taking riding lessons three times a week, and within six months she was the owner of a 9-year-old Quarter Horse gelding, with Michael's blessing.

"Getting horses back into my life has been the greatest thing I've ever done for myself, and for my marriage," Kimberly said. "I think Michael has a lot more respect for me now. I only wish I hadn't waited so long to make him understand how important this is to me."

Most women are so naturally intuitive that picking up on the unspoken feelings and needs of others is second nature to us. Very few men, on the other hand, share the gift of women's intuition, no matter how loving and sensitive they might be. As a rule, they're just not very good mind readers. Compared to women, they're also less skilled at reading body language and interpreting indirect forms of communication. You can drop a hint the size of a boulder if you like, but you shouldn't be surprised if it goes completely unnoticed.

Because you obviously can't expect your husband or significant other to read your mind, it's necessary to make sure you have his full attention. Tell him how very important your dream is to you and what it means to you. If you can, give him a realistic idea about what it involves — it may be less expensive and less time consuming than he might suspect. If you need his help or support to achieve your dream, it's usually best to be very clear about what you want, and tell him exactly what he can do to help you. The same goes for your kids. In all likelihood your loved ones want you to be happy, and although they may be more than willing to help you, they may not even know where to begin. You have to tell them very specifically what they can do to help you achieve your dream.

Like Kimberly, Lauren's goal of becoming an equestrian was met with opposition, not from her husband, but from her parents.

"When I was a little girl, I was crazy about horses, but my parents wouldn't even think about letting me get near them, no matter how much I begged and pleaded," she said. "They were very protective, and they were terrified that I'd get hurt."

During Lauren's freshman year at Penn State University, she became friends with Renee, a young woman whose family owned a large Tennessee Walking Horse farm a few miles from the university.

"Renee and I spent every spare minute at the barn when school was in session, and her dad, Walter, gave us both full-time jobs on the farm every summer," Lauren remembered. "I absolutely loved taking care of the horses, just like I knew I would when I was a little girl."

In her sophomore year, Lauren changed her major from biology to animal husbandry. When she graduated from college, Walter offered her a job as farm manager.

"That was four years ago, and I'm still here, doing what I love to do best. As for my overly protective parents," Lauren chuckled, "they're still worried that I'm going to get hurt."

Parents who don't understand their daughters' love of horses can be harder to deal with than spouses or significant others, but the good news is that once you're an adult, they're more likely to step out of the way and let you make your own decisions. Like many other young women, Lauren found it necessary to put her dream aside until the time was right, and then she seized the opportunity to pursue her passion when it finally arose.

Finding Common Ground

Even if your family members don't share your love of horses, they obviously love you, and there's a good chance they enjoy your company. If you can find at least one aspect of horsemanship that interests your loved ones, you'll have a far better chance of gaining their support as you pursue your dreams.

Natalie's husband has always been very supportive of her interest in riding, but even before they were married, he made it clear he didn't share it.

WEEKLY SCHEDULE

TAKE A FEW MINUTES TO WRITE OUT YOUR TYPICAL WEEKLY SCHEDULE. Block out the hours already filled with work, sleep, and other necessary and important tasks and activities. If you're not sure if a task or activity is necessary or important, ask yourself which of your life priorities it sustains. If the answer is none, it might not be worth the investment of your time. When you're finished, you will have identified a few time slots — windows of opportunity — that potentially could be used to move you closer to your dream.

Monday

5:00 am _____

6:00 _____

7:00 _____

8:00 _____

9:00 _____

10:00 _____

11:00 _____

12:00 _____

1:00 pm _____

2:00 _____

3:00 _____

4:00 _____

5:00 _____

6:00 _____

7:00 _____

8:00 _____

9:00 _____

10:00 _____

11:00 _____

12:00 _____

1:00 am _____

2:00 _____

3:00 _____

4:00 _____

Tuesday

5:00 am _____

6:00 _____

7:00 _____

8:00 _____

9:00 _____

10:00 _____

11:00 _____

12:00 _____

1:00 pm _____

2:00 _____

3:00 _____

4:00 _____

5:00 _____

6:00 _____

7:00 _____

8:00 _____

9:00 _____

10:00 _____

11:00 _____

12:00 _____

1:00 am _____

2:00 _____

3:00 _____

4:00 _____

Wednesday

5:00 am _____

6:00 _____

7:00 _____

8:00 _____

9:00 _____

10:00 _____

11:00 _____

12:00 _____

1:00 pm _____

2:00 _____

3:00 _____

4:00 _____

5:00 _____

6:00 _____

7:00 _____

8:00 _____

9:00 _____

10:00 _____

11:00 _____

12:00 _____

1:00 am _____

2:00 _____

3:00 _____

4:00 _____

Thursday

5:00 am	_____
6:00	_____
7:00	_____
8:00	_____
9:00	_____
10:00	_____
11:00	_____
12:00	_____
1:00 pm	_____
2:00	_____
3:00	_____
4:00	_____
5:00	_____
6:00	_____
7:00	_____
8:00	_____
9:00	_____
10:00	_____
11:00	_____
12:00	_____
1:00 am	_____
2:00	_____
3:00	_____
4:00	_____

Friday

5:00 am	_____
6:00	_____
7:00	_____
8:00	_____
9:00	_____
10:00	_____
11:00	_____
12:00	_____
1:00 pm	_____
2:00	_____
3:00	_____
4:00	_____
5:00	_____
6:00	_____
7:00	_____
8:00	_____
9:00	_____
10:00	_____
11:00	_____
12:00	_____
1:00 am	_____
2:00	_____
3:00	_____
4:00	_____

Saturday

5:00 am _____

6:00 _____

7:00 _____

8:00 _____

9:00 _____

10:00 _____

11:00 _____

12:00 _____

1:00 pm _____

2:00 _____

3:00 _____

4:00 _____

5:00 _____

6:00 _____

7:00 _____

8:00 _____

9:00 _____

10:00 _____

11:00 _____

12:00 _____

1:00 am _____

2:00 _____

3:00 _____

4:00 _____

Sunday

5:00 am _____

6:00 _____

7:00 _____

8:00 _____

9:00 _____

10:00 _____

11:00 _____

12:00 _____

1:00 pm _____

2:00 _____

3:00 _____

4:00 _____

5:00 _____

6:00 _____

7:00 _____

8:00 _____

9:00 _____

10:00 _____

11:00 _____

12:00 _____

1:00 am _____

2:00 _____

3:00 _____

4:00 _____

"It used to bother me," admitted Natalie, a freelance writer from Champaign, Illinois. "I wanted riding to be something that Ronnie and I could do together as a couple. But he really didn't like being around horses at all, so I didn't try to force it on him. When our daughters got old enough to ride and they started competing in 4-H shows, Ronnie kind of got pulled into the horse world. He wasn't exactly kicking and screaming, but he was a little reluctant at first. The girls and I will probably never get him on a horse, but he's the best groom you could ever hope for. He takes great pride in his ability to turn out a horse to perfection, and he loves watching the girls show. Having horses has been a really good thing for our family."

Teresa, a college art teacher in Augusta, Georgia, faced a similar obstacle. Her husband, Jacob, has never been on a horse in his life, but he enjoys traveling with her to dressage competitions.

"He loves the road trips," Teresa said. "Jacob's a detail person, and he's great at planning and organizing. He takes care of all the paperwork, and he likes mapping out the best routes to all the shows. His favorite part is driving the 'big red rig,' as he calls it. The horse is mine, but the truck and the trailer are Jacob's. It's a great arrangement, because it frees me up to concentrate on riding and showing."

When You Stand in the Way of Your Dream

Sometimes, it's not others that keep you from pursuing your passion; it's you. Many women nurture a lifelong dream of riding, only to find that they're unprepared to take advantage of the opportunity to fulfill their dream when it finally arises. While fear and lack of self-confidence hold some women back, lack of physical fitness prevents others from realizing their dreams.

Maria, a computer programer from Scottsdale, Arizona, believes she was born loving horses. "My dad would make me stick horses when I was a little girl, and I trotted and galloped and neighed wherever I went," she said.

In spite of her longing to ride horses of real live flesh and blood instead of wood, Maria didn't get her chance until she was in her late 40s.

"Up till then, I had spent most of my adult life sitting in an office working at a computer, and I just hadn't kept myself in shape. When I finally got up enough courage to start taking riding lessons, I was devastated to find that I wasn't strong enough to even get on a horse," she admitted. "But there was no way I was going to give up, so I got to work."

Maria started exercising, focusing on strengthening her body and improving her balance. "I practiced climbing over a wooden fence at the barn over and over so I could get the feel of lifting myself up in the stirrup with my left leg and throwing my right leg over the saddle," she said. "I'm sure I looked pretty ridiculous, but I didn't care about that — I was on a mission."

Maria not only mastered the skill of mounting a horse, she went on to become an excellent rider. These days, she rides four or five hours a week.

"I'm so glad I didn't give up on my dream or on myself," she said. "I'm 52 now, and I think

I'm in better shape than I was as a teenager. For the first time in my life, I'm an athlete. I feel strong, like I can do just about anything."

Like Maria, 58-year-old Nancy has loved horses since she was a girl.

"I can't explain it," she said, "but I've loved horses and had a dream of riding for as long as I can remember, even before I had ever touched one."

Nancy nurtured her dream, but she didn't act on it for more than 50 years. First as an attorney, and later as a judge in Chicago, Nancy devoted her career to helping battered women and abused and neglected children.

"I put my dream aside and devoted my time and my life to raising my children and helping others," Nancy explained. "I'm a nurturer by nature, and I was so busy taking care of everyone else that I didn't take care of myself. I've been overweight my whole life, and I got even heavier as I got older."

When Nancy retired from the bench at age 57, she knew it was her turn.

"I always pictured myself on a horse, smiling and happy," she said. "I was ready to make that happen, but at the time I knew I was too heavy to ride."

With a weight loss goal of 100 pounds, Nancy overhauled her diet and started exercising. She and her husband also began exploring the local horse community, learning as much as they could. It was this activity that led them to Randy, a local horse owner who was happy to introduce Nancy and her husband to the world of horses.

"Randy offered to teach me about horses, so that I'd be comfortable around them, and they'd be comfortable around me," Nancy said. "He wasn't all that concerned about my weight — he told me that when I felt that I was ready to ride, he'd put me on a horse. It happened a lot sooner than I thought it would. Knowing that, finally, I was really going to get to ride a horse was an incredible motivator."

While Nancy worked hard to lose weight, she continued to study the basics of horsemanship with Randy.

"I had to learn everything from scratch," she said. "Things like how to approach a horse, how to lead it, and how to pick out its feet. It was a great experience."

When Nancy had lost about 40 pounds, she felt that she was ready to ride.

"The first time I rode a horse, I felt like I was flying — I felt so free," Nancy remembered. "It was the most incredible, wonderful sensation; far better than I had ever imagined it would be. That feeling is what keeps pushing me to get in even better shape. I haven't reached my goal weight yet, but I will. I haven't let up yet, and I'm working at it every day."

Sadly, many women let weight issues stand in the way of their dreams. Unless you aspire to be a jockey or you're determined to ride a miniature horse, there's really no weight limit for riders. Equestrians come in all shapes and sizes, and the same goes for horses. Regardless of your size, there's no shortage of horses that can be a good match for you. If you're heavier than you'd like to be, you'll undoubtedly feel better if you lose weight, but there's no need to deprive yourself of the chance to realize your dream in the meantime.

When Fear is a Factor

Sometimes, women stand in the way of their dreams by letting their fears get the best of them. At age 32, Allison, a homemaker from Duluth, Minnesota, was in great physical shape, but a previous riding accident had badly shaken her confidence.

"It happened after I'd been taking riding lessons for about five or six months, and I was making great progress," she said. "I've always been very athletic, and riding just seemed to come naturally to me. I had finally talked my instructor into letting me ride this big gelding named Skipper that I was really crazy about. He was a little more horse than I was used to, but I felt like I could handle him. The first time I cantered him around the ring, one of the barn cats jumped onto the rail and spooked him. I ended up on the ground with a broken wrist."

For the first time since she started riding, Allison began to doubt her potential as an equestrian.

"I'm kind of a control freak, and I felt totally out of control when Skipper spooked and I fell off," she said. "He just went out from under me, and I was terrified that something like that might happen again. You always hear that you're supposed to climb right back on a horse after you fall off, but I just couldn't make myself do it, even for several months after my wrist had healed."

Allison credits her instructor with helping her rebuild her confidence so that she could ride again.

"It wasn't because she pushed me to get back on a horse," Allison said. "It was because she didn't push me. She encouraged me to keep coming out to the barn to groom and feed and lunge Skipper and the other horses, and she told me that when I was ready to ride again, I'd know it. She was right."

I don't think I've ever met an experienced equestrian who hasn't taken a tumble or two from the saddle — myself included. When an incident or an accident shakes your confidence, it's important to backtrack to the point that you feel completely comfortable and move forward from there. If you feel comfortable trotting but not cantering, there's no harm in leaving the canter till later. If you're not ready to ride at all, you can do what Allison did: Go back to the ground work and focus on rebuilding your confidence with the help of a good riding instructor and a quiet, well-schooled horse.

Courage Breeds Confidence

If you want to know all the reasons you can't achieve your dream, you can ask just about anyone and they'll gladly enlighten you. Sadly, the vast majority of people will never even try to fulfill their own dreams in life, and, as a result, they can't imagine you might be able to accomplish yours. As the old saying goes, never let a poor man tell you how to become rich. By the same token, you should never let a bench-warmer tell you how to become — or even how not to become — a winner. If you need expert advice on how to succeed in your equestrian discipline, make sure you ask an expert.

An accomplished equestrian from Johnson City, Tennessee, Amy had competed in local horse shows since she was old enough to hang on to the saddle horn in the lead-line class. By her mid-20s, she was a force to be reckoned with on the local show circuit. Amy was proud of her success, but her dream was to show her Arabian gelding, Rocky, at the national level.

Unfortunately, the closest professional Arabian horse trainer was a good two-hour drive from Amy's barn. Even worse, the cost of having Rocky professionally conditioned and trained for a national competition would be about $600 a month plus expenses, with no guarantee the horse would make the cut. Suffering from a bad case of sticker shock, Amy decided she would condition, train, and show Rocky herself.

"Everyone kept telling me that there was no way I could do it on my own," she said. "They said it was impossible to compete with the big-name trainers."

Amy refused to listen to the nay-sayers. "I bought Rocky so I could enjoy him, not so I could ship him off and never see him," she said. "He knows me and he trusts me. I knew he would show better for me than he would for anyone else. Plus," she added, "I could think of a lot of other ways to spend six hundred bucks a month!"

Amy devised a plan to qualify Rocky for a national competition. She oversaw every aspect of the gelding's preparation: nutrition, conditioning, training, grooming, turnout time. For an entire year she worked harder than she ever had. Much to everyone's surprise but her own, she accomplished her goal.

"You might be an amateur," she said, "but the trick is not to look like one or act like one. Your horse has to be conditioned and groomed like a superstar. You have to carry yourself like a superstar and believe that you have as much right to be in the ring as anyone else, including the big-name trainers. When you're confident, your horse is confident."

In a class full of professionals, Amy's winning attitude didn't hurt her one bit. Not only did she and Rocky win the blue ribbon in the open gelding halter class, they beat out every other gelding at the show, earning the title of Supreme Champion Gelding. Not bad for a couple of amateurs.

"It's was an awesome feeling to set such a huge goal and then achieve it," she said. "It made me realize that I can accomplish whatever I decide to, as long as I'm willing to work hard enough and stick with it."

Becoming a horsewoman and an equestrian — at any level — isn't always easy or effortless. It requires patience and persistence, commitment and courage. It's a journey, rather than a destination. And like every other journey, there will be obstacles to overcome — both internal and external. How far you travel depends less on the number and size of these obstacles and more on your desire and determination to realize your dream.

equestrian longevity

RIDING THROUGH THE SEASONS OF LIFE

If you ask any equestrian who has been fortunate enough to grow up and grow old in the company of horses, she'll tell you what you may already know: Horses can enrich a woman's existence at every stage of her life.

Having shared my entire life with horses, I have no doubt they've made me a better, stronger person than I might have been otherwise. When I was a girl, horses gave me a reason to dream and a passion to pursue. Along with my parents, they were my earliest teachers, and from them I learned important lessons about love and loyalty, respect and responsibility. Horses enticed me to spend time outside and instilled in me a deep appreciation for the beauty and wonder of nature.

Growing up with horses, I learned that excuses never substitute for earnest effort and hard work and that practice and repetition of any skill lead to competence and confidence. Although I was bolstered by my successes and humbled by my failures, I came to realize that both are temporary and tomorrow is another day.

During my teenage years, horses gave me a direction in life. They helped me realize that having a purpose was more important than being popular and that true beauty was more about attitude than appearance. Having learned to hold my ground with thousand-pound horses, I never had any problems handling 150-pound adolescent boys, no matter how irresistible they fancied themselves.

Growing up on a farm prepared me for the realities of childbirth and the responsibilities of motherhood. After caring for a couple dozen horses and managing a 30-stall barn, taking care of a few kids and a three-bedroom house didn't seem so daunting.

Over the past decade I've spent far more time and energy raising children than riding horses, but I wouldn't change a minute of it. Now that my boys are growing up and becoming more independent, I find I've come full circle. With more time on my hands, horses give me a reason to dream and a passion to pursue. They entice me to spend time outside, where I can appreciate the beauty and wonder of nature. Riding keeps me physically strong and mentally alert. It gives me an opportunity to engage in lifelong learning and master a skill. As I grow older, I suspect that my relationship with horses will take on a deeper meaning with each passing year. Horses are the keepers of my memories, and they hold the history of my life.

No matter what your age or stage of life, it

is never too early or too late to seek out the company of horses. I hope you will never let anyone — including yourself — tell you that you are too old to enjoy a relationship with a horse or that you've missed your chance to become a horsewoman. Even if you're returning to horses after a decades-long detour or even if you didn't discover your love for horses until later in life, it's never too late to pursue your passion and chase your dreams.

The Longevity Factor

The good news is that you probably have far more time to devote to your dreams than you might think. As a woman, you've got an excellent chance of enjoying a very long life — longer than your grandparents or even your parents. These days, women in the United States and in other developed countries have a greater life expectancy than ever before. In 1960, for example, the average American was 30 years old and could expect to live another 44 years. In 2000 the average American was considerably older, 35, and still could expect to live an additional 44 years.

These numbers are important because when you consider how old you are, what matters most is not necessarily the number of years you have already lived but rather the number of years that still lie before you. While the odds of enjoying a long and healthy life are definitely in your favor, longevity is guaranteed to no one, and it should never be taken for granted. The better care you take of yourself, the longer you're likely to live. If you're blessed with good genes and good health, and if you practice good habits, it's not unrealistic to look forward to celebrating birthdays well into your 90s.

As longevity continues to increase, women are staying relatively younger for longer. You may have heard it said that 50 is the new 40, and in terms of how young you feel and the number of meaningful, productive years that still lie before you, the statement is generally true. By the same token, 60 is the new 50; 70 is the new 60; and so on. This means you can continue to experience good health and maintain an active lifestyle well into your "golden" years, riding horses and engaging in other physically challenging pursuits once considered impossible — or at least inadvisable — for older women.

To take full advantage of these bonus years, you have to manage your physical health carefully and keep your body in good shape. It's also important to have the right mindset ahead of time, one that accepts growing older as a natural part of life. In spite of our nation's passionate love affair with youth, aging is not a disease nor is it a disability.

If you live long enough, you will eventually grow old, and if you're like most women, you probably find this reality far more desirable than the alternative. If you stay healthy as you age, you can continue to enjoy the company of horses just as much as you did in your younger years.

How healthy you are as a mature adult depends, to a large extent, on the health-related decisions you've made, the behaviors you've practiced, the habits you've acquired — and those you've avoided — over the course of your life. If your decisions, behaviors, and habits have been less than ideal in the past, don't despair. The human body is exceptionally forgiving and incredibly resilient. Making simple, positive changes in your diet, activity level, and attitude can improve your health dramatically at virtually any age.

One of the greatest benefits of taking good care of your health is that the positive effects tend to snowball. When you eat more nutritious foods and focus on improving your level of fitness, you'll become stronger and more energetic. Your moods will improve, and you'll become more optimistic. You'll find yourself searching for new ways to tweak your diet and step up your level of activity. The better you feel — both physically and emotionally — the more likely you'll be to take on new challenges, accomplish your goals, and realize your dreams. Regardless of your age, it's never too late to start making changes that will impact your life in positive ways. It is never too late to take the first step toward a future filled with horses, happiness, and good health.

BIBLIOGRAPHY

Chapter 2

Willett, W.C.; Manson, J.E.; Stampfer, M.J.; et al. Weight, weight change, and coronary heart disease in women. *JAMA,* 1995; 273;461-5.

Overweight, obesity, and health risk. National Task Force on the Prevention and Treatment of Obesity. *Arch Intern Med,* 2000; 160: 898-904.

Willett, W.C. Dietary fat plays a major role in obesity. *Obes Rev,* 2002; 3:59-68.

Cholesterol: What your level means. *American Academy of Family Physicians,* 1996-2006.

Albertazzi, P.; et al. The effect of dietary soy supplementation on hot flashes. *Obstet Gynecol* 1998; 91: 6-11.

Recommended Clinical Preventive Services for Adult Women. *American Academy of Family Physicians,* 2006.

Luscombe-March, N.D.; Noakes, M.; Wittert, G.A.; Keogh, J.B., Foster, P.; Clifton, P.M. Carbohydrate restricted diets high in either monounsaturated fat or protein are equally effective at promoting fat loss and improving blood lipids, *Am. J. Clinical Nutrition,* April 1, 2005; 81 (4): 762-772.

Prentice, R.L.; Caan, B.; Chlebowski, R.T.; et al. Low-fat dietary pattern and risk of invasive breast cancer: the Women's Health Initiative Randomized Controlled Dietary Modification Trial. *JAMA,* 2006; 295:639-42.

Osteoporosis facts. *National Osteoporosis Foundation.*

Papadimitropoulos, E.; Wells, G.; Shea, B.; et al. Meta-analyses of therapies for postmenopausal osteoporosis. *Endocr Rev,* 2002; 23:560-9.

Manson, J.E.; Hsia, J.; Johnson, K.C.; et al. Estrogen plus progestin and the risk of coronary heart disease. *N Engl J Med,* 2003; 349:523-34.

Centers for Disease Control and Prevention. National diabetes fact sheet. U.S. Department of Health and Human Services, Centers for Disease Control and Prevention: Atlanta, GA, 2004.

Cardiovascular and renal benefits of dry bean and soybean intake. *Am. J. Clin Nutr,* 1999; 70 (3): 464S-474.

Matthews, K.A.; Meilahn, E.; Kuller, L.H.; et al. Menopause and risk factors for coronary heart disease. *N Engl J Med,* 1989; 321 (10): 641-6.

Poehlman, E.T.; Toth, M.J.; Gardner, A.W. Changes in energy balance and body composition at menopause: a controlled longitudinal study. *Ann Intern Med,* 1994; 123 (9): 673-5.

Wing, R.R.; Matthews, K.A.; Kuller, L.H.; et al. Weight gain at the time of menopause. *Arch Intern Med,* 1991; 151: (1): 97-102.

Tchernof, A.; Peohlman, E.T. Effects of the menopause transition on body fatness and body fat distribution. *Obes Res* 1998; 6(3): 246-54.

Kuller, L.H. Hormone replacement therapy and coronary heart disease: a new debate. *Med Clin North Am,* 2000; 84(1): 181-98.

Appel, L.J. Nonpharmacologic therapies that reduce blood pressure: a fresh perspective. *Clin Cardiol,* 1999; 22 (S III): 1111-15.

Menopausal Hormone Therapy: Summary of a scientific workshop. *An Int Med,* 2003; 138: 361-4.

Carroll, D. Non-hormonal therapies for hot flashes in menopause, *American Family Physician* 2006; 73 (3): 457-64.

Kronenberg, F.; Fugh-Berman, A. Complementary and alternative medicine for menopausal symptoms: a review of randomized, controlled trials. *Ann Intern Med,* 2002; 137: 805-13.

McMichael-Phillips, D.F.; Harding, C.; Morton, M., et al. Effects of soy protein supplementation on epithelial proliferation in the histologically normal human breast. *Am J Clin Nutr,* 1998; 68: 1431S-1435S.

Kreijkamp-Kaspers, S.; Kok, L.; Grobbee, D.E.; et al. Effect of soy protein containing isoflavones on cognitive function, bone mineral density, and plasma lipids in postmenopausal women: a randomized controlled trial. *JAMA,* 2004; 292: 65-74.

Health claims: Soy protein and risk of coronary heart disease. *Code of Federal Regulations* 21CFR101.82 (2001).

Sacks, F.M.; Lichtenstein, A.; Van Horn, L.; Harris, W.; Kris-Etherton, P.; Winston, M. Soy Protein, Isoflavones, and Cardiovascular Health. An American Heart Association Science Advisory for Professionals From the Nutrition Committee. *Circulation* 2006.

Anderson, J.W.; Johnstone, B.M.; Cook-Newell, M.E. Meta-analysis of the effects of soy protein intake on serum lipids. *N Engl J Med,* 1995; 333: 276-82.

Krebs, E.E.; Ensrud, K.E.; MacDonald, R.; Wilt, T.J. Phytoestrogens for treatment of menopausal symptoms: a systematic review. *Obstet Gynecol,* 2004: 104: 824-36.

Olendzki, B; Speed, C; Domino, F.J.; Nutritional assessment and counseling for prevention and treatment of cardiovascular disease. *American Family Physician*, 2006; 73 (2): 257-264.

Effect of hormone therapy on risk of heart disease may vary by age and years since menopause. National Institutes of Health, April 3, 2007.

Chapter 3

Salmeron, J.; Hu, F.B.; Manson, J.E.; Stampfer, M.J.; Colditz, G.A.; Rimm, E.B.; Willett, W.C. Dietary fat intake and risk of type 2 diabetes in women. *Am J Clin Nutr,* 2001; 73 (6): 1019-26.

Food Labeling: Trans Fatty Acids in Nutrition Labeling. Government Publishing Office.

Bessesen, D.N. The role of carbohydrates in insulin resistance. *J Nutr,* 2001; 121 (10): 2782S-2786S.

Jenkins, D.J.; Kendall, C.W.; Augustin, L.S.; Franceschi, S.; et al. Glycemic index: overview of implications in health and disease. *Am J Clin Nutr,* 2002; 76(1): 266S-73S.

Fuchs, C.S.; Giovannucci, E.L.; Colditz, G.A.; et al. Dietary fiber and the risk of colorectal cancer and adenoma in women. *N Engl J Med,* 1999; 340: 169-76.

Pereira, M.A.; O'Reilly, E.; Augustsson, K.; et al. Dietary fiber and risk of coronary heart disease: a pooled analysis of cohort studies. *Arch Intern Med,* 2004; 164: 370-6.

Van Horn, L. Fiber, lipids, and coronary heart disease. A statement for healthcare professionals from the Nutrition Committee, American Heart Association. *Circulation,*1997; 95: 2701-4.

Institute of Medicine: Dietary reference intakes for energy, carbohydrate, fiber, fat, fatty acids, cholesterol, protein, and amino acids. Washington, DC: *National Academies Press*, 2002.

Revealing Trans Fats, U.S. Food and Drug Administration, U.S. Department of Health and Human Services, 2004.

Litin, L.; Sacks, F. Trans-fatty-acid content of common foods. *N Engl J Med,* 1993; 329: 1969-1970.

Griel, A.E.; Ruder, E.H.; Kris-Etherton, P.M.The changing roles of dietary carbohydrates: from simple to complex. *Arterioscler Thromb Vasc Biol,* 2006; 26 (9): 1958-1965.

Castro, I.A.; Barroso, L.P.; Sinnecker, P. Functional foods for coronary heart disease risk reduction: a meta-analysis using a multivariate approach. *Am J Clin Nutr,* 2005; 82 (1): 32-40.

Beresford, S.A.; Johnson, K.C.; Ritenbaugh, C.; et al. Low-fat dietary pattern and risk of colorectal cancer: the Women's Health Initiative Randomized Controlled Dietary Modification Trial. *JAMA,* 2006; 295: 643-54.

Howard, B.V.; Van Horn, L.; Hsia, J.; et al. Low-fat dietary pattern and weight change over 7 years: the Women's Health Initiative Randomized Controlled Dietary Modification Trial. *JAMA,* 2006; 295:39-49.

Brown L.; Rosner, B.; Willett, W.W.; Sacks, F.M. Cholesterol-lowering effects of dietary fiber: a meta-analysis. *Am J Clin Nutr,* 1999; 69: 30-42.

Liu, S. Insulin resistance, hyperglycemia and risk of major chronic diseases—a dietary perspective. *Proc Nutrit Soc Austral,* 1998; 22:140.

Liese, A.D.; Roach, A.K.; Sparks, K.C.; Marquart, L.; D'Agostino, R.B.; Mayer-Davis, E.J. Whole grain intake and insulin sensitivity: the Insulin Resistance Atherosclerosis Study. *Am J Clin Nutr,* 2003; 78: 965-71.

Chandalia, M.; Abhimanyu, G.; von Bergenmann, K.; et al. Beneficial effects of high dietary fiber intake in patients with type II diabetes mellitus. *New Engl J Med,* 2000; 42: 1392-8.

Jensen, C.; Haskell, W.; Whittam, J. Long-term effects of water-soluble dietary fiber in the management of hypercholesterolemia in healthy men and women. *Am J Cardiol,* 1997; 79: 34-7.

Anderson, J.; Gustafason, N.; Bryant, C.; Tietyen-Clark, J. Dietary fiber and diabetes: a comprehensive review and practical application. *J Am Diet Assoc,* 1987; 87: 1189-97.

Hunter, J.E.; Applewhite, T.H. Reassessment of trans fatty acid availability in the U.S. diet. *Am J Clin Nutr,* 1991; 54: 363-369.

Shapiro, S. Do trans fatty acids increase the risk of coronary heart disease? A critique of the epidemiologic evidence. *Am J Clin Nutr,* 1997; 66(S): 1011S -1017S.

Hu, F.B.; Stampfer, M.J.; Manson, J.E.; et al. Dietary fat intake and the risk of coronary heart disease in women. *N Engl J Med,* 1997; 337:1491-1499.

Mensink, R.P.M.; Katan, M.B. Effect of dietary trans fatty acids on high-density and low-density lipoprotein cholesterol levels in healthy subjects. *N Engl J Med,* 1990; 323: 439-45.

Kirs-Etherton, P.M.; Harris, W.S.; Appel, J.L. Fish consumption, fish oil, omega-3 fatty acids and cardiovascular disease. *Circulation,* 2002; 106: 2747-57.

Willet, W.C.; MacMahon, B. Diet and cancer—and overview. *N Engl J Med,* 1984; 310: 633-8.

Smith-Warner, S.A.; Spiegelman, D.; Adami, H.O.; et al. Types of dietary fat and breast cancer: a pooled analysis of cohort studies. *Int J Cancer,* 2001; 92: 767-74.

Burke, V.; Hodgson, J.M.; Beilin, L.J.; Giangiulioi, N.; Rogers, P.; Puddey, I.B. Dietary protein and soluble fiber reduce ambulatory blood pressure in treated hypertensives. *Hypertension,* 2001; 38 (4): 821-826.

Chandalia, M.; Garg, A.; Lutjohann, D.; von Bergmann, K.; Grundy, S.M.; Brinkley, L.J. Beneficial effects of high dietary fiber intakes in patients with type 2 diabetes mellitus. *N Eng J Med,* 2000; 342: 1392-1398.

Pentice, R.L.; Caan, B.; Chlebowski, R.T.; et al. Low-fat dietary pattern and risk of invasive breast cancer: the Women's Health Initiative Randomized Controlled Dietary Modification Trial. *JAMA,* 2006; 295:629-42.

Mozaffarian, D.; Pischon, T.; Hankinson, S.E.; et al. Dietary intake of trans fatty acids and systemic inflammation in women. *JAMA,* 1999; 281:1387-94.

Hu, F.B.' Manson, J.E.; Willett, W.C. Types of dietary fat and risk of coronary heart disease among women. *Lancet,*1993; 341: 581-5.

Hu, F.B.; Manson, J.E.; Willett, W.C. Types of dietary fat and risk of coronary heart disease: a critical review. *J Am Coll Nutr,* 2001; 20:5-19.

Chapter 4

Clinton, S.K. Lycopene: chemistry, biology, and implications for human health and disease. *Nutr Rev,* 1998; 56 (2): 35-51.

Franceschi, S.; Bidoli, E.; La Vecchia, C. Tomatoes and risk of digestive-tract cancers. *Cancer,* 1994; 59: 181-4.

Gerster, H. The potential role of lycopene for human health. *J Am Coll Nutr* 1997; 16 (2): 109-26.

Hu, F.B.; Cho, E.; Rexrode, K.M.; Albert, C.M.; Manson, J.E. Fish and long-chain omega-3 fatty acid intake and risk of coronary heart disease and total mortality in diabetic women. *Circulation,* 2003; 107: 1852-7.

Pereira, M.A.; Liu, S. Types of carbohydrates and risk of cardiovascular disease. *J Women's Health,* 2003; 12: 115-22.

Saris, W.; Astrup, A.; Prentice, A.; Zunft, H.; Formiguera, X.; et al. Randomized controlled trial of changes in dietary carbohydrate/fat ratio and simple vs complex carbohydrates on body weight and blood lipids: the CARMEN study. *Int J Obes,* 2000; 24 (10): 1310-18.

McKeown, N.; Meigs, J.; Liu, S.; Wilson, P.; Jacques, P. Whole grain intake is favorably associated with metabolic risk factors for diabetes and cardiovascular disease in the Framingham Offspring Study. *Am J Clin Nut,* 2002; 76: 390-8.

Liu, S.; Willett, W.C.; Stampfer, M.J.; et al. A prospective study of dietary glycemic load, carbohydrate intake, and risk of coronary heart disease in US women. *Am J Clin Nutr,* 2000; 71: 1455-61.

2005 Dietary Guidelines for Americans. Center for Nutrition Policy and Promotion, U.S. Department of Agriculture.

Hung, H.C.; Joshipura, K.J.; Jiang, R.; et al. Fruit and vegetable intake and risk of major chronic disease. *J Natl Cancer Inst,* 2004; 96: 1577-84.

Djousse, L.; Arnett, D.K.; Coon, H.; Province, M.A.; et al. Fruit and vegetable consumption and LDL cholesterol: The National Heart, Lung, and Blood Institute Family Heart Study. *Am J Clin Nutr,* 2004; 79: 213-7.

Rice-Evans, C.A. The relative antioxidant activities of plant-derived polyphenoic flavonoids. *Free Radical Res,* 1995; 4: 3785-93.

Meyer, K.; Kushi, D.; Slavin, J.; et al. Carbohydrates, dietary fiber, and incident type 2 diabetes in older women. *Am J Clin Nutr,* 2000; 71: 921-30.

Wrolstad, R.E. The Possible Health Benefits of Anthocyanin Pigments and Polyphenolics, The Linus Pauling Institute, 2001.

Quinn, E. Exercise and Fluid Replacement: The American College of Sports Medicine Position Stand, 2006.

Jayaprakasam, B.; Shaiju, K.V.; Olson, L.K.; Nair, M.G.; Insulin Secretion by Bioactive Anthocyanins and Anthocyanidins Present in Fruits. *J Agric Food Chem*, 2005; 53 (1), 28-31.

Liu, S.; Manson, J.E.; Stampfer, M.J.; et al. A prospective study of whole grain intake and risk of type 2 diabetes mellitus in women. *Am J Pub Health,* 2000; 90:1409-1415.

Anderson, J.W. Whole grains protect against atherosclerotic cardiovascular disease. *Proc Nutr Soc,* 2003; 62: 135-42.

Hu, F.B.; Stampfer, M.J. Nut consumption and risk of coronary heart disease: a review of epidemiologic evidence. *Curr Atheroscler Rep,* 1999; 1: 204-9.

Albert, C.M.; Hennekens, C.H.; O'Donnell, C.J.; Ajani, U.A.; Carey, V.J.; Willet, W.C.; et al. Fish consumption and risk of sudden cardiac death. *JAMA,* 1998; 279: 23-8.

Natow A, Heslin J. *The Complete Food Counter.* Pocket Books, New York; 2006.

Chapter 5

Blumenthal, M.; Goldberg, A.; Brinckmann, J. *Herbal Medicine: Expanded Commission E Monographs.* Newton, MA: *Integrative Medicine Communications,* 2000: 314-321.

Mosekilde, L. Vitamin D and the elderly. *Clin Endocrinol*, 2005; 62(3): 265-281.

Zemel, M.B. Calcium modulation of adiposity, *Obes Res*, 2003; 11: 375-376.

Zemel, M.B. Regulation of adiposity and obesity risk by dietary calcium: mechanisms and implications *J Am Coll Nutr*, 2001; 21:146S-156S.

Zemel, M.B.; Morgan, K. Interaction between calcium, dairy and dietary macronutrients in modulating body composition in obese mice, 2002; *FASEB J* 16, A369.

Zemel, M.B.; Thompson, W.; Zemel, P.; Nocton, A.M.; Milstead, A.; Morris, K.; Campbell, P. Dietary calcium and dairy products accelerate weight and fat loss during energy restriction in obese adults, *Am J Clin Nutr*, 2002; 75(S2), 342S.

Turnbull, W.H.; Thomas, H.G. The effect of a Plantago ovata seed containing preparation on appetite variables, nutrient and energy intake. *Int J Obes Relat Metab Disord*, 1995;19:338-342.

Manson, J.E.; Gaziano, J.M.; Spelsberg, A.; et al. A secondary prevention trial of antioxidant vitamins and cardiovascular disease in women. Rationale, design and methods. The WACS Research Group. *Ann Epidemiol*, 1995; 5: 261-9.

Carr, A.C.; Frei, B. Toward a new recommended dietary allowance for vitamin C based on antioxidant and health effects in humans. *Am J Clin Nutr*, 1999; 69: 1086-107.

Holick, M.F. Vitamin D: importance in the prevention of cancers, type 1 diabetes, heart disease, and osteoporosis. *Am J Clin Nutr, 2004*; 79: 362-71.

Rimm, E.B.; Stampfer, M.J. Antioxidants for vascular disease. *Med Clin North Am*, 2000; 84: 239-49.

Kris-Etherton, P.M.; Lichtenstein, A.H.; Howard, B.V.; et al. AHA science advisory: antioxidant vitamin supplements and cardiovascular disease. *Circulation*, 2004; 10: 637-641.

Glucosamine and Chondroitin: What do NIH study results mean for your patients? *Consultant*, 2006 (5) 603-604.

McAlindon, T.E.; LaValley, M,P.; Gulin, J.P.; Felson, D.T. Glucosamine and chondroitin for treatment of osteoarthritis: a systematic quality assessment and meta-analysis. *JAMA*, 2000; 283: 1469-1475.

Richy, F.; Bruyere, O.; Ethgen, O.; et al. Structural and symptomatic efficacy of glucosamine and chondroitin in knee osteoarthritis: a comprehensive meta-analysis. *Arch Intern Med*, 2003; 163: 1514-1522.

Evans, J. Multivitamin benefits scrutinized by NIH Panel, *Fam Prac News*, 2006: 6:10.

McLean, R,M. Magnesium and its therapeutic uses: a review. *Am J Med*, 1994; 96: 63-76.

Zhang, Y.H.; Kramer, T.R.; Taylor, P.R.; et al. Possible immunologic involvement of antioxidants in cancer prevention. *Am J Clin Nutr*, 1995; 62 (S): 1477S-1482S.

Lawvere, S.; Mahoney, M. St. John's Wort. *American Family Physician*, 2005; 72 (11): 2249-54.

Wu, C.H.; et al. Epidemiological evidence of increased bone mineral density in habitual tea drinkers. *Arch Intern Med*, 2002; 162:1001-6

Holick, M.F. Vitamin D: importance in the prevention of cancers, type 1 diabetes, heart disease, and osteoporosis. *Am J Clin Nutr*, 2004; 79 (3): 362-371.

Holick, M.F. Evolution and function of vitamin D. *Can Res*, 2003; 164:3-28.

Diplock, A.T. Antioxidants and disease prevention. *Mol Aspects Med*, 1994; 15: 293-376.

Hercberg, S.; Galan, P.; Preziosi, P.; Alfarez, M.J.; Vazquez, C. The potential role of antioxidant vitamins in preventing cardiovascular disease and cancer. *Nutr*, 1998: 14:513-520.

Martinez, M.E.; Willett, W.C. Calcium, vitamin D, and colorectal cancer: a review of the epidemiologic evidence. *Cancer Epidemiol Biomarkers Prev*, 1998; 7:163-8.

Hyman, J.; Baron, J.A.; Dain, B.J.; et al. Dietary and supplemental calcium and the recurrence of colorectal adenomas. *Cancer Epidemiol Biomarkers Prev*, 1998; 7:291-5.

Cappuccio, F.P.; Elliott, P.; Allender, P.S.; Pryer, J.; Follman, D.A.; Cutler, J.A. Epidemiologic association between dietary calcium intake and blood pressure: a meta-analysis of published data. *Am J Epidemiol*, 1995; 142: 935-45.

Anderson, J.; Allgood, L.; Turner, J.; et al. Effects of psyllium on glucose and serum lipid responses in men with type 2 diabetes and hypercholesterolemia. *Am J Clin Nutr*, 1999; 70: 466-73.

Silvam, P.G. Protection against Helicobacter pylori and other bacterial infections by garlic. *J Nutr*, 2001; 131:1106S-08S.

Bordnitz, M.H.; Pscale, J.V.; Derslice, L.V. Flavor components of garlic extract. *J Agr Food Chem*, 1977;19 (2): 273-275.

Lawson, L.D.; Ransom, D.K.; Hughes, B.G. Inhibition of whole blood platelet aggregation by compounds in garlic clove extracts and commercial garlic products. *Throm Res*, 1992;65:141-156.

Amagase, H.; Petesch, B.; Matsuura, H.; Kasuga, S.; Itakura, Y. Intake of garlic and its bioactive components. *J Nutr*, 2001; 131 3(S): 955S-962S.

Ashraf, W.; Park, F.; Lof, J.; Quigley, E.M. Effects of psyllium therapy on stool characteristics, colon transit and anorectal function in chronic idiopathic constipation. *Aliment Pharmacol Ther*, 1995; 9: 649-647.

Steinberg, D. Antioxidant vitamins and coronary heart disease. *N Engl J Med* 1993; 328: 1487-1489.

Chisolm, G.M.; Steinberg, D. The oxidative modification hypothesis of atherogenesis: an overview. *Free Radic Biol Med*, 2000; 28: 1815-1826.

Podmore, I.D.; Griffiths, H.R.; Herbert, K.E.; et al. Vitamin C exhibits pro-oxidant properties. *Nature*, 1998: 392-559.

Lozada, C.J. Glucosamine in osteoarthritis: questions remain. *Cleveland Clin J Med*, 2007; 74 (1): 65-71.

Villareal, D.tT.; Holloszy, J.O.; Kohrt, W,M. Effects of DHEA replacement on bone mineral density and body composition in elderly women and men. *Clin Endocrinol*, 2000; 53: 561-568.

Flynn, M.A.; Weaver-Sterholtz, D.; Sharpe-Timms, K.L.; Allen, S.; Krause, G. Dehydroepiandrosterone replacement in aging humans. *J Clin Endocrinol Metab*, 1999; 84: 1527-1533.

Fairfield, K.M.; Fletcher, R.H. Vitamins for chronic disease prevention in adults. *JAMA*, 2002; 287: 3116-26.

Rimm, E.B.; Williams, P.; Fosher, K.; Criqui, M; Stampfer, M.J. Moderate alcohol intake and lower risk of coronary heart disease: meta-analysis of effects on lipids and haemostatic factors. *BMJ*, 1999; 319: 1523-8.

Chen, W.Y.; Colditz, G.A.; Rosner, B.; et al. Use of postmenopausal hormones, alcohol, and risk for invasive breast cancer. *Ann Intern Med*, 2002; 137: 798-801.

Rimm, E.B.; Klatsky, A.; Grobbee, D.; Stampfer, M.J. Review of moderate alcohol consumption and reduced risk of coronary heart disease: is the effect due to beer, wine or spirits? *BMJ*, 1996; 312: 731-6.

Stampfer, M.J.; Colditz, G.A.; Willet, W.C.; Speizer, F.E.; Hennekens, C.H. A prospective study of moderate alcohol consumption and the risk of coronary disease and stroke in women. *N Engl J Med*, 1988; 319: 267-273.

Popa, A. Ginkgo biloba and memory, Pharmacotherapy Update, *The Cleveland Clinic*, 2002; 5: 1-5.

Thys-Jacobs, S.; Starkey, P.; Bernstein, D.; Tian, J. Calcium carbonate and the premenstrual syndrome: effects on premenstrual and menstrual symptoms. Premenstrual Syndrome Study Group. *Am J Obstet Gynecol*, 1998; 179:444-452.

Sherwood, R.A.; Rocks, B.F.; Stewart, A.; Saxton, R.S. Magnesium and the premenstrual syndrome. *Ann Clin Biochem*, 1986; 23: (Pt 6): 667-670.

Berger, J.S.; Roncaglioni, M.C.; Avanzini, F.; Pangrazzi, I.; Tognoni, G.; Brown, D.L. Aspirin for the primary prevention of cardiovascular events in women and men. *JAMA*, 2006; 295:306-311.

Lauer, M.S. Aspirin for primary prevention of coronary events, *N Engl J Med*, 2002; 346 (19): 1468-1474.

Dietary Reference Intakes: Estimated Average Requirements for Groups, Food and Nutrition Board, Institute of Medicine, National Academy of Sciences, 2002.

Street, D.A.; Comstock, G.W.; Salkeld, R.M.; et al. Serum antioxidants and myocardial infarction. *Circulation*, 1994; 90: 1154-61.

Britton, A.; Marmot, M. Different measures of alcohol consumption and risk of coronary heart disease and all-cause mortality: 11 year follow-up of the Whitehall II Cohort Study. *Addiction*, 2004; 99: 109-16.

Physician's Desk Reference for Herbal Medicines. Medical Economics Company, Montvale, NJ, 1998.

European Scientific Cooperative on Phytotherapy. Monographs on the medicinal uses of plant drugs. March 1996.

Chapter 6

Hu, F.B.; Manson, J.E.; Stampfer, M.J.; et al. Diet, lifestyle, and the risk of type 2 diabetes mellitus in women. *N Engl J Med*, 2001; 345: 790-7.

Knowler, W.C.; Barret-Connor, E.; Fowler, S.E.; et al. Reduction in the incidence of type 2 diabetes with lifestyle intervention or metformin. *N Engl J Med*, 2002; 346: 393-403.

Tuomilehto, J.; Lindstrom, J.; Eriksson, J.G.; et al. Prevention of type 2 diabetes mellitus by changes in lifestyle among subjects with impaired glucose tolerance. *N Engl J Med*, 2001; 344: 1343-50.

Hu, F.B.; Sigal, R.J.; Rich-Edwards, J.W.; et al. Walking compared with vigorous physical activity and risk of type 2 diabetes in women: a prospective study. *JAMA*, 1999; 282: 1433-9.

Waxman, A. Prevention of chronic diseases: WHO global strategy on diet, physical activity and health. *Food Nutr Bull*, 2003; 24: 281-4.

Chapter 10

Sanderson, W.C. and Scherbov, S. 2005. Average remaining lifetimes can increase as human populations age. *Nature* 435: 811-813 (June 9, 2005).

ACKNOWLEDGEMENTS

Writing *Riding for Life* has been an incredibly rewarding experience for me, and I am very grateful to Jacqueline Duke, editor at Eclipse Press, for the opportunity. I'm also indebted to Kimberly Brown and Stephanie Church at *The Horse: Your Guide to Equine Healthcare*, and to Gail and Doug Prather for giving me a leg up in the beginning.

For their support and patience, I owe special thanks and lots of love to my wonderful husband, Robin Peavler, M.D.; to my three amazing sons, Oakley, Gatlin, and Chad; and to my lovely new daughter-in-law, Lindsey. I am forever indebted to my dear friend and photographer extraordinaire, Kimberly Miller, and her staff at fotochick.com, and to my friends Carmela Roush, Mary Austin, Nancy Rectenwald, and Gayle Santich.

Finally, I extend my deepest gratitude to all the wise and wonderful horsewomen (and a few good horsemen) who generously shared their expertise, experience, and insight with me as I wrote this book: Alice Page, Amy Austin, Amy Long, Faith Meredith, Dr. Elizabeth Hammerman, Robin Ashley Hood, Edward C. Horton Jr., the Honorable Nancy Sidote Salyers, Martha Martin, Marty Tuley, Mark Crawford, Ph.D., Brooke Sable, Justine Hand, Connie Matherly, Elaine Hensley, Becky Talbert, Tammy Zigo, Susan Boatwright, Lisa Gentry, Rachel Alana, Kimberly Chadwick, Lauren Lawton, Natalie Goldstein, Teresa Barber, Maria Perez Smith, Nancy Vesper, Andrea Lord, Robbie Hambright, Marcia Davis, Bonnie Kreitler, Nancy Crumley, Karen Capik, Gwen Costner, Allison Greer, Randy Mullins, and Jeff Dawson.

Cover photo by Jacques Toffi
Photos by Kimberly Miller of fotochick.com

ABOUT THE AUTHOR

Rallie McAllister was raised on Thirteen Oaks, an Arabian horse farm in Tennessee that has produced numerous U.S., Canadian, and German regional and national champions in its 30-year history. Prior to attending medical school, McAllister owned and operated her own training facility, training horses for farms in Tennessee, North Carolina, Florida, and South Carolina. At its peak, the training center was home to approximately 80 performance horses.

A board-certified family physician since 1998, McAllister earned her medical degree at James H. Quillen College of Medicine at East Tennessee State University in 1995 and completed her residency training in family medicine in 1997. McAllister also holds master's degrees in public health and environmental health.

She is author of several other health and wellness books and writes a nationally syndicated newspaper column, *Your Health*, that reaches millions of readers across the country. McAllister's articles appear on dozens of health-related Web sites as well. She also hosted *Rallie on Health*, a weekly regional health magazine on WJHL News Channel 11, which aired over a five-state area, and *No Bones About It*, a weekly radio talk show.

Currently, McAllister lives on a small farm in Nicholasville, Kentucky, and enjoys riding her four horses. As a physician, she serves as a consultant, designing and implementing worksite wellness programs in large corporations. Her focus is on preventive medicine, including nutrition, exercise, weight management, and motivational approaches to facilitating lifestyle changes.